FOLK-TALES
OF THE
BRITISH ISLES

FOLK-TALES
OF THE
BRITISH
ISLES

Chosen and with an Introduction by
KEVIN CROSSLEY–HOLLAND

Wood-engravings by
HANNAH FIRMIN

Pantheon Books, New York

Originally published in Great Britain in 1985 by
The Folio Society Limited,
and in 1986 by Faber & Faber Limited, London.

Folk-tales of the British Isles.
Bibliography: p. 391.
1. Tales—Great Britain.
I. Crossley-Holland, Kevin.
GR141.F645   1988   398.2'0941   87-42826
ISBN 0-394-56328-X
0-394-75553-7 (pbk.)

Manufactured in the United States of America

First American Edition

OR MY FATHER

Yr hên wr llwyd o'r cornel
Gan ei dad a glywodd chwedel,
A chan ei dad fe glywodd yntau
Ac ar ei ôl mi gofiais innau.

The grey old man in the corner
Of his father heard a story,
Which from his father he had heard,
And after them I have remembered.

ONTENTS

INTRODUCTION ≋≋≋≋≋≋≋≋≋≋≋≋≋≋≋≋≋ 1

FAIRIES ≋≋≋≋≋≋≋≋≋≋≋≋≋≋≋≋≋ 9

The Legend of Knockgrafton, *Ireland, Thomas Crofton*
   Croker 16
Tom Tit Tot, *England, Edward Clodd* 22
The Lady of Llyn y Fan Fach, *Wales, Sir John Rhys* 28
The Fairy Horse Dealer, *Isle of Man, George Waldron* 37
The Woman of the Sea, *Shetland, Helen Waddell* 39
The Young Tamlane, *Scotland, Sir Walter Scott* 43
Brewery of Eggshells, *Wales, Joseph Jacobs* 55
Yallery Brown, *England, Alan Garner* 57
The Soul Cages, *Ireland, Thomas Keightley* 65
Departure of the Fairies, *Scotland, Hugh Miller* 78

ORIGINS AND CAUSES ≋≋≋≋≋≋≋≋≋≋≋≋≋≋ 83

Assipattle and the Muckle Mester Stoor Worm, *Orkney,*
   Ernest W. Marwick 86

Contents

Origin of the Welsh, *Wales, P. H. Emerson*   93
The Origin of the Wrekin, *England, Charlotte Burne and
    Georgina Jackson*   98
Fior Usga, *Ireland, Thomas Crofton Croker*   100
Origin of the Arms of the Island, *Isle of Man, Joseph Train*   104
Byard's Leap, *England, S. O. Addy*   105

KINGS AND HEROES 〰〰〰〰〰〰〰〰〰〰   109

Fionn in Search of His Youth, *Ireland, Sean O'Sullivan*   114
Diarmaid and Grainne, *Scotland, John Francis Campbell*   118
Knight to Knight, *England, Sybil Marshall*   123
The Sleeping Warriors, *Wales, Elijah Waring*   129

FABULOUS BEASTS 〰〰〰〰〰〰〰〰〰〰   135

The Dragon of Wantley, *England, Anon (Jacqueline
    Simpson)*   139
The Black Dog of the Wild Forest, *Gypsy (Welsh), Francis
    Groome*   145
The Spirit Horse, *Ireland, Thomas Crofton Croker*   150
The Black Bull of Norroway, *Scotland, Robert Chambers*   154

NURSERY AND JOCULAR 〰〰〰〰〰〰〰〰   161

The Story of the Three Bears, *England, Robert Southey*   165
The Wee Bunnock, *Scotland, Robert Chambers*   170
Munachar and Manachar, *Ireland, Douglas Hyde*   175
The Cow on the Roof, *Wales, T. Gwynn Jones*   180
The Three Wise Men of Gotham, *England, W. A.
    Clouston*   183

Contents

GHOSTS ≋≋≋≋≋≋≋≋≋≋≋≋≋≋≋≋≋ 187

The Ghosts and the Game of Football, *Ireland, Patrick Kennedy* 192
The Bewitched Sixareen, *Shetland, Ernest W. Marwick* 196
The Great Giant of Henllys, *Wales, Anon (Athenaeum)* 201
Croglin Grange, *England, Augustus Hare* 203
The Men in the Turnip Field, *England, Ruth Tongue* 208
Lamplighter's Dream, *England, W. H. Barrett* 209

FABLES AND ANIMAL TALES ≋≋≋≋≋≋≋≋≋ 217

The Fox and the Wild Goose, *Scotland, John Francis Campbell* 220
How the Wolf Lost his Tail, *Scotland, John Francis Campbell* 221
The Fox and the Geese, *England, Joseph Cundall* 223
Two Women or Twelve Men, *Ireland, Sean O'Sullivan* 230
The Long-Lived Ancestors, *Wales, P. H. Emerson* 231

GIANTS AND STRONG MEN ≋≋≋≋≋≋≋≋≋ 235

The Son of the King of Erin and the Giant of Loch Léin, *Ireland, Jeremiah Curtin* 239
A Legend of Black Gang Chyne, *Isle of Wight, Abraham Elder* 251
Tom Hickathrift, *England, Joseph Jacobs* 257
The Blacksmith and the Horseman, *Ireland, Sean O'Sullivan* 263
The History of Jack and the Bean-Stalk, *England, Benjamin Tabart* 265

Contents

HISTORICAL 〰〰〰〰〰〰〰〰〰〰〰〰〰〰 281

Garlatha, *Harris (Hebrides), John Gregorson Campbell* 285
Beth Gêlert, *Wales, William Robert Spencer* 288
Whittington, *England, W. Carew Hazlitt* 291
The Wildman, *England, Kevin Crossley-Holland* 297
Ivar and Matilda, *Isle of Man, A. W. Moore* 300
Cromwell and O'Donnell, *Ireland, Sean O'Sullivan* 303

SAINTS AND DEVILS 〰〰〰〰〰〰〰〰〰〰〰〰 311

The Fiend Master, *Wales, Wirt Sikes* 315
King O'Toole and his Goose, *Ireland, Samuel Lover* 317
The Man that Sold his Soul to the Devil, *Scotland,*
    Hamish Henderson 322
The Crowza Stones, *England, Robert Hunt* 324
The Demon Cat, *Ireland, Jane F. Wilde* 327

ENCHANTMENT 〰〰〰〰〰〰〰〰〰〰〰〰〰〰 331

The Three Heads of the Well, *England, James Orchard*
    Halliwell 336
The Story of Tom Thumb, *England, James Reeves* 341
Daniel O'Rourke, *Ireland, Thomas Crofton Croker* 346
Rashin Coatie, *Scotland, Andrew Lang* 355
Frosty, *Gypsy (Welsh), Dora E. Yates* 358
Bewitched Butter, *Ireland, W. B. Yeats* 362
The Soul as a Butterfly, *Ireland, Sean O'Sullivan* 373
Black Annis, *England, Ruth Tongue* 376
The Paddo, *Scotland, Robert Chambers* 379
The King o' the Cats, *England, Joseph Jacobs* 382

Contents

ENVOI 〰〰〰〰〰〰〰〰〰〰〰〰〰〰〰 387

Why Everyone Should be Able to Tell a Story, *Scotland,*
   John Lorne Campbell 388

BIBLIOGRAPHY 〰〰〰〰〰〰〰〰〰〰〰 391

CKNOWLEDGEMENTS

The Folio Society would like to thank the following authors, publishers and owners of copyright for permission to reproduce stories from their collections:

W.H. Barrett: *More Tales from the Fens:* Routledge & Kegan Paul PLC

Alan Garner: *The Hamish Hamilton Book of Goblins:* Hamish Hamilton Limited

Hamish Henderson: *A Dictionary of British Folk Tales:* Routledge & Kegan Paul PLC

Angus MacLellan and John Lorne Campbell: *Stories from South Uist:* John Lorne Campbell

Sybil Marshall: *Everyman's Book of English Folk Tales:* J.M. Dent & Son Limited

Ernest W. Marwick: *The Folklore of Orkney and Shetland:* B.T. Batsford Limited

Sean O'Sullivan: *Folk Tales of Ireland:* Chicago University Press

Helen Waddell: *The Princess Splendour:* Mary M. Martin

Dora E. Yates: *A Book of Gypsy Folk-Tales:* The National Library of Wales

James Reeves: *English Fables and Fairy Stories:* John Johnson Limited

Introduction

The world in which Shakespeare wrote *A Midsummer Night's Dream*, printed in 1600, may well have been a place seething with folk customs, superstitions and enthralling tales. But the decline of the folk-tale, and it has been a most unconscionable time dying, was certainly already underway. Writing later in that same turbulent century, the sociable and scatty antiquary John Aubrey astutely reported in his 'Remaines of Judaisme and Gentilisme':

> Before Printing, Old-wives Tales were ingeniose, and since Printing came in fashion, till a little before the Civill-warres, the ordinary sort of People were not taught to reade. Now-a-dayes Bookes are common, and most of the poor people understand letters; and the many good Bookes, and variety of Turnes of Affaires, have putt all the old Fables out of doors: and the divine art of Printing and Gunpowder have frighted away Robin-goodfellow and the Fayries.

During the second half of the following century, the Industrial Revolution rapidly eroded rural life and continuities. The sons and daughters of people who never had occasion to stray more than a mile or two from their own villages, and for whom a trek to the county town – perhaps for a fair – was an annual event, gravitated to new mill and mining towns, or emigrated. This process, and the further advance of literacy that followed Sir Robert Peel's Education Act of 1834, naturally accelerated the demise of folk beliefs and the tales in which they were dressed. So that the Dublin bookseller Patrick Kennedy was articulating the fears of everyone who cared about roots when he wrote in 1866:

Taking into consideration the diminishing of our population by want and emigration, and the general diffusion of book learning, such as it is, and the growing taste for the rubbishy tales of the penny and halfpenny journals, we have in these latter times been haunted with the horrid thought that the memory of tales heard in boyhood would be irrecoverably lost.

This is the background against which one must set the resourceful, diverse and utterly invaluable work of folklorists during the nineteenth and twentieth centuries. For John Aubrey and the antiquaries who preceded and succeeded him, men such as William Camden and John Stow, John Brand and Joseph Strutt, were not so much interested in tales as beliefs and customs. They were students of Popular Antiquities – remains of the mental and physical past – of which folklore constituted only one part; and their omnium gatherums of descriptions of physical remains, brief biographies, legends and lore, drew far more extensively on earlier literary sources than on oral tradition.

The story of how, at the beginning of the nineteenth century, certain antiquaries began to turn their energies to fieldwork is vivid and exciting. As with the first years of any major endeavour, in our own time space exploration and open heart surgery, it was a time of big personalities, public argument and pioneering spirit.

First in Ireland and Scotland, then in England, still later in Wales, brilliant amateurs, inspired by the example of Wilhelm and Jacob Grimm in Germany, devoted summers or even whole years to the collection of folk-tales. As the decades passed, they became ever more concerned with precision; they were meticulous about the words themselves, recording them exactly as they heard them; they were meticulous about their sources and the circumstances of collection. They began to interpret the tales collected, to compare them with analogies and variants found in countries east and west, to argue over whether they all derived from one source, one master tale as it were, or whether they were of independent growth. What began as a serious hobby

2

had become, during the second part of the nineteenth century, a science.

The folklore movement in the British Isles reached its apotheosis in the years following the foundation of the Folk-Lore Society in 1878. The quarterly journal *Folk-Lore* was packed with information, speculation and provocation; the Society's annual conference was the scene of brilliant papers and fierce argument; polymaths and poets and publishers trod the stage alongside professional folklorists. Folk-tales were seen not only as worthy of study in their own right but as springboards for the creative – especially the literary – imagination and as illustrations of human behaviour that, with but little doctoring, would appeal to children.

Like so much else, this excitement was snuffed out by the First World War. What Richard Dorson calls 'a brilliant chapter of intellectual history' came to an end. In the last sixty years, folk studies have necessarily been more muted although names such as Iona and Peter Opie, Katharine Briggs and Ruth Tongue are evidence of enduring life in the body. The slow transition from fieldwork to scholarship is, however, irreversible. While tales will continue to be created for as long as there are people to tell and listen to them, and more fieldwork remains to be done especially amongst urban communities, the truth is that newspapers, radio and television have dealt severe blows to the oral tradition. People are no longer much good at entertaining themselves; they expect to be entertained.

The purpose of this anthology is firstly to illustrate the extraordinary range and quality of tales collected in the field in the British Isles; secondly, through these tales, to exemplify the work of as many of the great storytellers and collectors as possible; and thirdly, to show the literary reteller of tales at work in verse and prose: in short, to offer as representative an anthology of the folk-tales of the British Isles as seems possible. Each storyteller, collector and writer is briefly introduced in the paragraphs at the head of the book's twelve sections.

How to divide anthologies into manageable and meaningful

sections is often a vexed question. While recognising the force of Katharine Briggs' distinction between folk legend (an account of something believed to have happened) and folk narrative (folk fiction, told for edification or delight), and making use of it in the penultimate section, I have otherwise disregarded it as inappropriate to this anthology. Rather, I have divided the tales thematically (although in a number of cases a tale could equally well fit into two sections). Within each section, I have not arranged the tales or their collectors and retellers chronologically but with an eye for what makes the most satisfying artistic progression.

For in the end, it is the tales that matter most, not the scholarly paraphernalia they inspire. Here is a huge pageant of kings and heroes, horsedealers, hunchbacks and numbskulls, changelings and imps and bogles, ghosts and giants, dragons, magic bulls and black dogs, devils and witches; and here too are love and hate, hope and fear, courage and cowardice, patience and impetuosity, humour and humility. Folk-tales may offer us strange company and lead us on strange journeys, but their destinations seem to us entirely familiar. They are doorstep stories leading to a better understanding of ourselves and our own world. This, and our natural love of story, are the reasons for the folk-tale's perennial appeal.

So I come to my own doorstep and the matter of acknowledgments. Firstly, my thanks to Sue Bradbury and John Letts of The Folio Society and Phyllis Hunt of Faber & Faber for their faith in commissioning this anthology, prudent advice during its compilation and fortitude in waiting for it. To Debbie Felgate, my thanks for her diligence in typing it. For their courteous assistance, gratitude to the staff of the London Library; without its existence, the preparation of a book of this kind, involving a very great deal of reading, would be virtually impossible. In learning about the nineteenth century folklorists, Richard Dorson's history, *The British Folklorists* (Routledge and Kegan Paul, 1968) has been my indispensable companion. To the Winchester School of Art and the Arts Council of Great Britain, a grateful acknowledgement of the Fellowship in Writing for the years 1983 and 1984 during which I assembled and edited the anthology. My wife Gillian has, as usual, had to bear most of the daily brunt. To share a writer's life may be stimulating but is also very exacting and I am deeply grateful to her for her temperance and her sustaining belief in me.

I first heard so many of these tales from my father; he told them to me and my sister as we lay in our bunk beds, to still us before sleep. Sometimes he accompanied his tellings with the Welsh harp, and of fairy music he knows as much as any mortal may. To him this book is dedicated.

KEVIN CROSSLEY-HOLLAND

AIRIES

Fairies

'...Little as a dwarf, keen-eyed as a hawk, and of easy prepossessing manners.' So writes Sir Walter Scott of Thomas Crofton Croker (1798–1854), the Irish-born Admiralty clerk whose *Fairy Legends and Traditions from the South of Ireland* (1825) was the first volume of folk-tales in the British Isles not culled from an amalgam of sources but expressly collected in the field. For his part Crofton Croker was thrilled to meet the great Scottish antiquary and novelist, and in a letter to his sister proudly records him as saying, 'I am glad to see you, Mr Croker, you and I are not unknown to each other . . . You are our (I speak of the Celtic nations) great authority now on Fairy Superstition, and have made Fairy Land your kingdom . . .'

The thirty-eight tales in *Fairy Legends* were an immediate critical and sales success. The publisher John Murray encouraged Crofton Croker to return to Cork, Waterford and Limerick in search of more material, and the founding fathers of nineteenth-century folklore, Wilhelm and Jacob Grimm, translated the book into German. Although Crofton Croker was prepared to doctor his tales in a way that later folklorists considered intrusive and unscientific, and tended to stereotype characters (see Yeats's comments on p.311–12), he is esteemed by folklorists not only for the basic authenticity of his tales but for his illuminating notes in which he describes his sources and the circumstances in which the tales were collected, and also interprets aspects of them.

So, for *The Legend of Knockgrafton* (a tale I remember hearing from my father at the age of four or five), Crofton Croker prints 'this rude melody, which is certainly, from its construction, very ancient' and tells us that it is 'commonly sung by every skilful narrator of the tale, to render the recitation more effective'.

Crofton Croker also provides a useful gloss on the name of the

The 'rude melody' from 'The Legend of Knockgrafton'

first hunchback. 'Lusmore, literally the *great herb,* is specifically applied to that graceful and hardy plant the *digitalis purpurea,* usually called by the peasantry Fairy Cap "from the supposed resemblance of its bells to this part of fairy dress".' *The Legend of Knockgrafton* introduces us to what might be called the price of disrespect. There are certain rules that must be observed by humans who have dealings with fairies, and those who ignore them do so at their peril. As we pass through this section, meeting kindly fairies, imps and evil fairies, as well as people of the sea, it is a theme we will encounter again.

Tom Tit Tot is a delicious Suffolk variant of a tale also found in Germany, Ireland, Finland and Denmark, and first collected by the brothers Grimm ('Rumpelstilzchen') in their *Kinder- und Hausmärchen* (1812). It was written down by Mrs A. Walter Thomas who had heard it as a girl from her old West Suffolk nurse, and first printed in the *Ipswich Journal* in 1878. Here, it later caught the eye of Edward Clodd (1840-1930), a banker who lived in London and Aldeburgh and became President of the Folk-Lore Society in 1895. Already interested in name magic (the belief that power resides in a name), Clodd made it the subject first of an article for the *Folk-Lore Journal* and then of his monograph *Tom Tit Tot, an Essay on Savage Philosophy in Folk-Tale* (1898), a comparative work on name spells in primitive magic.

There is so much humour in the telling of this tale that Tom Tit Tot himself, an irresistible creation, seems more impish than sinister. Mrs Walter Thomas and her sister, Miss L. A. Fison, also recorded a little-known sequel to *Tom Tit Tot* in which the heroine has no sooner rid herself of 'that snaisty little black impet' than her king-husband demands she spin *five* skeins every day, a dilemma only resolved with the help of a crafty word-spinning gypsy.

Sir John Rhys (1840-1916) is the cornerstone of Welsh folk studies. Elected to the first chair in Celtic at Oxford in 1877 and subsequently Principal of Jesus College, he was firstly a philologist who, like so many Victorian scholars, entertained a host of interests – the history of religion, archaeology, ethnology, and ultimately folklore. Inspired by John Francis Campbell's *Popular Tales of the West Highlands*, and well aware that increasing literacy and the dislocation of rural communities was leading to a breakdown of oral tradition, Rhys collected a large body of material in the field and by letter about the fairy people – *y Twlwyth Teg* – over a period of thirty years. What his massive *Celtic Folklore* (2 volumes, 1901) reveals, however, is that Welsh oral tradition was nothing like as rich as its Celtic counterparts in

Scotland and Ireland, a discovery all the more unexpected and disappointing when one thinks of the quite extraordinary imaginative colour, folk belief and energy in *The Mabinogion*.

Nevertheless, there are several magnificent Welsh tales in *Celtic Folklore* – all presented in a number of variants – and one of them is the Carmarthenshire legend of *The Lady of Llyn y Fan Fach*. The recognition test, the taboo of the three blows, and the aetiological element of the 'well-marked furrow ... which remains to this day' combine in a story which perfectly shows how marriages between human and supernatural beings will never last for long, and leave the human partner with a terrible sense of loss. The version printed here was taken by Rhys from *The Physicians of Myddvai* (1861) which examines the fascinating historical sequel to the tale – the tale in itself of how Rhiwallon and his sons became physicians to the Lord of Llandovery and Dynefor Castles 'who gave them rank, lands, and privileges at Myddvai for their maintenance in the practice of their art and science, and the healing and benefit of those who should seek their help', and how physicians continued to practise at Myddvai until the third decade of the eighteenth century.

One may read *The Fairy Horse Dealer* as a simple morality tale in praise of integrity (the Manxman has no way of telling that the purchaser is a supernatural being until after the deal has been completed) or as a lesson on the importance of rectitude in dealings with the fairies. It is one of a number of short tales collected by George Waldron, an English civil servant sent to Man to report on its export and import activities, *The History and Description of the Isle of Man* (1744).

The natural affection that exists between humans and seals has given rise to many folk-tales and folk beliefs, none of them more haunting than that of *The Woman of the Sea*, a story claimed by a number of the Northern Isles and here attributed to Unst in Shetland. The tale-type has affinities with *The Lady of Llyn y Fan Fach*, for here is another union between male mortal and female fairy that is not destined to last, while in some versions the seal woman also returns like the lady of the lake to give her children

12

medical knowledge. The tradition that there are still a few families with webbed fingers or toes, or horny skin on their hands and feet, indicating descent from a seal-woman is still current in the north of Scotland.

Helen Waddell (1889-1965) used her great gifts as a historian, novelist and translator to make the Middle Ages live and sing for the non-specialist. Readers who are familiar with her enchanting tales of the early Celtic saints in *Beasts and Saints* will not be surprised at *The Woman of the Sea*'s simplicity and grace.

Early British folklore – and more especially Scottish folklore – derived both direction and prestige from Sir Walter Scott's (1771–1832) association with it. More wide-ranging than the brothers Grimm in his interests and talents, and internationally known for his historical romances, the Waverley Novels, he was an immensely prolific man as well as a generous friend ready to provide material and regularly correspond with those with like interests. His first major work, *The Minstrelsy of the Scottish Border* (1802), inspired by Bishop Percy's *Reliques of Ancient English Poetry* (1765), contained a wealth of historical, traditional and romantic ballads, Border lore, physical antiquities and literary invention, but balanced a respect for the old antiquarian tradition with an enthusiasm for the living oral tradition in a way that stimulated and influenced those who followed him into the field. His subsequent folklore publications included *Border Antiquities of England and Scotland* (1814-17) and *Letters on Demonology and Witchcraft* (1830).

Scott collated several printed copies of *The Young Tamlane* with oral recitations he had himself collected to achieve the version reprinted here, and noted that the ballad was still popular in Ettrick Forest and that 'in no part of Scotland, indeed, has the belief in fairies maintained its ground with more pertinacity than in Selkirkshire'. The ballad teems with folk beliefs about the fairies. 'Here' in Katharine Briggs's words

we have the summoning of a spirit by breaking the branch of a tree sacred to him, the *fairy rade* with its jingling bells at

Hallowe'en, the time most sacred to fairies, the fairy *knowe*, the *teind* to Hell, so characteristic of Scottish Fairyland – the rescue from Fairyland by holding fast, the *shape-shifting* of the captive, and the essential ill-will of the Fairy Queen.

Another longstanding belief about the fairies was that from time to time they stole human children, to strengthen their own stock, to pay them over as tithes to Hell, or simply because they found human beauty irresistible. This is what underlies the short tale *Brewery of Eggshells* taken by Joseph Jacobs (1854–1916) from the *Cambrian Quarterly Magazine* (1830) and included by him in *Celtic Fairy Tales* (1892).

Jacobs was equally influential as a Jewish historian and as a folklorist. He persuasively argued the diffusionist theory that variants of a tale found in different countries derived from a single original source against the view of survivalists such as Andrew Lang that such tales were of independent growth; he wrote introductory essays to several editions of fables; he edited the journal *Folk-Lore* in its heyday from 1889 until 1900; and he won wide popularity with his five books of tales (two Celtic, two English and one Indian) retold for children.

Yallery Brown introduces us to that kind of fairy with whom it is unwise to have any traffic at all. It is one of the strikingly atmospheric group of tales collected by Mrs M. C. Balfour in the Lincolnshire Cars – the fens of Lindsey – and printed by her in three numbers of *Folk-Lore* in 1891. The broad dialect of the original makes very difficult reading and the version printed here is by Alan Garner, one of the leading writers for children at work today, whose own novels have regularly drawn on folk beliefs and who calls *Yallery Brown* 'the most powerful of all English folk tales'.

Thomas Keightley (1789–1872), who grew up in County Kildare before gravitating to London and Grub Street, provided Thomas Crofton Croker with four tales and many notes which Croker used in *Fairy Tales and Legends* without giving him coin or credit for it; after Keightley had protested in public, Croker confined himself in later editions to the tales he had personally collected. We can however be grateful to Croker for awakening in Keightley a passionate interest in the world of faerie. Keightley's *The Fairy Mythology* (1828), in which he set himself 'to collect, arrange, classify and give under one point of view the various ideas and legends respecting the Fairies and similar beings of the popular creed, which lie scattered in a variety of books and a variety of languages', is a pioneering work, written at a time when comparative folklore was still in its infancy.

In it, Keightley confessed that the genial tale of *The Soul Cages* (which was first published by Croker) had not been collected in the field but was partly based on a German tale (in which, in his underwater house, a waterman shows a peasant a number of pots turned upside down, and tells him they contain the souls of drowned people) and partly pure invention. But Keightley also noted that he later discovered the tale was 'well-known on the coast of Cork and Wicklow'. As ever, truth is stranger than fiction.

Several tales tell of the *Departure of the Fairies,* more often than not because they cannot stand the sound of church bells. Rudyard Kipling's 'Dymchurch Flit' in *Puck of Pook's Hill* is a memorable literary treatment of this theme. The short version printed here is included by Hugh Miller (1802–1856) in *Old Red Sandstone* (1841); and he says that the events described took place at the Burn of Eathie in Aberdeenshire. Miller himself, ambitious, brooding and untidy, came from Cromarty. Primarily thought of in his own time as a geologist and theologian, he is best remembered as a folklorist. His *Scenes and Legends of the North of Scotland* (1835), inspired by Sir Walter Scott, and the autobiographical *My School and Schoolmasters* (1854) together reveal, in the words of Richard Dorson, 'what the whole literature of folklore rarely divulges, the place that folk tradition occupies in the life of a town, and in the life of a man'.

The Legend of Knockgrafton

THERE was once a poor man who lived in the fertile glen of
Aherlow, at the foot of the gloomy Galtee mountains, and he had
a great hump on his back: he looked just as if his body had been
rolled up and placed upon his shoulders; and his head was
pressed down with the weight so much, that his chin, when he
was sitting, used to rest upon his knees for support. The country
people were rather shy of meeting him in any lonesome place,
for though, poor creature, he was as harmless and as inoffensive
as a new-born infant, yet his deformity was so great, that he
scarcely appeared to be a human creature, and some ill-minded
persons had set strange stories about him afloat. He was said to
have a great knowledge of herbs and charms; but certain it was
that he had a mighty skilful hand in plaiting straw and rushes
into hats and baskets, which was the way he made his liveli-
hood.

Lusmore, for that was the nickname put upon him by reason
of his always wearing a sprig of the fairy cap, or lusmore (the
foxglove), in his little straw hat, would ever get a higher penny

for his plaited work than any one else, and perhaps that was the reason why some one, out of envy, had circulated the strange stories about him. Be that as it may, it happened that he was returning one evening from the pretty town of Cahir towards Cappagh, and as little Lusmore walked very slowly, on account of the great hump upon his back, it was quite dark when he came to the old moat of Knockgrafton, which stood on the right-hand side of his road. Tired and weary was he, and noways comfortable in his own mind at thinking how much farther he had to travel, and that he should be walking all the night; so he sat down under the moat to rest himself, and began looking mournfully enough upon the moon, which

> *Rising in clouded majesty, at length,*
> *Apparent queen, unveil'd her peerless light,*
> *And o'er the dark her silver mantle threw.*

Presently there rose a wild strain of unearthly melody upon the ear of little Lusmore; he listened, and he thought that he had never heard such ravishing music before. It was like the sound of many voices, each mingling and blending with the other so strangely, that they seemed to be one, though all singing different strains, and the words of the song were these: *Da Luan, Da Mort, Da Luan, Da Mort, Da Luan, Da Mort,** when there would be a moment's pause, and then the round of melody went on again.

Lusmore listened attentively, scarcely drawing his breath lest he might lose the slightest note. He now plainly perceived that the singing was within the moat, and though at first it had charmed him so much, he began to get tired of hearing the same round sung over and over so often without any change; so availing himself of the pause when the *Da Luan, Da Mort,* had been sung three times, he took up the tune and raised it with the words *augus Da Cadine,*[†] and then went on singing with the voices inside of the moat, *Da Luan, Da Mort,* finishing the melody, when the pause again came, with *augus Da Cadine.*

*Monday, Tuesday. †Wednesday.

17

The fairies within Knockgrafton, for the song was a fairy melody, when they heard this addition to their tune, were so much delighted, that with instant resolve it was determined to bring the mortal among them, whose musical skill so far exceeded theirs, and little Lusmore was conveyed into their company with the eddying speed of a whirlwind.

Glorious to behold was the sight that burst upon him as he came down through the moat, twirling round and round and round with the lightness of a straw, to the sweetest music that kept time to his motion. The greatest honour was then paid him, for he was put up above all the musicians, and he had servants 'tending upon him, and everything to his heart's content, and a hearty welcome to all; and in short he was made as much of as if he had been the first man in the land.

Presently Lusmore saw a great consultation going forward among the fairies, and, notwithstanding all their civility, he felt very much frightened, until one stepping out from the rest came up to him and said:

> *'Lusmore! Lusmore!*
> *Doubt not, nor deplore,*
> *For the hump which you bore*
> *On your back is no more;*
> *Look down on the floor,*
> *And view it, Lusmore!'*

When these words were said, poor little Lusmore felt himself so light, and so happy, that he thought he could have bounded at one jump over the moon, like the cow in the history of the cat and the fiddle; and he saw, with inexpressible pleasure, his hump tumble down upon the ground from his shoulders. He then tried to lift up his head, and he did so with becoming caution, fearing that he might knock it against the ceiling of the grand hall, where he was; he looked round and round again with the greatest wonder and delight upon everything, which appeared more and more beautiful; and overpowered at beholding such a resplendent scene, his head grew dizzy, and his eyesight became dim. At last he fell into a sound sleep, and when he awoke he found that it was broad daylight, the sun shining brightly, the birds singing sweet; and that he was lying just at the foot of the moat of Knockgrafton, with the cows and sheep grazing peaceably round about him. The first thing Lusmore did, after saying his prayers, was to put his hand behind to feel for his hump, but no sign of one was there on his back, and he looked at himself with great pride, for he had now become a well-shaped, dapper little fellow; and more than that, found himself in a full suit of new clothes, which he concluded the fairies had made for him.

Towards Cappagh he went, stepping out as lightly, and springing up at every step as if he had been all his life a dancing-master. Not a creature who met Lusmore knew him without his hump, and he had great work to persuade everyone that he was the same man – in truth he was not, so far as outward appearance went.

Of course it was not long before the story of Lusmore's hump got about, and a great wonder was made of it. Through the country, for miles round, it was the talk of every one, high and low.

One morning as Lusmore was sitting contented enough at his cabin door, up came an old woman to him, and asked if he could direct her to Cappagh?

'I need give you no directions, my good woman,' said Lusmore, 'for this is Cappagh; and whom may you want here?'

'I have come', said the woman, 'out of Decie's country, in the county of Waterford, looking after one Lusmore, who, I have heard tell, had his hump taken off by the fairies: for there is a son of a gossip of mine who has got a hump on him that will be his death; and may be, if he could use the same charm as Lusmore, the hump may be taken off him. And now I have told you the reason of my coming so far: 'tis to find out about this charm, if I can.'

Lusmore, who was ever a good-natured little fellow, told the woman all the particulars, how he had raised the tune for the fairies at Knockgrafton, how his hump had been removed from his shoulders, and how he had got a new suit of clothes into the bargain.

The woman thanked him very much, and then went away quite happy and easy in her own mind. When she came back to her gossip's house, in the county Waterford, she told her everything that Lusmore had said, and they put the little hump-backed man, who was a peevish and cunning creature from his birth, upon a car, and took him all the way across the country. It was a long journey, but they did not care for that, so the hump was taken from off him; and they brought him, just at nightfall, and left him under the old moat of Knockgrafton.

Jack Madden, for that was the humpy man's name, had not been sitting there long when he heard the tune going on within the moat much sweeter than before; for the fairies were singing it the way Lusmore had settled their music for them, and the song was going on: *Da Luan, Da Mort, Da Luan, Da Mort, Da Luan, Da Mort, augus Da Cadine*, without ever stopping. Jack Madden, who was in a great hurry to get quit of his hump, never thought of waiting until the fairies had done, or watching for a fit opportunity to raise the tune higher again than Lusmore had: so having heard them sing it over seven times without stopping, out he bawls, never minding the time, or the humour of the tune, or how he could bring his words in properly, *augus Da Cadine, augus Da Hena*,* thinking that if one day was good, two were better; and that if Lusmore had one new suit of clothes given him, he should have two.

No sooner had the words passed his lips than he was taken up and whisked into the moat with prodigious force; and the fairies came crowding round about him with great anger, screeching and screaming, and roaring out, 'who spoiled our tune? who spoiled our tune?' and one stepped up to him above all the rest and said:

---

*Wednesday, Thursday.

'Jack Madden! Jack Madden!
Your words came so bad in
The tune we feel glad in;
This castle you're had in,
That your life we may sadden;
Here's two humps for Jack Madden!'

And twenty of the strongest fairies brought Lusmore's hump and put it down upon poor Jack's back, over his own, where it became fixed as firmly as if it was nailed on with twelve-penny nails, by the best carpenter that ever drove one. Out of their castle they then kicked him, and in the morning when Jack Madden's mother and her gossip came to look after their little man, they found him half dead, lying at the foot of the moat, with the other hump upon his back. Well to be sure, how they did look at each other! but they were afraid to say anything, lest a hump might be put upon their own shoulders. Home they brought the unlucky Jack Madden with them, as downcast in their hearts and their looks as ever two gossips were; and what through the weight of his other hump, and the long journey, he died soon after, leaving, they say, his heavy curse to any one who would go to listen to fairy tunes again.

Tom Tit Tot

WELL, once upon a time there were a woman and she baked five pies. And when they come out of the oven, they was that overbaked, the crust were too hard to eat. So she says to her darter:

'Maw'r,'* says she, 'put you them there pies on the shelf an' leave 'em there a little, an' they'll come agin' – she meant, you know, the crust 'ud get soft.

But the gal, she says to herself, 'Well, if they'll come agin, I'll ate 'em now.' And she set to work and ate 'em all, first and last.

Well, come supper time the woman she said, 'Goo you and git one o' them there pies. I dare say they've came agin now.'

The gal she went an' she looked, and there warn't nothin' but the dishes. So back she come and says she, 'Noo, they ain't come agin.'

'Not none on 'em?' says the mother.

'Not none on 'em,' says she.

'Well, come agin, or not come agin,' says the woman, 'I'll ha' one for supper.'

*Short for *mawther*: daughter, maid.

22

'But you can't, if they ain't come,' says the gal.

'But I can,' says she. 'Goo you and bring the best of 'em.'

'Best or worst,' says the gal, 'I've ate 'em all, and you can't ha' one till that's come agin.'

Well, the woman she were wholly bate, and she took her spinnin' to the door to spin, and as she span she sang:

> '*My darter ha' ate five, five pies today –*
> *My darter ha' ate five, five pies today.*'

The king he were a comin' down the street an' he hard her sing, but what she sang he couldn't hare, so he stopped and said:

'What were that you was a singun of, maw'r?'

The woman, she were ashamed to let him hare what her darter had been a doin', so she sang, 'stids o' that:

> '*My darter ha' spun five, five skeins today –*
> *My darter ha' spun five, five skeins today.*'

'S'ars o' mine!' said the king, 'I never heerd tell of anyone as could do that.'

Then he said: 'Look you here, I want a wife, and I'll marry your darter. But look you here,' says he, ''leven months out o' the year she shall have all the vittles she likes to eat, and all the gownds she likes to git, and all the cumpny she likes to hev; but the last month o' the year she'll ha' to spin five skeins iv'ry day, an' if she doon't, I shall kill her.'

'All right,' says the woman: for she thowt what a grand marriage that was. And as for them five skeins, when te come tew, there'd be plenty o' ways of gettin' out of it, and likeliest, he'd ha' forgot about it.

Well, so they was married. An' for 'leven months the gal had all the vittles she liked to eat, and all the gownds she liked to git, an' all the cumpny she liked to hev.

But when the time was gettin' oover, she began to think about them skeins an' to wonder if he had 'em in mind. But not one word did he say about 'em, an' she whoolly thowt he'd forgot 'em.

Howsivir, the last day o' the last month, he takes her to a room she'd niver set eyes on afore. There worn't nothin' in it but a spinnin' wheel and a stool. An' says he, 'Now, me dear, hare yow'll be shut in tomorrow with some vittles and some flax, and if you hain't spun five skeins by the night, yar hid'll goo off.'

An' awa' he went about his business.

Well, she were that frightened. She'd allus been such a gatless mawther, that she didn't se much as know how to spin, an' what were she to dew tomorrer, with no one to come nigh her to help her. She sat down on a stool in the kitchen, and lork! how she did cry!

Howsivir, all on a sudden she hard a sort of a knockin' low down on the door. She upped and oped it, an' what should she see but a small little black thing with a long tail. That looked up at her right kewrious, an' that said:

'What are yew a cryin' for?'

'Wha's that to yew?' says she.

'Niver yew mind,' that said, 'but tell me what you're a cryin' for.'

'That oon't dew me noo good if I dew,' says she.

'Yew doon't know that,' that said, an' twirled that's tail round.

'Well,' says she, 'that oon't dew no harm, if that doon't dew no good,' and she upped and told about the pies an' the skeins an' everything.

'This is what I'll dew,' says the little black thing: 'I'll come to yar winder iv'ry mornin' an' take the flax an' bring it spun at night.'

'What's your pay?' says she.

That looked out o' the corners o' that's eyes an' that said: 'I'll give you three guesses every night to guess my name, an' if you hain't guessed it afore the month's up, yew shall be mine.'

Well, she thowt she'd be sure to guess that's name afore the month was up. 'All right,' says she, 'I agree.'

'All right,' that says, an' lork! how that twirled that's tail.

24

Well, the next day, har husband he took her inter the room, an' there was the flax an' the day's vittles.

'Now, there's the flax,' says he, 'an' if that ain't spun up this night off goo yar hid.' An' then he went out an' locked the door.

He'd hardly goon, when there was a knockin' agin the winder.

She upped and she oped it, and there sure enough was the little oo'd thing a settin' on the ledge.

'Where's the flax?' says he.

'Here te be,' says she. And she gonned it to him.

Well, come the evening', a knockin' come agin to the winder. She upped an' she oped it, and there were the little oo'd thing, with five skeins of flax on his arm.

'Here te be,' says he, an' he gonned it to her.

'Now, what's my name?' says he.

'What, is that Bill?' says she.

'Noo, that ain't,' says he. An' he twirled his tail.

'Is that Ned?' says she.

'Noo, that ain't,' says he. An' he twirled his tail.

'Well, is that Mark?' says she.

'Noo, that ain't,' says he. An' he twirled his tail harder, an' awa' he flew.

Well, when har husban' he come in: there was the five skeins riddy for him. 'I see I shorn't hev for to kill you tonight, me dare,' says he. 'Ycw'll hev yar vittles and yar flax in the mornin',' says he, an' away he goes.

Well, ivery day the flax an' the vittles, they was browt, an' ivery day that there little black impet used for to come mornin's and evenin's. An' all the day the mawther she set a trying' fur to think of names to say to it when te come at night. But she niver hot on the right one. An' as that got towarts the ind o' the month, the impet that began for to look soo maliceful, an' that twirled that's tail faster an' faster each time she gave a guess.

At last te come to the last day but one. The impet that come at night along o' the five skeins, an' that said:

'What, hain't yew got my name yet?'

'Is that Nicodemus?' says she.

'Noo, t'ain't,' that says.

'Is that Sammle?' says she.

'Noo, t'ain't,' that says.

'A-well, is that Methusalem?' says she.

'Noo, t'ain't that norther,' he says.

Then that looks at her with that's eyes like a cool o' fire, an' that says, 'Woman, there's only tomorrer night, an' then yar'll be mine !' An' away te flew.

Well, she felt that horrud. Howsomediver, she hard the king a coming along the passage. In he came, an' when he see the five skeins, he says, says he !

'Well, me dare,' says he, 'I don't see but what yew'll ha' your skeins ready tomorrer night as well, an' as i reckon I shorn't ha' to kill you, I'll ha' supper in here tonight.' So they brought supper, an' another stool for him, and down the tew they sat.

Well, he hadn't eat but a mouthful or so, when he stops and begins to laugh.

'What is it?' says she.

'A-why,' says he, 'I was out a-huntin' today, an' I got away to a place in the wood I'd never seen afore. An' there was an old chalk pit. An' I heerd a sort of a hummin', kind o'. So I got off my hobby, an' I went right quiet to the pit, an' I looked down. Well, what should there be but the funniest little black thing yew iver set eyes on. An' what was that a dewin' on, but that had a little spinnin' wheel, an' that were a spinnin' wonnerful fast, an' a twirlin' that's tail. An' as that span, that sang:

> '*Nimmy nimmy not,*
> *My name's Tom Tit Tot.*'

Well, when the mawther heerd this, she fared as if she could ha' jumped outer her skin for joy, but she di'n't say a word.

Next day, that there little thing looked soo maliceful when he come for the flax. An' when night came, she heerd that a knockin' agin the winder panes. She oped the winder, an' that come right in on the ledge. That were grinnin' from are to are, an' Oo ! tha's tail were twirlin' round so fast.

'What's my name?' that says, as that gonned her the skeins.

'Is that Solomon?' she says, pretendin' to be afeard.

'Noo, t'ain't,' that says, an' that come fudder inter the room.

'Well, is that Zebedee ?' says she agin.

'Noo, t'ain't,' says the impet. An' then that laughed an' twirled that's tail till yew cou'n't hardly see it.

'Take time, woman,' that says; 'next guess, an you're mine.' An' that stretched out that's black hands at her.

Well, she backed a step or two, an' she looked at it, and then she laughed out, an' says she, a pointin' of her finger at it:

> 'Nimmy nimmy not,
> Yar name's Tom Tit Tot.'

Well, when that hard her, that shruck awful an' awa' that flew into the dark, an' she niver saw it noo more.

The Lady of Llyn y Fan Fach

WHEN the eventful struggle made by the Princes of South Wales to preserve the independence of their country was drawing to its close in the twelfth century, there lived at Blaensawdde near Llanddeusant, Carmarthenshire, a widowed woman, the relict of a farmer who had fallen in those disastrous troubles.

The widow had an only son to bring up, but Providence smiled upon her, and despite her forlorn condition, her live stock had so increased in course of time, that she could not well depasture them upon her farm, so she sent a portion of her cattle to graze on the adjoining Black Mountain, and their most favourite place was near the small lake called Llyn y Fan Fach, on the north-western side of the Carmarthenshire Fans.

The son grew up to manhood, and was generally sent by his mother to look after the cattle on the mountain. One day, in his peregrinations along the margin of the lake, to his great astonishment, he beheld, sitting on the unruffled surface of the water, a lady; one of the most beautiful creatures that mortal eyes ever beheld, her hair flowed gracefully in ringlets over her shoulders,

28

the tresses of which she arranged with a comb, whilst the glassy surface of her watery couch served for the purpose of a mirror, reflecting back her own image. Suddenly she beheld the young man standing on the brink of the lake, with his eyes riveted on her, and unconsciously offering to herself the provision of barley bread and cheese with which he had been provided when he left his home.

Bewildered by a feeling of love and admiration for the object before him, he continued to hold out his hand towards the lady, who imperceptibly glided near to him, but gently refused the offer of his provisions. He attempted to touch her, but she eluded his grasp, saying:

> 'Cras dy fara;
> Nid hawdd fy nala.'
>
> *Hard baked is thy bread!*
> *'Tis not easy to catch me.*

and immediately dived under the water and disappeared, leaving the love-stricken youth to return home, a prey to disappointment and regret that he had been unable to make further acquaintance with one, in comparison with whom the whole of the fair maidens of Llanddeusant and Myddfai* whom he had ever seen were as nothing.

*Myddfai parish was, in former times, celebrated for its fair maidens, but whether they were descendants of the Lady of the Lake or otherwise cannot be determined. An old pennill records the fact of their beauty thus:

> *Mae eira gwyn*
> *Ar ben y bryn,*
> *A'r glasgoed yn y Ferdre,*
> *Mae bedw mân*
> *Ynghoed Cwm-brân,*
> *A merched glân yn Myddfe.*

Which may be translated,

> *There is white snow*
> *On the mountain's brow,*
> *And greenwood at the Verdre,*
> *Young birch so good*
> *In Cwm-brân wood,*
> *And lovely girls in Myddfe.*   [J.R.]

On his return home the young man communicated to his mother the extraordinary vision he had beheld. She advised him to take some unbaked dough or 'toes' the next time in his pocket, as there must have been some spell connected with the hard-baked bread, or 'Bara cras', which prevented his catching the lady.

Next morning, before the sun had gilded with its rays the peaks of the Fans, the young man was at the lake, not for the purpose of looking after his mother's cattle, but seeking for the same enchanting vision he had witnessed the day before; but all in vain did he anxiously strain his eyeballs and glance over the surface of the lake, as only the ripples occasioned by a stiff breeze met his view, and a cloud hung heavily on the summit of the Fan, which imparted an additional gloom to his already distracted mind.

Hours passed on, the wind was hushed, and the clouds which had enveloped the mountain had vanished into thin air before the powerful beams of the sun, when the youth was startled by seeing some of his mother's cattle on the precipitous side of the acclivity, nearly on the opposite side of the lake. His duty impelled him to attempt to rescue them from their perilous position, for which purpose he was hastening away, when, to his inexpressible delight, the object of his search again appeared to him as before, and seemed much more beautiful than when he first beheld her. His hand was again held out to her, full of unbaked bread, which he offered with an urgent proffer of his heart also, and vows of eternal attachment. All of which were refused by her, saying:

> 'Llaith dy fara!
> Ti ni fynna.'
>
> *Unbaked is thy bread!*
> *I will not have thee.*

But the smiles that played upon her features as the lady vanished beneath the waters raised within the young man a

30

hope that forbade him to despair by her refusal of him, and the recollection of which cheered him on his way home. His aged parent was made acquainted with his ill-success, and she suggested that his bread should next time be but slightly baked, as most likely to please the mysterious being of whom he had become enamoured.

Impelled by an irresistible feeling, the youth left his mother's house early next morning, and with rapid steps he passed over the mountain. He was soon near the margin of the lake, and with all the impatience of an ardent lover did he wait with a feverish anxiety for the reappearance of the mysterious lady.

The sheep and goats browsed on the precipitous sides of the Fan; the cattle strayed amongst the rocks and large stones, some of which were occasionally loosened from their beds and suddenly rolled down into the lake; rain and sunshine alike came and passed away; but all were unheeded by the youth, so wrapped up was he in looking for the appearance of the lady.

The freshness of the early morning had disappeared before the sultry rays of the noonday sun, which in its turn was fast verging towards the west as the evening was dying away and making room for the shades of night, and hope had wellnigh abated of beholding once more the Lady of the Lake. The young man cast a sad and last farewell look over the waters, and, to his astonishment, beheld several cows walking along its surface. The sight of these animals caused hope to revive that they would be followed by another object far more pleasing; nor was he disappointed, for the maiden reappeared, and to his enraptured sight, even lovelier than ever. She approached the land, and he rushed to meet her in the water. A smile encouraged him to seize her hand; neither did she refuse the moderately baked bread he offered her; and after some persuasion she consented to become his bride, on condition that they should only live together until she received from him three blows without a cause,

Tri ergyd diachos.

Three causeless blows.

31

And if he ever should happen to strike her three such blows she would leave him for ever. To such conditions he readily consented, and would have consented to any other stipulation, had it been proposed, as he was only intent on then securing such a lovely creature for his wife.

Thus the Lady of the Lake engaged to become the young man's wife, and having loosed her hand for a moment she darted away and dived into the lake. His chagrin and grief were such that he determined to cast himself headlong into the deepest water, so as to end his life in the element that had contained in its unfathomed depths the only one for whom he cared to live on earth. As he was on the point of committing this rash act, there emerged out of the lake *two* most beautiful ladies, accompanied by a hoary-headed man of noble mien and extraordinary stature, but having otherwise all the force and strength of youth. This man addressed the almost bewildered youth in accents calculated to soothe his troubled mind, saying that as he proposed to marry one of his daughters, he consented to the union, provided the young man could distinguish which of the two ladies before him was the object of his affections. This was no easy task, as the maidens were such perfect counterparts of each other that it seemed quite impossible for him to choose his bride, and if perchance he fixed upon the wrong one all would be for ever lost.

Whilst the young man narrowly scanned the two ladies, he could not perceive the least difference betwixt the two, and was almost giving up the task in despair, when one of them thrust her foot a slight degree forward. The motion, simple as it was, did not escape the observation of the youth, and he discovered a trifling variation in the mode with which their sandals were tied. This at once put an end to the dilemma, for he, who had on previous occasions been so taken up with the general appearance of the Lady of the Lake, had also noticed the beauty of her feet and ankles, and on now recognizing the peculiarity of her shoe-tie he boldly took hold of her hand.

'Thou hast chosen rightly,' said her father; 'be to her a kind and faithful husband, and I will give her, as a dowry, as many sheep, cattle, goats, and horses as she can count of each without heaving or drawing in her breath. But remember, that if you prove unkind to her at any time, and strike her three times without a cause, she shall return to me, and shall bring all her stock back with her.'

Such was the verbal marriage settlement, to which the young man gladly assented, and his bride was desired to count the number of sheep she was to have. She immediately adopted the mode of counting by *fives*, thus: One, two, three, four, five – One, two, three, four, five; as many times as possible in rapid succession, till her breath was exhausted. The same process of reckoning had to determine the number of goats, cattle, and horses respectively; and in an instant the full number of each came out of the lake when called upon by the father.

The young couple were then married, by what ceremony was not stated, and afterwards went to reside at a farm called Esgair Llaethdy, somewhat more than a mile from the village of Myddfai, where they lived in prosperity and happiness for several years, and became the parents of three sons, who were beautiful children.

Once upon a time there was a christening to take place in the neighbourhood, to which the parents were specially invited. When the day arrived the wife appeared very reluctant to attend the christening, alleging that the distance was too great for her to walk. Her husband told her to fetch one of the horses which were grazing in an adjoining field. 'I will,' said she, 'if you will bring me my gloves which I left in our house.' He went to the house and returned with the gloves, and finding that she had not gone for the horse jocularly slapped her shoulder with one of them, saying, 'go! go! (*dos dos*), when she reminded him of the understanding upon which she consented to marry him – that he was not to strike her without a cause – and warned him to be more cautious for the future.

On another occasion, when they were together at a wedding, in the midst of the mirth and hilarity of the assembled guests, who had gathered together from all the surrounding country, she burst into tears and sobbed most piteously. Her husband touched her on her shoulder and inquired the cause of her weeping: she said, 'Now people are entering into trouble, and your troubles are likely to commence, as you have the *second* time stricken me without a cause.'

Years passed on, and their children had grown up, and were particularly clever young men. In the midst of so many worldly blessings at home the husband almost forgot that there remained only *one* causeless blow to be given to destroy the whole of his prosperity. Still he was watchful lest any trivial occurrence should take place which his wife must regard as a breach of their marriage contract. She told him, as her affection for him was unabated, to be careful that he would not, through some inadvertence, give the last and only blow, which, by an unalterable destiny, over which she had no control, would separate them for ever.

It, however, so happened that one day they were together at a funeral, where, in the midst of the mourning and grief at the house of the deceased, she appeared in the highest and gayest spirits, and indulged in immoderate fits of laughter, which so shocked her husband that he touched her, saying, 'Hush! hush! don't laugh.' She said that she laughed 'because people when they die go out of trouble,' and, rising up, she went out of the house, saying, 'The last blow has been struck, our marriage contract is broken, and at an end! Farewell!' Then she started off towards Esgair Llaethdy, where she called her cattle and other stock together, each by name. The cattle she called thus:

> 'Mu wlfrech, Moelfrech,
> Mu olfrech, Gwynfrech,
> Pedair cae tonn-frech,
> Yr hen wynebwen.
> A'r las Geigen,
> Gyda'r Tarw Gwyn
> O lys y Brenin;
> A'r llo du bach,

34

Sydd ar y bach,
Dere dithau, yn iach adre!'

Brindled cow, white speckled,
Spotted cow, bold freckled,
The four field sward mottled,
The old white-faced,
And the grey Geingen,
With the white bull,
From the court of the king;
And the little black calf
Tho' suspended on the hook,
Come thou also, quite well home!

They all immediately obeyed the summons of their mistress. The 'little black calf', although it had been slaughtered, became alive again, and walked off with the rest of the stock at the command of the lady. This happened in the spring of the year, and there were four oxen ploughing in one of the fields; to these she cried:

'Pedwar eidion glas
Sydd ar y maes,
Deuwch chwithau
Yn iach adre!'

The four grey oxen,
That are on the field,
Come you also
Quite well home!

Away the whole of the live stock went with the Lady across Myddfai Mountain, towards the lake from whence they came, a distance of above six miles, where they disappeared beneath its waters, leaving no trace behind except a well-marked furrow, which was made by the plough the oxen drew after them into the lake, and which remains to this day as testimony to the truth of this story.

What became of the affrighted ploughman, whether he was left on the field when the oxen set off, or whether he followed

35

them to the lake, has not been handed down to tradition; neither has the fate of the disconsolate and half-ruined husband been kept in remembrance. But of the sons it is stated that they often wandered about the lake and its vicinity, hoping that their mother might be permitted to visit the face of the earth once more, as they had been apprised of her mysterious origin, her first appearance to their father, and the untoward circumstances which so unhappily deprived them of her maternal care.

In one of their rambles, at a place near Dol Howel, at the Mountain Gate, still called 'Llidiad y Meddygon', The Physicians' Gate, their mother appeared suddenly, and accosted her eldest son, whose name was Rhiwallon, and told him that his mission on earth was to be a benefactor to mankind by relieving them from pain and misery, through healing all manner of their diseases; for which purpose she furnished him with a bag full of medical prescriptions and instructions for the preservation of health. That by strict attention thereto he and his family would become for many generations the most skilful physicians in the country. Then, promising to meet him when her counsel was most needed, she vanished. But on several occasions she met her sons near the banks of the lake, and once she even accompanied them on their return home as far as the place still called 'Pant-y-Meddygon', The Dingle of the Physicians, where she pointed out to them the various plants and herbs which grew in the dingle, and revealed to them their medicinal qualities or virtues; and the knowledge she imparted to them, together with their unrivalled skill, soon caused them to attain such celebrity that none ever possessed before them. And in order that their knowledge should not be lost, they wisely committed the same to writing, for the benefit of mankind throughout all ages.

The Fairy Horse Dealer

A MANXMAN, who had the reputation of the utmost integrity, being desirous of disposing of a horse he had at that time no great occasion for, and riding him to market for that purpose, was accosted, in passing over the mountains, by a little man in a plain dress, who asked him if he would sell his horse. ''Tis the design I am going on,' replied the person who told the story.

On which the other desired to know the price.

'Eight pounds,' said he.

'No,' resumed the purchaser, 'I will give no more than seven; which, if you will take, here is your money.'

The owner thinking he had bid pretty fair, agreed with him, and the money being told out, the one dismounted and the other got on the back of the horse, which he had no sooner done than both beast and rider sunk into the earth immediately, leaving the person who made the bargain in the utmost terror and consternation. As soon as he had a little recovered himself, he went directly to the parson of the parish, and related what had passed, desiring he would give his opinion whether he ought to make use of the money he had received or not. To which he replied that, as he had made a fair bargain, and in no way circumvented, nor endeavoured to circumvent, the buyer, he saw no reason to believe, in case it was an evil spirit, it could have any power over him. On this assurance, he went home well satisfied, and nothing afterwards happened to give him any disquiet concerning this affair.

The Woman of the Sea

ONE clear summer night, a young man was walking on the sand by the sea on the Isle of Unst. He had been all day in the hayfields and was come down to the shore to cool himself, for it was the full moon and the wind blowing fresh off the water.

As he came to the shore he saw the sand shining white in the moonlight and on it the sea-people dancing. He had never seen them before, for they show themselves like seals by day, but on this night, because it was midsummer and a full moon, they were dancing for joy. Here and there he saw dark patches where they had flung down their sealskins, but they themselves were as clear as the moon itself, and they cast no shadow.

He crept a little nearer, and his own shadow moved before him, and of a sudden one of the sea-people danced upon it. The dance was broken. They looked about and saw him and with a cry they fled to their sealskins and dived into the waves. The air was full of their soft crying and splashing.

But one of the fairy people ran hither and thither on the sands, wringing her hands as if she had lost something. The young man looked and saw a patch of darkness in his own shadow. It was a seal's skin. Quickly he threw it behind a rock and watched to see what the sea-fairy would do.

She ran down to the edge of the sea and stood with her feet in the foam, crying to her people to wait for her, but they had gone too far to hear. The moon shone on her and the young man thought she was the loveliest creature he had ever seen. Then she began to weep softly to herself and the sound of it was so pitiful that he could bear it no longer. He stood upright and went down to her.

'What have you lost, woman of the sea?' he asked her.

She turned at the sound of his voice and looked at him, terrified. For a moment he thought she was going to dive into the sea. Then she came a step nearer and held up her two hands to him.

'Sir,' she said, 'give it back to me and I and my people will give you the treasure of the sea.' Her voice was like the waves singing in a shell.

'I would rather have you than the treasure of the sea,' said the young man. Although she hid her face in her hands and fell again to crying, more hopeless than ever, he was not moved.

'It is my wife you shall be,' he said. 'Come with me now to the priest, and we will go home to our own house, and it is yourself shall be mistress of all I have. It is warm you will be in the long winter nights, sitting at your own hearth stone and the peat burning red, instead of swimming in the cold green sea.'

She tried to tell him of the bottom of the sea where there comes neither snow nor darkness of night and the waves are as warm as a river in summer, but he would not listen. Then he threw his cloak around her and lifted her in his arms and they were married in the priest's house.

He brought her home to his little thatched cottage and into the kitchen with its earthen floor, and set her down before the hearth in the red glow of the peat. She cried out when she saw the fire, for she thought it was a strange crimson jewel.

'Have you anything as bonny as that in the sea?' he asked her, kneeling down beside her and she said, so faintly that he could scarcely hear her, 'No.'

'I know not what there is in the sea,' he said, 'but there is nothing on land as bonny as you.' For the first time she ceased her crying and sat looking into the heart of the fire. It was the first thing that made her forget, even for a moment, the sea which was her home.

All the days she was in the young man's house, she never lost the wonder of the fire and it was the first thing she brought her children to see. For she had three children in the twice seven years she lived with him. She was a good wife to him. She baked his bread and she spun the wool for the fleece of his Shetland sheep.

He never named the seal's skin to her, nor she to him, and he thought she was content, for he loved her dearly and she was happy with her children. Once, when he was ploughing on the headland above the bay, he looked down and saw her standing on the rocks and crying in a mournful voice to a great seal in the water. He said nothing when he came home, for he thought to himself it was not to wonder at if she were lonely for the sight of her own people. As for the seal's skin, he had hidden it well.

There came a September evening and she was busy in the house, and the children playing hide-and-seek in the stacks in the gloaming. She heard them shouting and went out to them.

'What have you found?' she said.

The children came running to her. 'It is like a big cat,' they said, 'but it is softer than a cat. Look!' She looked and saw her seal's skin that was hidden under last year's hay.

She gazed at it, and for a long time she stood still. It was warm dusk and the air was yellow with the afterglow of the sunset. The children had run away again, and their voices among the stacks sounded like the voices of birds. The hens were on the roost already and now and then one of them clucked in its sleep. The air was full of little friendly noises from the sleepy talking of the swallows under the thatch. The door was open and the warm smell of the baking of bread came out to her.

She turned to go in, but a small breath of wind rustled over the stacks and she stopped again. It brought a sound that she had heard so long she never seemed to hear it at all. It was the sea whispering down on the sand. Far out on the rocks the great waves broke in a boom, and close in on the sand the little waves slipped racing back. She took up the seal's skin and went swiftly down the track that led to the sands. The children saw her and cried to her to wait for them, but she did not hear them. She was just out of sight when their father came in from the byre and they ran to tell him.

'Which road did she take?' said he.

'The low road to the sea,' they answered, but already their father was running to the shore. The children tried to follow him, but their voices died away behind him, so fast did he run.

As he ran across the hard sands, he saw her dive to join the big seal who was waiting for her, and he gave a loud cry to stop her. For a moment she rested on the surface of the sea, then she cried with her voice that was like the waves singing in a shell, 'Fare ye well, and all good befall you, for you were a good man to me.'

Then she dived to the fairy places that lie at the bottom of the sea and the big seal with her.

For a long time her husband watched for her to come back to him and the children; but she came no more.

The Young Tamlane

O I forbid ye, maidens a',
  That wear gowd on your hair,
To come or gae by Carterhaugh;
  For young Tamlane is there.

There's nane, that gaes by Carterhaugh,
  But maun leave him a wad;
Either goud rings, or green mantles,
  Or else their maidenheid.

But up then spake her, fair Janet,
  The fairest o' a' her kin;
'I'll come and gang to Carterhaugh,
  And ask nae leave o' him.'

Janet has kilted her green kirtle,
  A little aboon her knee;
And she has braided her yellow hair,
  A little aboon her bree.

43

And she's away to Carterhaugh,
  And gaed beside the wood;
And there was sleeping young Tamlane,
  And his steed beside him stood.

She pu'd the broom flower frae the bush,
  And strewed it on's white hause bane;
And that was to be a witter* true,
  That maiden she had gane.

'O where was ye, my milk white steed,
  That I did love sae dear,
That wadna watch, and waken me,
  When there was maiden here?'

'I stamped wi' my foot, master,
  I gar'd my bridle ring;
But no kin' thing would waken ye,
  Till she was past and gane.'

'And wae betide ye, my gray goshawk,
  That I did love sae well;
That wadna watch, and waken me,
  When my love was here hersell!'

'I clapped wi' my wings, master,
  And ay my bell I rang;
And ay cried, "Waken, waken, master,
  Afore your true love gang."'

'But haste, and haste, my good white steed,
  To come the maiden till;
Or a' the birds, in good green wood,
  O' your flesh shall hae their fill.'

*Token.

44

Fairies

'Ye needna burst your good white steed,
 By running o'er the howm;
Nae hare runs swifter o'er the lea,
 Nor your love ran thro' the broom.'

Fair Janet, in her green cleiding,
 Returned upon the morn;
And she met her father's ae brother,
 The laird of Abercorn.

'I'll wager, I'll wager, I'll wager wi' you,
 Five hunder merk and ten,
I'll maiden gang to Carterhaugh,
 And maiden come again.'

She princked hersell, and prin'd hersell,
 By the ae light of the moon;
And she's away to Carterhaugh,
 As fast as she could win.

And when she cam to Carterhaugh,
 She gaed beside the wall;
And there she fand his steed standing,
 But away was himsell.

She hadna pu'd a red red rose,
 A rose but barely three,
Till up and starts a wee wee man,
 At Lady Janet's knee.

Says, 'Why pu' ye the rose, Janet?
 What gars ye break the tree?
Or why come ye to Carterhaugh,
 Withoutten leave o' me!'

Says, 'Carterhaugh it is mine ain;
  My daddie gave it me;
I'll come and gang to Carterhaugh,
  And ask nae leave o' thee.'

He's ta'en her by the milk-white hand,
  And by the grass-green sleeve;
He's led her to the fairy ground,
  And spier'd at her nae leave.

When she came to her father's ha',
  She looked pale and wan;
They thought she's dried some sair sickness,
  Or been wi' some leman.

She didna comb her yellow hair,
  Nor make meikle o' her heid;
And ilka thing, that lady took,
  Was like to be her deid.

Its four-and-twenty ladies fair
  Were in her father's ha';
Whan in there came the fair Janet,
  The flower amang them a'.

Four-and-twenty ladies fair
  Were playing at the chess;
And out there came the fair Janet,
  As green as any grass.

Out and spake an auld gray-headed knight,
  Lay o'er the castle wa' —
'And ever alas! for thee, Janet,
  But we'll be blamed a'.'

Fairies

'Now had your tongue, ye auld gray knight!
   And an ill deid may ye die!
Father my bairn on whom I will,
   I'll father nane on thee.'

Out then spake her father dear,
   And he spoke meek and mild –
'And ever alas! my sweet Janet,
   I fear ye gae with child.'

'And if I be with child, father,
   Mysell maun bear the blame;
There's ne'er a knight, about your ha',
   Shall hae the bairnie's name.

'If my love were an earthly knight,
   As he's an elfin grey,
I wadna gie my ain true love
   For nae lord that ye hae.'

'Is it to a man o' might, Janet,
   Or is it to a man o' mean?
Or is it unto young Tamlane,
   That's wi' the Fairies gane?'

''Twas down by Carterhaugh, father,
   I walked beside the wa;
And there I saw a wee wee man,
   The least that e'er I saw.

'His legs were skant a shathmont* lang,
   Yet umber was his thie;
Between his brows there was ae span,
   And between his shoulders, thrie.

*The length of the hand, when clenched, with the thumb erect.

Fairies

'He's ta'en and flung a meikle stane,
  As far as I could see;
I could na, had I been Wallace wight,
  Hae lifted it to my knee.

'"O wee wee man, but ye be strang!
  Where may thy dwelling be?"
"Its down beside yon bonny bower;
  Fair lady, come and see."

'On we lap, and away we rade,
  Down to a bonny green;
We lighted down to bait our steed,
  And we saw the Fairy Queen.

'With four-and-twenty at her back,
  Of ladies clad in green;
Tho' the King of Scotland had been there,
  The worst might hae been his Queen.

'On we lap, and away we rade,
  Down to a bonny ha';
The roof was o' the beaten goud,
  The floor was of chrystal a'.

'And there were dancing on the floor,
  Fair ladies jimp and sma';
But, in the twinkling o' an eye,
  They sainted* clean awa'.

'And, in the twinkling of an eye,
  The wee wee man was gane;
And he says, gin he binna won by me,
  He'll ne'er be won by nane.'

*Vanished.

48

Fairies

Janet's put on her green cleiding,
   Whan near nine months were gane;
And she's awa to Carterhaugh,
   To speak wi' young Tamlane.

And when she came to Carterhaugh,
   She gaed beside the wall;
And there she saw the steed standing,
   But away was himsell.

She hadna pu'd a double rose,
   A rose but only twae,
When up and started young Tamlane,
   Says 'Lady, thou pu's nae mae!

'Why pu' ye the rose, Janet,
   Within this garden green?
And a' to kill the bonnie babe,
   That we got us between.'

'The truth ye'll tell to me, Tamlane;
   A word ye mauna lie;
Gin e'er ye was in haly chapel,
   Or sained* in Christentie.'

'The truth I'll tell to thee, Janet;
   A word I winna lie;
A knight me got, and a lady me bore,
   As well as they did thee.

'Roxburgh was my grandfather;
   Took me with him to bide;
And, as we frae the hunting came,
   This harm did me betide.

*Hallowed.

Fairies

'Roxburgh was a hunting knight,
  And loved hunting well;
And, on a cauld and frosty day,
  Down frae my horse I fell.

'The Queen o' Fairies keppit* me,
  In yon green hill to dwell;
And I'm a fairy, lyth and limb;
  Fair lady, view me well.

'And pleasant is the fairy land;
  But, an eiry tale to tell!
Ay, at the end o' seven years,
  We pay the teind to hell;
And I'm sae fair and fu' o' flesh,
  I'm fear'd it be mysell.

'This night is Hallowe'en, Janet;
  The morn is Hallowday;
And, gin ye dare your true love win,
  Ye have nae time to stay.

'The night it is good Hallowe'en,
  When fairy folk will ride;
And they, that wad their true love win,
  At Miles Cross they maun bide.'

'But how shall I thee ken, Tamlane?
  Or how shall I thee knaw?
Amang so many unearthly knights,
  The like I never saw?'

*Caught.

Fairies

'The first company that passes by,
  Say na, and let them gae;
The next company that passes by,
  Say na, and do right sae;
The third company that passes by,
  Then I'll be ane o' thae.

'First let pass the black, Janet,
  And syne let pass the brown;
But grip ye to the milk-white steed,
  And pu' the rider down.

'For I ride on the milk-white steed,
  And ay nearest the town;
Because I was a christened knight,
  They gave me that renown.

'My right hand will be gloved, Janet,
  My left hand will be bare;
And thae's the tokens I gie thee,
  Nae doubt I will be there.

'They'll turn me in your arms, Janet,
  An ulder and a snuke;
But had me fast, let me not pass,
  Gin ye wad be my maik.

'They'll turn me in your arms, Janet,
  An adder and an ask;
They'll turn me in your arms, Janet,
  A bale* that burns fast.

'They'll turn me in your arms, Janet,
  A red hot gad o' iron;

*A faggot.

Fairies

But had me fast, let me not pass,
    For I'll do you no harm.

'First, dip me in a stand o' milk,
    And then in a stand o' water;
But had me fast, let me not pass,
    I'll be your bairn's father.

'And next they'll shape me in your arms,
    A toad, but and an eel;
But had me fast, nor let me gang,
    As you do love me weel.

'They'll shape me in your arms, Janet,
    A dove, but and a swan;
And last they'll shape me in your arms,
    A mother-naked man:
Cast your green mantle over me –
    I'll be mysell again.'

Gloomy, gloomy, was the night,
    And eiry* was the way,
As fair Janet, in her green mantle,
    To Miles Cross she did gae.

About the dead hour o' the night,
    She heard the bridles ring;
And Janet was as glad o' that,
    As any earthly thing!

And first gaed by the black black steed,
    And then gaed by the brown;
But fast she gript the milk-white steed,
    And pu'd the rider down.

*Producing supernatural dread.

Fairies

She pu'd him frae the milk-white steed,
　And loot the bridle fa';
And up there raise an erlish* cry –
　'He's won amang us a'!'

They shaped him in fair Janet's arms,
　An esk[†], but and an adder;
She held him fast in every shape,
　To be her bairn's father.

They shaped him in her arms at last,
　A mother-naked man;
She wrapt him in her green mantle,
　And sae her true love wan.

Up then spake the Queen o' Fairies,
　Out o' a bush o' broom –
'She that has borrowed young Tamlane,
　Has gotten a stately groom.'

Up then spake the Queen o' Fairies,
　Out o' a bush of rye –
'She's ta'en awu the bonniest knight,
　In a' my companie.

'But, had I kenn'd, Tamlane,' she says,
　'A lady wad borrowed thee –
I wad ta'en out they twae gray een,
　Put in twae een o' tree.

'Had I but kenn'd, Tamlane,' she says,
　'Before ye came frae hame –
I wad ta'en out your heart o' flesh,
　Put in a heart o' stane.

*Ghastly.　†Newt.

53

Fairies

'Had I had but the wit yestreen,
    That I hae coft* the day —
I'd paid my kane seven times to hell,
Ere you'd been won away!'

*Bought.

Brewery of Eggshells

IN TRENEGLWYS there is a certain shepherd's cot known by the name of Twt y Cymrws because of the strange strife that occurred there. There once lived there a man and his wife, and they had twins whom the woman nursed tenderly. One day she was called away to the house of a neighbour at some distance. She did not much like going and leaving her little ones all alone in a solitary house, especially as she had heard tell of the good folk haunting the neighbourhood.

Well, she went and came back as soon as she could, but on her way back she was frightened to see some old elves of the blue petticoat crossing her path though it was midday. She rushed home, but found her two little ones in the cradle and everything seemed as it was before.

But after a time the good people began to suspect that something was wrong, for the twins didn't grow at all.

The man said: 'They're not ours.'

The woman said: 'Whose else should they be?'

And so arose the great strife so that the neighbours named the cottage after it. It made the woman very sad so one evening she made up her mind to go and see the Wise Man of Llanidloes, for he knew everything and would advise her what to do.

So she went to Llanidloes and told the case to the Wise Man. Now there was soon to be a harvest of rye and oats, so the Wise Man said to her, 'When you are getting dinner for the reapers, clear out the shell of a hen's egg and boil some potage in it, and then take it to the door as if you meant it as a dinner for the reapers. Then listen if the twins say anything. If you hear them speaking of things beyond the understanding of children, go back and take them up and throw them into the waters of Lake Elvyn. But if you don't hear anything remarkable, do them no injury.'

So when the day of the reap came the woman did all that the Wise Man ordered, and put the eggshell on the fire and took it off and carried it to the door, and there she stood and listened. Then she heard one of the children say to the other:

> 'Acorn before oak I knew,
> An egg before a hen,
> But I never heard of an eggshell brew
> A dinner for harvest men.'

So she went back into the house, seized the children and threw them into the Llyn, and the goblins in their blue trousers came and saved their dwarfs and the mother had her own children back and so the great strife ended.

Yallery Brown

I'VE heard tell as how the bogles and boggarts were main bad in the old times, but I can't rightly say as I ever saw any of them myself; not rightly bogles, that is, but I'll tell you about Yallery Brown. If he wasn't a boggart, he was main near it, and I knew him myself. So it's all true – strange and true I tell you.

I was working on the High Farm to then, and nobbut a lad of sixteen or maybe eighteen years; and my mother and folks dwelt down by the pond yonder, at the far end of the village.

I had the stables and such to see to, and the horses to help with, and odd jobs to do, and the work was hard, but the pay good. I reckon I was an idle scamp, for I couldn't abide hard work, and I looked forward all the week to Sundays, when I'd walk down home, and not go back till darklins.

By the green lane I could get to the farm in a matter of twenty minutes, but there used to be a path across the west field yonder, but the side of the spinney, and on past the fox cover and so to the ramper, and I used to go that way. It was longer for one thing, and I wasn't never in a hurry to get back to the work, and it was still and pleasant like of summer nights, out in the broad silent fields, mid the smell of the growing things.

Folk said as the spinney was haunted, and for sure I have seen lots of fairy stones and rings and that, along the grass edge; but I never saw nowt in the way of horrors and boggarts, let alone Yallery Brown, as I said before.

One Sunday, I was walking across the west field. It was a beautiful July night, warm and still, and the air was full of little sounds, as if the trees and grass were chattering to their selves. And all to once there came a bit ahead of me the pitifullest greetin I've ever heard, sob, sobbing, like a bairn spent with fear, and near heart-broken; breaking off into a moan, and then rising again in a long, whimpering wailing that made me feel sick nobbut to hark to it. I was always fond of babbies, too, and I began to look everywhere for the poor creature.

'Must be Sally Bratton's,' I thought to myself. 'She was always a flighty thing, and never looked after it. Like as not, she's flaunting about the lanes, and has clean forgot the babby.'

But though I looked and looked I could find nowt. Nonetheless the sobbing was at my very ear, so tired like and sorrowful that I kept crying out, 'Whisht, bairn, whisht! I'll take you back to your mother if you'll only hush your greetin.'

But for all my looking I could find nowt. I keekit under the hedge by the spinney side, and I clumb over it, and I sought up and down by, and mid the trees, and through the long grass and weeds, but I only frightened some sleeping birds, and stinged my own hands with the nettles. I found nowt, and I fair gave up to last; so I stood there, scratching my head, and clean beat with it all. And presently the whimpering got louder and stronger in the quietness, and I thought I could make out words of some sort.

I harkened with all my ears, and the sorry thing was saying all mixed up with sobbing:

'Oh, oh! The stone, the great big stone! Oh, oh! The stone on top!'

Naturally I wondered where the stone might be, and I looked

again, and there by the hedge bottom was a great flat stone, near buried in the mools, and hid in the cotted grass and weeds. One of those stones as were used to call the Strangers' Tables. The Strangers danced on them at moonlight nights, and so they were never meddled with. It's ill luck, you know, to cross the Tiddy People.

However, down I fell on my knee-bones by the stone, and harkened again. Clearer nor ever, but tired and spent with greetin came the little sobbing voice.

'Ooh! Ooh! The stone, the stone on top.'

I was misliking to meddle with the thing, but I couldn't stand the whimpering babby, and I tore like mad at the stone, till I felt it lifting from the mools, and all to once it came with a sigh, out of the damp earth and the tangled grass and growing things. And there, in the hole, lay a tiddy thing on its back, blinking up at the moon and at me.

It was no bigger than a year-old brat, but it had long cotted hair and beard, twisted round and round its body, so as I couldn't see its clouts. And the hair was all yaller and shining and silky, like a bairn's; but the face of it was old, and as if it were hundreds of years since it was young and smooth. Just a heap of wrinkles, and two bright black eyes in the mid, set in a lot of shining yaller hair; and the skin was the colour of the fresh turned earth in the Spring – brown as brown could be, and its bare hands and feet were brown like the face of it.

The greetin had stopped, but the tears were standing on its cheek, and the tiddy thing looked mazed like in the moonshine and the night air. It was wondering what I'd do, but by and by it scrambled out of the hole, and stood looking about it, and at myself. It wasn't up to my knee, but it was the queerest creature I ever set eyes on. Brown and yaller all over; yaller and brown, as I told you before, and with such a glint in its eyes, and such a wizened face, that I felt feared on it, for all that it was so tiddy and old.

The creature's eyes got some used to the moonlight, and presently it looked up in my face as bold as ever was.

'Tom,' it says, 'you're a good lad.'

As cool as you can think, it says, 'Tom, you're a good lad,' and its voice was soft and high and piping like a little bird twittering.

I touched my hat, and began to think what I had ought to say: but I was clemmed with fright, and I couldn't open my gob.

'Houts!' says the thing again. 'You needn't be feared of me; you've done me a better turn than you know, my lad, and I'll do as much for you.'

I couldn't speak yet, but I thought: 'Lord! For sure it's a bogle!'

'No!' it says, quick as quick, 'I'm not a bogle, but you'd best not ask me what I am; anyways, I'm a good friend of yours.'

My very knee-bones struck, for certainly an ordinary body couldn't have known what I'd been thinking to myself, but it looked so kind like, and spoke so fair, that I made bold to get out, a bit quavery like:

'Might I be asking to know your honour's name?'

'Hm,' it says, pulling its beard, 'as for that,' and it thought a bit, 'ay so,' it went on at last, 'Yallery Brown you may call me; Yallery Brown. It's my nature, you see. And as for a name, it will do as well as any other. Yallery Brown, Tom, Yallery Brown's your friend, my lad.'

'Thank you, master,' says I, quite meek like.

'And now,' he says, 'I'm in a hurry tonight, but tell me quick, what shall I do for you? Will you have a wife? I can give you the rampingest lass in the town. Will you be rich? I'll give you gold as much as you can carry. Or will you have help with your work? Only say the word.'

I scratched my head. 'Well, as for a wife, I have no hankering after such. They're but bothersome bodies, and I have women folk to home as will mend my clouts. And for gold; that's as may be,' for, you see, I thought he was talking only, and may be he couldn't do as much as he said, 'but for work – there, I can't abide work, and if you'll give me a helping hand in it, I'll thank you.'

'Stop,' says he, quick as lightning. 'I'll help you, and welcome, but if ever you say that to me – if ever you thank me, do you see?

60

– you'll never see me more. Mind that now. I want no thanks, I'll have no thanks, do you hear?' And he stamped his tiddy foot on the earth and looked as wicked as a raging bull.

'Mind that now, great lump as you be,' he went on, calming down a bit, 'and if ever you need help, or get into trouble, call on me and just say, "Yallery Brown, come from the mools, I want thee!" and I shall be with you to once. And now,' says he, picking up a dandelion puff, 'good night to you.' And he blowed it up, and it all came in my eyes and ears.

Soon as I could see again, the tiddy creature was gone, and but for the stone on end, and the hole at my feet, I'd have thought I'd been dreaming.

Well, I went home and to bed, and by the morning I'd near forgot all about it. But when I went to the work, there was none to do! All was done already! The horses seen to, the stables cleaned out, everything in its proper place, and I'd nowt to do but sit with my hands in my pockets.

And so it went on day after day, all the work done by Yallery Brown, and better done, too, than I could have done it myself. And if the master gave me more work, I sat down by, and the work did itself, the singeing irons, or the besom, or what not, set to, and with never a hand put to them would get through in no time. For I never saw Yallery Brown in daylight; only in the darklins I have seen him hopping about, like a will-o-the-wyke without his lanthorn.

To first, it was mighty fine for me. I'd nowt to do, and good pay for it; but by and by, things began to go arsy-varsy. If the work was done for me, it was undone for the other lads. If my buckets were filled, theirs were upset. If my tools were sharpened, theirs were blunted and spoiled. If my horses were clean as daisies, theirs were splashed with muck. And so on. Day in, day out, it was always the same. And the lads saw Yallery Brown flitting about of nights, and they saw the things working without hands of days, and they saw as my work was done for me, and theirs undone for them, and naturally they began to look shy on me, and they wouldn't speak or come near me, and they carried tales to the master, and so things went from bad to worse.

For – do you see? – I could do nothing myself. The brooms wouldn't stay in my hand, the plough ran away from me, the hoe kept out of my grip. I'd thought oft as I'd do my own work after all, so as may be Yallery Brown would leave me and my neighbours alone. But I couldn't. I could only sit by and look on, and have the cold shoulder turned on me, whiles the unnatural thing was meddling with the others, and working for me.

To last, things got so bad that the master gave me the sack, and if he hadn't, I do believe as all the rest of the lads would have sacked him, for they swore as they'd not stay on the same garth with me. Well, naturally I felt bad. It was a main good place, and good pay, too; and I was fair mad with Yallery Brown, as had got me into such a trouble. So before I knew, I shook my fist in the air and called out as loud as I could:

'Yallery Brown, come from the mools; thou scamp, I want thee!'

You'll scarce believe it, but I'd hardly brung out the words as I felt something tweaking my leg behind, while I jumped with the smart of it. And soon as I looked down there was the tiddy thing, with his shining hair, and wrinkled face, and wicked, glinting black eyes.

I was in a fine rage, and should liked to have kicked him, but it was no good, there wasn't enough of him to get my boot against.

But I said to once: 'Look here, master, I'll thank you to leave me alone after this, do you hear? I want none of your help, and I'll have nowt more to do with you – see now.'

The horrid thing brak out with a screeching laugh, and pointed his brown finger at me.

'Ho ho, Tom!' says he. 'You've thanked me, my lad, and I told you not, I told you not!'

'I don't want your help, I tell you!' I yelled at him. 'I only want never to see you again, and to have nowt more to do with you. You can go!'

The thing only laughed and screeched and mocked, as long as

I went on swearing, but as soon as my breath gave out, 'Tom, my lad,' he says, with a grin, 'I'll tell you summat, Tom. True's true I'll never help you again, and call as you will, you'll never see me after today; but I never said as I'd leave you alone, Tom, and I never will, my lad! I was nice and safe under the stone, Tom, and could do no harm; but you let me out yourself, and you can't put me back again! I would have been your friend and worked for you if you had been wise; but since you are no more than a born fool, I'll give you no more than a born fool's luck; and when all goes arsy-varsy, and everything a gee – you'll mind as it's Yallery Brown's doing, though happen you didn't see him. Mark my words, will you?'

And he began to sing, dancing round me, like a bairn with his yaller hair, but looking older nor ever with his grinning wrinkled bit of a face:

> 'Work as you will,
> You'll never do well;
> Work as you might,
> You'll never gain owt:
> For harm and mischief and Yallery Brown
> You've let out yourself from under the stone.'

Ay! He said those very words, and they have ringed in my ears ever since, over and over again, like a bell tolling for the burying. And it was the burying of my luck – for I never had any since. However, the imp stood there mocking and grinning at me, and chuckling like the old devil's own wicked self.

And man! – I can't rightly mind what he said next. It was all cussing and swearing and calling down misfortune on me; but I was so mazed in fright that I could only stand there, shaking all over me, and staring down at the horrid thing; and I reckon if he'd gone on long, I'd have tumbled down in a fit. But by and by, his yaller shining hair – I can't abide yaller hair since that – rose up in the air, and wrapped itself round him, while he looked for all the world like a great dandelion puff; and he floated away on the wind over the wall and out of sight, with a parting skirl of his wicked voice and sneering laugh.

I tell you, I was near dead with fear, and I can't scarcely tell how I ever got home at all, but I did somehow, I suppose.

Well, that's all; it's not much of a tale, but it's true, every word of it, and there's others besides me as have seen Yallery Brown and known his evil tricks – and did it come true, you say? But it did sure! I have worked here and there, and turned my hand to this and that, but it always went a gee, and it is all Yallery Brown's doing. The children died, and my wife didn't; the beasts never fatted, and nothing ever did well with me. I'm going old now, and I shall must end my days in the house, I reckon; but till I'm dead and buried, and happen even afterwards, there'll be no end to Yallery Brown's spite at me. And day in and day out I hear him saying, whiles I sit here trembling:

> 'Work as you will,
> You'll never do well;
> Work as you might,
> You'll never gain owt;
> For harm and mischief and Yallery Brown
> You've let out yourself from under the stone.'

The Soul Cages

JACK DOGHERTY lived on the coast of the County Clare. Jack was a fisherman, as his father and his grandfather before him had been. Like them, too, he lived all alone (but for the wife), and just in the same spot, too. People used to wonder why the Dogherty family were so fond of that wild situation, so far away from all human kind, and in the midst of huge scattered rocks, with nothing but the wide ocean to look upon. But they had their own good reasons for it.

The place was just, in short, the only spot on that part of the coast where anybody could well live; there was a neat little creek, where a boat might lie as snug as a puffin in her nest, and out from this creek a ledge of sunken rocks ran into the sea. Now, when the Atlantic, according to custom, was raging with a storm, and a good westerly wind was blowing strong on the coast, many's the richly-laden ship that went to pieces on these rocks; and then the fine bales of cotton and tobacco, and such like things; and the pipes of wine, and the puncheons of rum, and the casks of brandy, and the kegs of Hollands that used to come ashore. Why, bless you! Dunbeg Bay was just like a little estate to the Doghertys.

Not but that they were kind and humane to a distressed sailor, if ever one had the good luck to get to land; and many a time, indeed, did Jack put out in his little *corragh*, that would breast the billows like any gannet to lend a hand towards bringing off the crew from a wreck. But when the ship was gone to pieces, and the crew were all lost, who would blame Jack for picking up all he could find? 'And who's the worse of it?' said he. 'For as to the king, God bless him! everybody knows he's rich enough already, without gettin' what's floatin' in the say.'

Jack, though such a hermit, was a good-natured, jolly fellow. No other, sure, could ever have coaxed Biddy Mahony to quit her father's snug and warm house in the middle of the town of Ennis, and to go so many miles off to live among the rocks, with the seals and sea-gulls for her next door neighbours. But Biddy knew what's what, and she knew that Jack was the man for a woman who wished to be comfortable and happy; for, to say nothing of the fish, Jack had the supplying of half the gentlemen's houses of the country with the Godsends that came into the bay. And she was right in her choice, for no woman ate, drank, or slept better, or made a prouder appearance at chapel on Sundays than Mrs Dogherty.

Many a strange sight, it may well be supposed, did Jack see, and many a strange sound did he hear, but nothing daunted him. So far was he from being afraid of Merrows, or such like beings, that the very first wish of his heart was fairly to meet with one. Jack had heard that they were mighty like Christians, and that luck had always come out of an acquaintance with them. Never, therefore, did he dimly discern the Merrows moving along the face of the waters in their robes of mist, but he made direct for them; and many a scolding did Biddy, in her own quiet way, bestow upon Jack for spending his whole day out at sea, and bringing home no fish. Little did poor Biddy know the fish Jack was after.

It was rather annoying to Jack that, though living in a place where the Merrows were as plenty as lobsters, he never could get a right view of one. What vexed him more was, that both his father and grandfather had often and often seen them, and he even remembered hearing, when a child, how his grandfather, who was the first of the family that had settled down at the Creek, had been so intimate with a Merrow, that, only for fear of vexing the priest, he would have had him stand for one of his children. This, however, Jack did not well know how to believe.

Fortune at length began to think that it was only right that Jack should know as much as his father and grandfather knew. Accordingly, one day, when he had strolled a little farther than usual along the coast to the northward, just as he was turning a point, he saw something, like to nothing he had ever seen before, perched upon a rock at a little distance out to sea: it looked green in the body, as well as he could discern at that distance, and he would have sworn, only the thing was imposs-ible, that it had a cocked hat in his hand. Jack stood, for a good half hour straining his eyes and wondering at it, and all the time the thing did not stir hand or foot. At last Jack's patience was quite worn out, and he gave a loud whistle and a hail, when the Merrow (for such it was) started up, put the cocked hat on its head, and dived down, head foremost, from the rock.

Jack's curiosity was now excited, and he constantly directed his steps toward the point; still he could never get a glimpse of the sea-gentleman with the cocked hat; and with thinking and thinking about the matter, he began at last to fancy he had been only dreaming. One very rough day, however, when the sea was running mountains high, Jack determined to give a look at the Merrow's rock, (for he had always chosen a fine day before), and then he saw the strange thing cutting capers upon the top of the rock, and then diving down, and then coming up, and then diving down again. Jack had now only to choose his time, (that is, a good blowing day), and he might see the man of the sea as often as he pleased. All this, however, did not satisfy him – 'much will have more' – he wished now to get acquainted with the Merrow, and even in this he succeeded. One tremendous blustery day, before he got to the point whence he had a view of the Merrow's rock, the storm came on so furiously that Jack was obliged to take shelter in one of the caves which are so numerous along the coast, and there, to his astonishment, he saw, sitting before him, a thing with green hair, long green teeth, a red nose, and pig's eyes. It had a fish's tail, legs with scales on them, and short arms like fins. It wore no clothes, but had the cocked hat under its arm, and seemed engaged thinking very seriously about something. Jack, with all his courage, was a little daunted; but now or never, thought he; so up he went boldly to the cogitating fish-man, took off his hat, and made his best bow.

'Your sarvint, sir,' said Jack.

'Your servant, kindly, Jack Dogherty,' answered the Merrow.

'To be shure, thin, how well your honour knows my name,' said Jack.

'Is it I not know your name, Jack Dogherty? Why, man, I knew your grandfather long before he was married to Judy Regan, your grandmother. Ah, Jack, Jack, I was fond of that grandfather of yours; he was a mighty worthy man in his time. I never met his match above or below, before or since, for sucking in a shellful of brandy. I hope, my boy,' said the old fellow, 'I hope you're his own grandson.'

'Never fear me for that,' said Jack; 'if my mother only reared me on brandy, 'tis myself that 'ud be a suckin infant to this hour.'

'Well, I like to hear you talk so manly; you and I must be better acquainted, if it were only for your grandfather's sake. But, Jack, that father of yours was not the thing; he had no head at all, not he.'

'I'm shure,' said Jack, 'sense your honour lives down undher the wather, you must be obleeged to dhrink a power to keep any hate in you, at all at all, in such a cruel, damp, cowld place. Well, I often hard of Christhens dhrinkin' like fishes – and might I be so bould as to ax where you get the sperits?'

'Where do you get them yourself, Jack?' said the Merrow, with a knowing look.

'Hubbubboo,' cries Jack, 'now I see how it is; but I suppose, sir, your honour has got a fine dhry cellar below to keep them in.'

'Let me alone for that,' said the Merrow, with another knowing look. 'I'm shure', continued Jack, 'it must be mighty well worth the luking at.'

'You may say that, Jack, with your own pretty mouth,' said the Merrow; 'and if you meet me here next Monday, just at this time of the day, we will have a little more talk with one another about the matter.'

Jack and the Merrow parted the best friends in the world; and on Monday they met, and Jack was not a little surprised to see that the Merrow had two cocked hats with him, one under each arm. 'Might I make so bould as to ask you, sir,' said Jack, 'why yer honour brought the two hats wid you today? You wouldn't, shure, be goin' to giv' me one o' them, to keep for the curosity of the thing?'

'No, no, Jack,' said he, 'I don't get my hats so easily, to part with them that way; but I want you to come down and eat a bit of dinner with me, and I brought you the hat to dive with.'

'The Lord bless and presarve us!' cried Jack, in amazement, 'would you want me to go down to the bottom of the salt say ocean? Shure I'd be smoothered and choked up wid the wather, to say nothin' of bein' dhrownded! And what would poor Biddy do for me, and what would she say?'

'And what matter what she says, you pinkeen you? Who cares for Biddy's squalling? It's long before your grandfather would have talked in that way. Many's the time he stuck that same hat on his head, and dived down boldly after me, and many's the snug bit of dinner, and good shellful of brandy, he and I had together, below under the water.'

'Is it raally, sir, and no joke?' said Jack; 'why, thin, sorra' be from me for ivir and a day afther, if I'll be a bit a worse man nor my grandfather was! So here goes; but play me fair now. Here's nick or nothin'!' cried Jack.

'That's your grandfather all over,' said the old fellow. 'So come along, my boy, and do as I do.'

69

They both left the cave, walked into the sea, and then swam a piece until they got to the rock. The Merrow climbed to the top of it, and Jack followed him. On the far side it was as straight as the wall of a house, and the sea looked so deep that Jack was almost cowed.

'Now, do you see, Jack,' said the Merrow, 'just put this hat on your head, and mind to keep your eyes wide open. Take hold of my tail, and follow after me, and you'll see what you'll see.'

In he dashed, and in dashed Jack after him boldly. They went and they went, and Jack thought they'd never stop going. Many a time did he wish himself sitting at home by the fireside with Biddy: yet, where was the use of wishing now, when he was so many miles as he thought below the waves of the Atlantic? Still he held hard by the Merrow's tail, slippery as it was. And, at last, to Jack's great surprise, they got out of the water, and he actually found himself on dry land at the bottom of the sea. They landed just in front of a nice little house that was slated very neatly with oyster-shells; and the Merrow, turning about to Jack welcomed him down. Jack could hardly speak, what with wonder, and what with being out of breath with travelling so fast through the water. He looked about him, and could see no living things, barring crabs and lobsters, of which there were plenty walking leisurely about on the sand. Overhead was the sea like a sky, and the fishes like birds swimming about in it.

'Why don't you speak, man?' said the Merrow: 'I dare say you had no notion that I had such a snug little concern as this? Are you smothered, or choked, or drowned, or are you fretting after Biddy, eh?'

'Oh! not mysilf, indeed,' said Jack, showing his teeth with a good-humoured grin, 'but who in the world 'ud ivir ha' thought uv seein' sich a thing?'

'Well, come along, my lad, and let's see what they've got for us to eat.'

Jack was really hungry, and it gave him no small pleasure to perceive a fine column of smoke rising from the chimney, announcing what was going on within. Into the house he followed the Merrow, and there he saw a good kitchen, right well provided with everything. There was a noble dresser, and plenty of pots and pans, with two young Merrows cooking. His host then led him into the *room,* which was furnished shabbily enough. Not a table or chair was there in it; nothing but planks and logs of wood to sit on, and eat off. There was, however, a good fire blazing on the hearth – a comfortable sight to Jack.

'Come, now, and I'll show you where I keep – you know what,' said the Merrow, with a sly look; and opening a little door, he led Jack into a fine long cellar, well filled with pipes and kegs, and hogsheads, and barrels. 'What do you say to that, Jack Dogherty? – Eh! – Maybe a body can't live snug down under the water!'

'The divil the doubt of that', said Jack, 'anyhow.'

They went back to the room, and found dinner laid. There was no tablecloth, to be sure – but what matter? It was not always Jack had one at home. The dinner would have been no discredit to the first house in the county on a fast-day. The choicest of fish, and no wonder, was there. Turbots, and soles, and lobsters, and oysters, and twenty other kinds, were on the planks at once, and plenty of foreign spirits. The wines, the old fellow said, were too cold for his stomach. Jack ate and drank till he could eat no more: then, taking up a shell of brandy,

'Here's to your honour's good health, sir,' said he, 'though beggin' your pardon, it's mighty odd, that as long as we're acquainted, I don't know your name yit.'

'That's true, Jack,' replied he; 'I never thought of it before, but better late than never. My name is Coomara.'

'Coomara! And a mighty dacint sort of a name it is, too,' cried Jack, taking another shellful: 'here's, then, to your good health, Coomara, and may you live these fifty years.'

'Fifty years!' repeated Coomara; 'I'm obliged to you, indeed; if you had said five hundred, it would have been something worth wishing.'

'By the laws, sir,' said Jack, 'yez live to a powerful great age here undher the wather! Ye knew my grandfather, and he's dead and gone betther nor sixty years. I'm shure it must be a mighty healthy place to live in.' 'No doubt of it; but come, Jack keep the liquor stirring.'

Shell after shell did they empty, and to Jack's exceeding surprise, he found the drink never got into his head, owing, I suppose, to the sea being over them, which kept their noddles cool. Old Coomara got exceedingly comfortable, and sang several songs; but Jack, if his life had depended on it, never could remember any of them. At length said he to Jack, 'Now, my dear boy, if you follow me, I'll show you my curosities!'

He opened a little door, and led Jack into a large room, where Jack saw a great many odds and ends that Coomara had picked up at one time or another. What chiefly took his attention, however, were things like lobster-pots, ranged on the ground along the wall.

'Well, Jack, how do you like my curosities?' said old Coo.

'Upon my sowkins, sir,' said Jack, 'they're mighty well worth the lukin' at; but might a body make so bould as to ax what thim things like lobster-pots are?'

'Oh, the soul-cages, is it?'

'The what, sir?'

'These things here that I keep the souls in.'

'Arrah! what sowls, sir?' said Jack in amazement: 'shure the fish ha' got no sowls in them?'

'Oh, no,' replied Coo, quite coolly, 'that they haven't; but these are the souls of drowned sailors.'

'The Lord presarve us from all harm!' muttered Jack, 'how in the world did you conthrive to get thim?'

'Easily enough. I've only when I see a good storm coming on, to set a couple of dozen of these, and then, when the sailors are drowned, and the souls get out of them under the water, the poor things are almost perished to death, not being used to the cold; so they make into my pots for shelter, and then I have them snug, and fetch them home, and keep them here dry and warm; and is it not well for them, poor souls, to get into such good quarters?'

72

Jack was so thunderstruck he did not know what to say, so he said nothing. They went back into the dining-room, and had some more brandy, which was excellent, and then, as Jack knew that it must be getting late, and as Biddy might be uneasy, he stood up, and said he thought it was time for him to be on the road.

'Just as you like, Jack,' said Coo, 'but take a *doch an durrus* before you go; you've a cold journey before you.'

Jack knew better manners than to refuse the parting glass. 'I wondher' said he, 'will I ivir be able to make out my way home.'

'What should ail you,' said Coo, 'when I show you the way?'

Out they went before the house, and Coomara took one of the cocked hats, and put it on Jack's head the wrong way, and then lifted him up on his shoulder that he might launch him up into the water.

'Now,' says he, giving him a heave, 'you'll come up just in the same spot you came down in; and, Jack, mind and throw me back the hat.'

He canted Jack off his shoulder, and up he shot like a bubble – whirr, whirr, whiz – away he went up through the water, till he came to the very rock he had jumped off, where he found a landing-place, and then in he threw the hat, which sunk like a stone.

The sun was just going down in the beautiful sky of a calm summer's evening. The evening star was seen brightly twinkling in the cloudless heaven, and the waves of the Atlantic flashed in a golden flood of light. So Jack, perceiving it was getting late, set off home; but when he got there, not a word did he say to Biddy of where he had spent his day.

The state of the poor souls cooped up in the lobster-pots, gave Jack a great deal of trouble, and how to release them cost him a great deal of thought. He at first had a mind to speak to the priest about the matter; but what could the priest do, and what did Coo care for the priest? Besides, Coo was a good sort of an old fellow, and did not think he was doing any harm. Jack had a regard for him too, and it also might not be much to his own

credit if it were known that he used to go dine with the Merrows
under the sea. On the whole, he thought his best plan would be
to ask Coo to dinner, and to make him drunk, if he was able, and
then to take the hat and go down and turn up the pots. It was
first of all necessary, however, to get Biddy out of the way; for
Jack was prudent enough, as she was a woman, to wish to keep
the thing secret from her.

Accordingly, Jack grew mighty pious all of a sudden, and said
to Biddy, that he thought it would be for the good of both their
souls if she was to go and take her rounds at Saint John's Well,
near Ennis. Biddy thought so too, and accordingly off she set one
fine morning at day dawn, giving Jack a strict charge to have an
eye to the place. The coast being clear, away then went Jack to
the rock to give the appointed signal to Coomara, which was,
throwing a big stone into the water; Jack threw, and up sprang
Coo.

'Good morrow, Jack,' said he; 'what do you want with me?'

'Jist nothin' at all to spake about, sir,' replied Jack; 'only to
come and take pot-luck wid me, now that Biddy's out of the way;
if I might make so free as to ax you, an' shure it's myself that's
afther doin' so.'

'It's quite agreeable, Jack, I assure you; what's your hour?'

'Any time that's most convanient to yoursilf, sir: say one
o'clock, that you may go home, if you wish it, wid the daylight.'

'I'll be with you,' said Coo, 'never fear me.'

Jack went home and dressed a noble fish dinner, and got out
plenty of his best foreign spirits, enough for that matter to make
twenty men drunk. Just to the minute came Coo, with his cocked
hat under his arm. Dinner was ready; they sat down, and ate
and drank manfully. Jack thinking of the poor souls below in the
pots, plied old Coo well with brandy, and encouraged him to
sing, hoping to put him under the table, but poor Jack forgot that
he had not the sea over his own head now to keep it cool. The
brandy got into it and did his business for him, and Coo reeled
off home, leaving his entertainer as dumb as a haddock on a
Good Friday.

Jack never woke till the next morning, and then he was in a sad way.

"Tis no use at all for me thinkin' to make that ould Rapperee dhrunk,' said Jack; 'an' how in this world can I help the poor sowls out o' the lobster pots.' After ruminating nearly the whole day, a thought struck him. 'I have it,' said he, slapping his thigh; 'I'll be bail Coo nivir saw a dhrop o' raal potyeen as ould as he is, an' that's the thing to settle him! Och! thin isn't it well that Biddy won't be home these two days yit; I can have another twist at him.'

Jack asked Coo again, and Coo laughed at him for having no better head; telling him, he'd never come up to his grandfather.

'Well, but thry me agin,' said Jack, 'and I'll be bail to dhrink you dhrunk and sober, and dhrunk agin.'

'Anything in my power', said Coo, 'to oblige you.'

All this dinner, Jack took care to have his own liquor watered, and to give the strongest brandy he had to Coo. At last, says he, 'Pray, sir, did you ivir dhrink any potyeen? any raal mountain-jew?'

'No,' says Coo; 'what's that, and where does it come from?'

'Oh! That's a sacret,' said Jack, 'but it's the right stuff; nivir believe me agin if it isn't fifty times better nor brandy or rum either. Biddy's brother jist sint me a prisent of a little dhrop, in exchange for some brandy, and we you're an ould frind o' the family, I kep it to thrate you wid.'

'Well, let's see what sort of thing it is,' said Coo.

The potyeen was the right sort. It was first-rate, and had the real smack on it. Coo was delighted with it; he drank and he sang, and he laughed and he danced, till he fell on the floor fast asleep. Then Jack, who had taken good care to keep himself sober, snapt up the cocked hat, ran off to the rock, leaped in, and soon arrived at Coo's habitation.

All was as still as a churchyard at midnight – not a Merrow young or old, was there. In he went and turned up the pots but nothing did he see, only he heard, he thought, a sort of a little whistle or chirp as he raised each of them. At this he was surprised, till he recollected what the priest had often said, that nobody living could see the soul, no more than they could see the wind or the air. Having now done all he could do for them he set the pots as they were before, and sent a blessing after the poor souls to speed them on their journey wherever they were going. He now began to think of returning; he put on the hat (as was right) the wrong way; but when he got out, he found the water so high over his head that he had no hopes of ever getting up into it now that he had not old Coomara to give him a lift. He walked about looking for a ladder, but not one could he find, and not a rock was there in sight. At last he saw a spot where the sea hung rather lower than anywhere else, so he resolved to try there. Just as he came to it, a big cod happened to put down his tail. Jack made a jump and caught hold of it, and the cod, all in amazement, gave a bounce and pulled Jack up. The minute the hat touched the water, pop away Jack was whisked; and up he shot like a cork, dragging the poor cod, that he forgot to let go, up with him tail foremost. He got to the rock in no time, and without a moment's delay hurried home rejoicing in the good deed he had done.

But meanwhile, there was fine work at home; for our friend Jack had hardly left the house on his soul-freeing expedition, when back came Biddy from her soul-saving one to the well. When she entered the house and saw the things lying *thrie-na heelah* on the table before her.

'Here's a purty job,' said she, 'that blackguard of mine – what ill-luck I had ivir to marry him – he's picked up some vagabone or other, while I was prayin' for the good of his sowl; and they've bin dhrinkin' up all the potyeen that my own brother gev' him, and all the sperits, to be shure, that he was to have sould to his honour.'

Then hearing an outlandish kind of grunt, she looked down and saw Coomara lying under the table. 'The blessed Vargin help an' save me', shouted she, 'if he hasn't made a rael baste of himself. Well, well, well to be shure, I often hard till of a man makin' a baste of himself wid dhrink, but I niver saw it afore! Oh hone, oh hone – Jack, honey, what 'ill I do wid you, or what 'ill I do widout you? How can any dacint woman ivir think of livin' wid a baste?'

With such like lamentations, Biddy rushed out of the house, and was going, she knew not where, when she heard the well known voice of Jack, singing a merry tune. Glad enough was Biddy to find him safe and sound, and not turned into a thing that was like neither fish nor flesh. Jack was obliged to tell her all; and Biddy, though she had half a mind to be angry with him for not telling her before, owned that he had done a great service to the poor souls. Back they both went most lovingly to the house, and Jack wakened up Coomara; and perceiving the old fellow to be rather dull, he bid him not be cast down, for 'twas many a good man's case; said it all came of his not being used to the potyeen, and recommended him, by way of cure, to swallow a hair of the dog that bit him. Coo, however, seemed to think he had had quite enough: he got up, quite out of sorts, and without having the good manners to say one word in the way of civility, he sneaked off to cool himself by a jaunt through the salt water.

Coomara never missed the souls. He and Jack continued the best friends in the world; and no one, perhaps, ever equalled Jack at freeing souls from purgatory; for he contrived fifty excuses for getting into the house below the sea, unknown to the old fellow; and then turned up the pots, and let out the souls. It vexed him, to be sure, that he could never see them; but as he knew the thing to be impossible, he was obliged to be satisfied. Their intercourse continued for several years. However, one morning, on Jack's throwing a stone, as usual, he got no answer. He flung another, and another; still there was no reply. He went away, and returned the next morning; but it was to no purpose. As he was without the hat, he could not go down to see what had become of Old Coo; but his belief was, that the old man, or the old fish, or whatever he was, had either died, or had removed away from that part of the country.

Departure of the Fairies

ON A SABBATH morning, all the inmates of a little hamlet had gone to church, except a herd-boy, and a little girl, his sister, who were lounging beside one of the cottages, when just as the shadow of the garden-dial had fallen on the line of noon, they saw a long cavalcade ascending out of the ravine, through the wooded hollow. It winded among the knolls and bushes, and turning round the northern gable of the cottage, beside which the sole spectators of the scene were stationed, began to ascend the eminence towards the south.

The horses were shaggy diminutive things, speckled dun and grey; the riders stunted, misgrown, ugly creatures, attired in antique jerkins of plaid, long grey clokes, and little red caps, from under which their wild uncombed locks shot out over their cheeks and foreheads. The boy and his sister stood gazing in utter dismay and astonishment, as rider after rider, each more uncouth and dwarfish than the other which had preceded it, passed the cottage and disappeared among the brushwood, which at that period covered the hill, until at length the entire

78

rout, except the last rider, who lingered a few yards behind the others, had gone by.

'What are you, little mannie? and where are ye going?' inquired the boy, his curiosity getting the better of his fears and his prudence.

'Not of the race of Adam,' said the creature, turning for a moment in its saddle, 'the people of peace shall never more be seen in Scotland.'

RIGINS AND
CAUSES

Origins and Causes

Folk-tales that explain beginnings, sometimes called aetiological tales, stand on the frontiers of myth. Like myth, they show us how things came to be – everything from how the world began to how the leopard got his spots; but unlike myth, they may be not so much articles of belief as entertainments. The stock characters of folk-tale may parade through the pages of an aetiological tale and it may well be set at a specific time.

The Orcadian story of *Assipattle and the Muckle Mester Stoor Worm* is virtually a cross-breed. The Stoor Worm that lies in the sea and coils its body round the earth is none other than the Midgard Serpent of Norse mythology, and the king whose land the Stoor Worm threatens claims descent from Odin, foremost of the gods. Yet here they inhabit the same world as the conventional lazy seventh son and the beautiful imperilled princess. The tale is as much about how Assipattle won the hand of Gem-de-lovely, and the kingdom into the bargain, as it is about how the Stoor Worm's teeth and body became island groups and land masses.

Assipattle was twice recorded by Walter Traill Dennison in the nineteenth century, once in dialect and once at great length. This retelling by Ernest Marwick, most celebrated of Orkney's folklorists in the last generation, takes its lead from those versions.

P. H. Emerson, best remembered for his photographs of rural life in East Anglia, lived on the island of Anglesey during the winter of 1891-92 and there collected the contents of his *Welsh Fairy-Tales and Other Stories* (1894). With its memory of the Trojan Wars and suggestion that the Celts were descendants of the Trojans, the tale of the *Origin of the Welsh* perpetuates the tradition recorded (and possibly initiated) by the twelfth-century

83

historian Geoffrey of Monmouth who, in his highly influential *History of the Kings of Britain*, depicted Brutus, great-grandson of the Trojan Aeneas, as founder of the British race: 'Brutus then called the island Britain from his own name, and his companions he called Britons. His intention was that his memory should be perpetuated by the derivation of the name.'

Several British folk-tales ascribe the position of hills and barrows to the work of the devil, among them *The Devil at Largo Law* (Fife), *The Devil's Lapful* (Somerset) and *The Devil's Spittleful* (Black Country). *The Origin of the Wrekin* closely resembles this last tale, but a weary giant takes the place of the devil. The tale was collected in Shropshire by Georgina Jackson. Her papers, unpublished during her lifetime, were edited by Charlotte Burne in 1883 under the title of *Shropshire Folk-Lore: A Sheaf of Gleanings* – a phrase which neatly expresses how county collectors at the end of the nineteenth century could still hope for handsome pickings provided they were persistent enough. In 1910, Charlotte Burne became the first female president of The Folk-Lore Society. She gave two significant presidential addresses on folklore method, and revised and expanded George Gomme's *A Handbook of Folklore*.

The idea of a lost village or town or land beneath the water is at once commonplace and peculiarly haunting. In his note on *Fior Usga*, Thomas Crofton Croker (whom we have already met as the collector of *The Legend of Knockgrafton*) suggests causes for the tales of this type:

> Stories of buildings beneath the waters have originated some in real events, as where towns have been swallowed by earthquakes, and lakes formed where they had stood; or where the sea, by gradual encroachment, has covered the land and the buildings on it; others, perhaps, from optical illusion, where the shadows of the mountains and the various and fantastic forms of the clouds are reflected from the calm and unruffled bosom of a lake.

And others, one may want to add, from a human longing for a

84

pure and timeless place, seemingly almost attainable, similar in kind to Avalon, Hy-Brasil and the Isles of the Blessed – an earthly paradise set in the western seas.

In *Fíor Usga*, however, the deluge of water is a purge and a punishment. The medieval Welsh topographer and historian Giraldus Cambrensis recorded the tradition that Lough Neagh had originally been a fountain which overflowed and drowned the neighbourhood so that, in the words of the poet Tom Moore, to whom Crofton Croker relayed this tale

> *On Lough Neagh's bank, as the fisherman strays*
> *When the clear cold eve's declining,*
> *He sees the round towers of other days*
> *In the wave beneath him shining.*

Joseph Train, a visitor to the island, compiled *An Historical and Statistical Account of the Isle of Man* in 1845. As *Origin of the Arms of the Island* may suggest, the folk material he assembled consisted not so much of developed tales as arresting snippets of belief, raw material. Perhaps he encountered the difficulty described by the great John Francis Campbell of Islay (see p.110) after his visit to Man in 1860: 'any attempt to extract a story, or search out a queer old custom, or a half-forgotten belief, seemed to act as a pinch of snuff does on a snail. The Manxman would not trust the foreigner with his secrets . . . '

Sidney Oldall Addy collected fifty-two tales from Yorkshire, Lincolnshire, Derbyshire and Nottinghamshire in the 1890s. Although he did not attempt to reproduce dialect, Addy said that 'As nearly as I could manage it, the tales are given in the words of the narrators', and this is usually evident in the swiftness and convincing cadences of his tales. Byard is only one of a number of fabulous horses whose footprints are stamped on Europe – not long ago, I inspected those of eight-legged Sleipnir in Iceland. A variant of *Byard's Leap* tells that if anyone attempts to fill the footprints up, they are always empty again next morning; man cannot do away with such magic, except perhaps through neglect.

Assipattle and the Muckle Mester Stoor Worm

ASSIPATTLE was the youngest of seven sons. He lived with his father and mother and brothers on a fine farm beside a burn. They all worked hard except Assipattle, who could be persuaded to do little. He lay beside the big open fire in the farm kitchen, caring nothing that he became covered with ashes. His father and mother shook their heads over him; his brothers cursed him for a fool and kicked him. Everyone hooted with mirth when Assipattle told, of an evening, stories of incredible battles in which he was the hero.

One day awful news reached the farm. It was said that the muckle mester Stoor Worm was coming close to land. The Stoor Worm was the most dreaded creature in all the world. People grew pale and crossed themselves when they heard his name, for he was the worst of 'the nine fearful curses that plague mankind'.

If the earth shook and the sea swept over the fields, it was Stoor Worm yawning. He was so long that there was no place for his body until he coiled it around the earth. His breath was so venomous that when he was angry and blew out a great blast of it every living thing within reach was destroyed and all the crops were withered. With his forked tongue he would sweep hills and villages into the sea, or seize and crush a house or ship so that he could devour the people inside.

When he came close to the country where Assipattle lived, and began to yawn, the people knew that he must be fed, otherwise he would get into a rage and destroy the whole land. The news was that the king had consulted a wise man, a spaeman, about what must be done. After thinking a while, the spaeman said that the only way to keep the Stoor Worm happy was to feed him on young virgins, seven of them each week. The people were horrified by this, but the danger was so appalling that they consented.

Every Saturday morning seven terrified girls were bound hand and foot and laid on a rock beside the shore. Then the monster raised his head from the sea and seized them in the fork of his tongue and they were seen no more.

As they listened to what the king's messenger, who had brought the news, had to tell, the faces of Assipattle's father and brothers grew grey and they trembled, but Assipattle declared he was ready to fight the monster. All through the years, he bragged, he had been saving his strength just for this. His brothers were furious and pelted him with stones, but his father said sadly, 'It's likely you'll fight the Stoor Worm when I make spoons from the horns of the moon.'

There were even more dreadful things for the messenger to relate. He said that the people of the country were so horrified by the deaths of the loveliest and most innocent girls that they demanded some other remedy. Once again the king consulted the spaeman, who declared at long last, with terror in his eyes, that the only way to persuade the monster to depart was to offer him the most beautiful girl in the land, the Princess Gem-de-lovely, the king's only child.

Gem-de-lovely was the king's heir and he loved her more than anyone else. But the people were so frantic with grief at the loss of their own children, that the king said with tears rolling down his cheeks, 'It is surely a wonderful thing that the last of the oldest race in the land, who is descended from the great god Odin, should die for her folk.'

There was only one possible way of saving the princess, so the king asked for sufficient time to send messengers to every part of his realm. They were to announce that the princess would become the wife of any man who was strong enough and brave enough to fight the monster and overcome him. The wedding gift to the champion would be the kingdom itself and the famous sword Sikkersnapper that the king had inherited from Odin.

Thirty champions had come to the palace [said the messenger who had halted his weary horse at Assipattle's farm], but only twelve of them remained after they had seen the Stoor Worm. Even they were sick with fear. It was certain that the king had no faith in them. Old and feeble as he was, he had taken the sword Sikkersnapper out of the chest behind the high table, and had sworn that he would fight the monster himself rather than let his daughter be destroyed. His boat was pulled down from its noust* and was anchored near the shore, so as to be ready when he needed it.

Assipattle listened eagerly to all this, but no one heeded him. The messenger mounted his horse and slowly rode away. Soon the father and mother went to bed. From where he lay in the ashes beside the flickering fire, Assipattle heard them saying that they would go next day to see the fight between the king and the monster. They would ride Teetgong, who was the swiftest horse in the land.

How was it that Teetgong could be made to gallop faster than any other horse? asked the mother. It was a long time before Assipattle's father would tell her, but at last, worn out by her questions, he said, 'When I want Teetgong to stand I give him a clap on the left shoulder; when I want him to run quickly I give

---

* A sheltered place above the reach of the tide.

him two claps on the right shoulder; and when I want him to gallop as fast as he can go I blow through the thrapple* of a goose that I always keep in my pocket. He has only to hear that and he goes like the wind.'

After a while there was silence and Assipattle knew that they were asleep. Very quietly he pulled the goose thrapple out of his father's pocket. He found his way to the stable, where he tried to bridle Teetgong. At first the horse kicked and reared, but when Assipattle patted him on his left shoulder he was as still as a mouse. When Assipattle got on his back and patted his right shoulder he started off with a loud neigh. The noise wakened the father, who sprang up and called his sons. All of them mounted the best horses they could find and set off in pursuit of the thief, little knowing that it was Assipattle.

The father, who rode fastest, almost overtook Teetgong, and he shouted to him,

> 'Hi, hi, ho!
> Teetgong wo.'

At that, Teetgong came at once to a halt. Assipattle put the goose thrapple to his mouth and blew as hard as he could. When Teetgong heard the sound he galloped away like the wind, leaving his master and the six sons far behind. The speed was such that Assipattle could hardly breathe.

It was almost dawn when Assipattle reached the coast where the Stoor Worm was lying. There was a dale between the hills. In the dale was a small croft house. Assipattle tethered his horse and slipped into the croft. An old woman lay in bed, snoring loudly. The fire had been rested,† and an iron pot stood beside it. Assipattle seized the pot. In it he placed a glowing peat from the fire. The woman did not waken as he crept quietly out of the house, but the grey cat which lay at the bottom of her bed yawned and stretched itself.

Down to the shore Assipattle hurried. Far out from the land

---

* Windpipe.
† Banked.

there was a dark high island, which was really the top of the Stoor Worm's head. But close to the shore a boat was rocking at anchor. A man stood up in the boat beating flukes,* for it was a cold morning. Assipattle shouted to the man, 'Why don't you come on shore to warm yourself?'

'I would if I could', replied the man, 'but the king's kamperman† would thrash me black and blue if I left the boat.'

'You had better stay then,' said Assipattle, 'a whole skin is better than a sarkful of sore bones. As for myself, I am going to light a fire to cook limpets for my breakfast.' And he began to dig a hollow in the ground for a fireplace.

He dug for a minute or two, then he jumped up crying, 'Gold! It must be gold! It's yellower than the corn and brighter than the sun!'

When the man in the boat heard this he jumped into the water and waded ashore. He almost knocked Assipattle down, so anxious was he to see the gold. With his bare hands he scratched the earth where Assipattle had been digging.

Meanwhile, Assipattle untied the painter and sprang into the boat with the pot in his hand. He was well out to sea when the man looked up from his digging and began to roar with madram.‡ The sun appeared like a red ball over the end of the valley as Assipattle hoisted his sail and steered towards the head of the monster. When he looked behind, he could see that the king and all his men had gathered on the shore. Some of them were dancing with fury, bawling at him to come back. He paid no heed, knowing that he must reach the Stoor Worm before the creature gave his seventh yawn.

The Stoor Worm's head was like a mountain and his eyes like round lochs, very deep and dark. When the sun shone in his eyes the monster wakened and began to yawn. He always gave seven long yawns, then his dreadful forked tongue shot out and

* Swinging his arms across his chest to warm himself.
† Seneschal.
‡ Rage.

seized any living thing that happened to be near. Assipattle steered close to the monster's mouth as he yawned a second time. With each yawn a vast tide of water was swept down the Stoor Worm's gullet. Assipattle and his boat were carried with it into the mighty cavern of a mouth, then down the throat, then along twisting passages like tremendous tunnels. Mile after mile he was whirled, with the water gurgling around him. At last the force of the current grew less, the water got shallower, and the boat grounded.

Assipattle knew that he had only a short while before the next yawn, so he ran, as he had never run in his life, around one corner after another until he came to the Stoor Worm's liver. He could see what he was about because all the inside of the monster was lit up by meeracles.*

He pulled out a muckle ragger† and cut a hole in the liver. Then he took the peat out of the pail and pushed it in the hole, blowing for all he was worth to make it burst into flame. He thought the fire would never take, and had almost given up hope, when there was a tremendous blaze and the liver began to burn and sputter like a Johnsmas bonfire. When he was sure that the whole liver would soon be burning, Assipattle ran back to his boat. He ran even faster than he had done before, and he reached it just in time, for the burning liver made the Stoor Worm so ill that he retched and retched. A flood of water from the stomach caught the boat and carried it up to the monster's throat, and out of his mouth, and right to the shore, where it landed high and dry.

Although Assipattle was safe and sound, no one had any thought for him, for it seemed that the end of the world had come. The king and his men, and Assipattle, and the man who had been in the boat, and the old woman, who had been wakened by the noise, and her cat, all scrambled up the hill to escape from the floods that rushed from the Stoor Worm's mouth.

* Phosphorescence.
† Large knife.

91

Bigger and bigger grew the fire. Black clouds of smoke swirled from the monster's nostrils, so that the sky was filled with darkness. In his agony he shot out his forked tongue until it laid hold of a horn of the moon. But it slipped off and fell with such a tredad* that it made a deep rift in the earth. The tide rushed into the rift between the Dane's land and Norrowa. The place where the end of the tongue fell is the Baltic Sea. The Stoor Worm twisted and turned in torment. He flung his head up to the sky, and every time it fell the whole world shook and groaned. With each fall, teeth dropped out of the vile spewing mouth. The first lot became the Orkney Islands; the next lot became the Shetland Islands; and last of all, when the Stoor Worm was nearly dead, the Faroe Islands fell with an almighty splash into the sea. In the end the monster coiled himself tightly together into a huge mass. Old folk say that the far country of Iceland is the dead body of the Stoor Worm, with the liver still blazing beneath its burning mountains.

After a long while the sky cleared and the sun shone, and the people came to themselves again. On the top of the hill the king took Assipattle into his arms and called him his son. He dressed Assipattle in a crimson robe, and put the fair white hand of Gem-de-lovely into the hand of Assipattle. Then he girded the sword Sikkersnapper on Assipattle. And he said that as far as his kingdom stretched, north, south, east and west, everything belonged to the hero who had saved the land and people.

A week later, Assipattle and Gem-de-lovely were married in the royal palace. Never was there such a wedding, for everyone in the kingdom was happy that the Stoor Worm would never trouble them again. All over the country there was singing and dancing. King Assipattle and Queen Gem-de-lovely were full of joy, for they loved each other so much. They had ever so many fine bairns; and if they are not dead, they are living yet.

* Violent impact.

Origin of the Welsh

MANY years ago there lived several wild tribes round the King of Persia's city, and the king's men were always annoying and harassing them, exacting yearly a heavy tribute. Now these tribes, though very brave in warfare, could not hold their own before the Persian army when sent out against them, so that they paid their yearly tribute grudgingly, but took revenge, whenever they could, upon travellers to or from the city, robbing and killing them.

At last one of the tribesmen, a clever old chieftain, thought of a cunning plan whereby to defeat the Persians, and free themselves from the yearly tribute. And this was his scheme:

The wild wastes where these tribes lived were infested with large birds called 'Rohs',* which were very destructive to human beings – devouring men, women, and children greedily whenever they could catch them. Such a terror were they that the tribes had to protect their village with high walls, and then they slept securely, for the Roh hunted by night. This old

---

* Pronounced softly.

chieftain determined to watch the birds, and find out their nesting-places; so he had a series of towers built, in which the watchmen could sleep securely by night. These towers were advanced in whatever direction the birds were seen to congregate by night. The observers reported that the Roh could not fly, but ran very swiftly, being fleeter than any horse.

At length, by watching, their nesting-places were found in a sandy plain, and it was discovered that those monstrous birds stole sheep and cattle in great numbers.

The chieftain then gave orders for the watchmen to keep on guard until the young birds were hatched, when they were commanded to secure fifty, and bring them into the walled town. The order was carried out, and one night they secured fifty young birds just out of the egg, and brought them to the town.

The old chieftain then told off fifty skilful warriors, a man to each bird, to his son being allotted the largest bird. These warriors were ordered to feed the birds on flesh, and to train them for battle. The birds grew up as tame as horses. Saddles and bridles were made for them, and they were trained and exercised just like chargers.

When the next tribute day came round, the King of Persia sent his emissaries to collect the tax, but the chieftains of the tribes insulted and defied them, so that they returned to the king, who at once sent forward his army.

The chieftain then marshalled his men, and forty-six of the Rohs were drawn up in front of the army, the chief getting on the strongest bird. The remaining four were placed on the right flank, and ordered at a signal to advance and cut off the army, should they retreat.

The Rohs had small scales, like those of a fish, on their necks and bodies, the scales being hidden under a soft hair, except on the upper half of the neck. They had no feathers except on their wings. So they were invulnerable except as to the eyes – for in those days the Persians only had bows and arrows, and light javelins. When the Persian army advanced, the Rohs advanced at lightning speed, and made fearful havoc, the birds murdering and trampling the soldiers under foot, and beating them down with their powerful wings. In less than two hours half the Persian army was slain, and the rest had escaped. The tribes returned to their walled towns, delighted with their victory.

When the news of his defeat reached the King of Persia he was wroth beyond expression, and could not sleep for rage. So the next morning he called for his magician.

'What are you going to do with the birds?' asked the king.

'Well, I've been thinking the matter over,' replied the magician.

'Cannot you destroy all of them?'

'No, your majesty, I cannot destroy them, for I have not the power; but I can get rid of them in one way; for though I cannot put out life, I have the power of turning one life into some other living creature.'

'Well, what will you turn them into?' asked the king.

'I'll consider tonight , your majesty,' replied the magician.

'Well, mind and be sure to do it.'

'Yes, I'll be sure to do it, your majesty.'

The next day, at ten, the magician appeared before the king, who asked:

'Have you considered well?'

'Yes, your majesty.'

'Well, how are you going to act?'

'Your majesty, I've thought and thought during the night, and the best thing we can do is to turn all the birds into fairies.'

'What are fairies?' asked the king.

'I've planned it all out, and I hope your majesty will agree.'

'Oh! I'll agree, as long as they never molest us more.'

'Well, your majesty, I'm going to turn them to fairies – small living creatures to live in caves in the bowels of the earth, and they shall only visit people living on the earth once a year. They shall be harmless, and hurt nothing; they shall be fairies, and do nothing but dance and sing, and I shall allow them to go about on earth for twenty-four hours once a year and play their antics, but they shall do no mischief.'

'How long are the birds to remain in that state?' asked the king.

'I'll give them two thousand years, your majesty; and at the end of that time they are to go back into birds, as they were before. And after the birds change from the fairy state back into birds, they shall never breed more, but die a natural death.'

So the tribes lost their birds, and the King of Persia made such fearful havoc amongst them that they decided to leave the country.

They travelled, supporting themselves by robbery, until they came to a place where they built a city, and called it Troy, where they were besieged for a long time.

At length the besiegers built a large caravan, with a large man's head in front; the head was all gilded with gold. When the caravan was finished they put a hundred and fifty of the best warriors inside, provided with food, and one of them had a trumpet. Then they pulled the caravan, which ran upon eight broad wheels, up to the gates of the city, and left it there, their army being drawn up in a valley near by. It was agreed that when the caravan got inside the gates the bugler should blow three loud blasts to warn the army, who would immediately advance into the city.

The men on the ramparts saw this curious caravan, and they began wondering what it was, and for two or three days they left it alone.

At last an old chieftain said:

'It must be their food.'

On the third day they opened the gates, and attaching ropes, began to haul it into the city; then the warriors leaped out, and the horn blew, and the army hurried up, and the town was taken after great slaughter; but a number escaped with their wives and children, and fled on to the Crimea, whence they were driven by the Russians, so they marched away along the sea to Spain, and bearing up through France, they stopped.

Some wanted to go across the sea, and some stayed in the heart of France: they were the Bretoons.* The others came on over in boats, and landed in England, and they were the first people settled in Great Britain: they were the Welsh.

* Bretons.

The Origin of the Wrekin

ONCE upon a time there was a wicked old giant in Wales, who, for some reason or other, had a very great spite against the Mayor of Shrewsbury and all his people, and he made up his mind to dam up the Severn, and by that means cause such a flood that the town would be drowned. So off he set, carrying a spadeful of earth, and tramped along mile after mile, trying to find the way to Shrewsbury. And how he missed it I cannot tell, but he must have gone wrong somewhere, for at last he got close to Wellington, and by that time he was puffing and blowing under his heavy load, and wishing he was at the end of his journey. By and by there came a cobbler along the road with a sack of old boots and shoes on his back, for he lived at Wellington, and went once a fortnight to Shrewsbury to collect his customers' old boots and shoes, and take them home with him to mend. And the giant called out to him. 'I say,' he said, 'how far is it to Shrewsbury?'

'Shrewsbury?' said the cobbler. 'What do you want at Shrewsbury?'

'Why,' said the giant, 'to fill up the Severn with this lump of earth I've got here. I've an old grudge against the mayor and the folks at Shrewsbury, and now I mean to drown them out and get rid of them all at once.'

'My word!' thought the cobbler. 'This will never do! I can't afford to lose my customers!' and he spoke up again. 'Eh!' he said. 'You'll never get to Shrewsbury, not today, *nor* tomorrow. Why, look at me! *I'm* just come from Shrewsbury, and I've had time to wear out all these old boots and shoes on the road since I started.' And he showed him his sack.

'Oh!' said the giant with a great groan. 'Then it's no use! I'm fairly tired out already, and I can't carry this load of mine any farther. I shall just drop it here and go back home.'

So he dropped the earth on the ground just where he stood, and scraped his boots on the spade, and off he went home again to Wales, and nobody ever heard anything of him in Shropshire after. But where he put down his load there stands the Wrekin to this day, and even the earth he scraped off his boots was such a pile that it made the little Ercall by the Wrekin's side.

Fior Usga

A LITTLE way beyond the Gallows Green of Cork, and just
outside the town, there is a great lough of water, where people
in the winter go and skate for the sake of diversion; but the sport
above the water is nothing to what is under it, for at the very
bottom of this lough there are buildings and gardens, far more
beautiful than any now to be seen, and how they came there was
in this manner.

Long before Saxon foot pressed Irish ground, there was a great
king, called Corc, whose palace stood where the lough now is, in
a round green valley, that was just a mile about. In the middle of
the courtyard was a spring of fair water, so pure, and so clear,
that it was the wonder of all the world. Much did the king rejoice
at having so great a curiosity within his palace; but as people
came in crowds from far and near to draw the precious water of
this spring, he was sorely afraid that in time it might become
dry; so he caused a high wall to be built up round it, and would
allow nobody to have the water, which was a very great loss to
the poor people living about the palace. Whenever he wanted
any for himself he would send his daughter to get it, not liking to

trust his servants with the key of the well-door, fearing they might give some away.

One night the king gave a grand entertainment, and there were many great princes present, and lords and nobles without end; and there were wonderful doings throughout the palace: there were bonfires, whose blaze reached up to the very sky; and dancing was there, to such sweet music, that it ought to have waked up the dead out of their graves; and feasting was there in the greatest plenty for all who came; nor was any one turned away from the palace gates – but 'you're welcome – you're welcome, heartily,' was the porter's salute for all.

Now it happened at this grand entertainment there was one young prince above all the rest mighty comely to behold, and as tall and as straight as ever eye would wish to look on. Right merrily did he dance that night with the old king's daughter, wheeling here, and wheeling there, as light as a feather, and footing it away to the admiration of every one. The musicians played the better for seeing their dancing; and they danced as if their lives depended upon it. After all this dancing came the supper; and the young prince was seated at table by the side of his beautiful partner, who smiled upon him as often as he spoke to her; and that was by no means so often as he wished, for he had constantly to turn to the company and thank them for the many compliments passed upon his fair partner and himself.

In the midst of this banquet one of the great lords said to King Corc, 'May it please your majesty, here is every thing in abundance that heart can wish for, both to eat and drink, except water.'

'Water!' said the king, mightily pleased at some one calling for that of which purposely there was a want: 'Water shall you have, my lord, speedily, and that of such a delicious kind, that I challenge all the world to equal it. Daughter,' said he, 'go fetch some in the golden vessel which I caused to be made for the purpose.'

The king's daughter, who was called Fior Usga, (which signifies in English, Spring Water,) did not much like to be told to perform so menial a service before so many people, and though she did not venture to refuse the commands of her father, yet hesitated to obey him, and looked down upon the ground. The king, who loved his daughter very much, seeing this, was sorry for what he had desired her to do, but having said the word, he was never known to recall it; he therefore thought of a way to make his daughter go speedily and fetch the water, and it was by proposing that the young prince her partner should go along with her. Accordingly, with a loud voice, he said, 'Daughter, I wonder not at your fearing to go alone so late at night; but I doubt not the young prince at your side will go with you.' The prince was not displeased at hearing this; and taking the golden vessel in one hand, with the other led the king's daughter out of the hall so gracefully that all present gazed after them with delight.

When they came to the spring of water, in the courtyard of the palace, the fair Usga unlocked the door with the greatest care, and stooping down with the golden vessel to take some of the water out of the well, found the vessel so heavy that she lost her balance and fell in. The young prince tried in vain to save her, for the water rose and rose so fast, that the entire courtyard was speedily covered with it, and he hastened back almost in a state of distraction to the king.

The door of the well being left open, the water, which had been so long confined, rejoiced at obtaining its liberty, rushed forth incessantly, every moment rising higher, and was in the hall of the entertainment sooner than the young prince himself, so that when he attempted to speak to the king he was up to his neck in water. At length the water rose to such a height, that it filled the entire of the green valley in which the king's palace stood, and so the present Lough of Cork was formed.

Yet the king and his guests were not drowned, as would now happen if such an awful inundation were to take place; neither was his daughter, the fair Usga, who returned to the banquet-hall the very next night after this dreadful event; and every night since the same entertainment and dancing goes on in the palace in the bottom of the lough, and will last until some one has the luck to bring up out of it the golden vessel which was the cause of all this mischief.

Nobody can doubt that it was a judgment upon the king for his shutting up the well in the courtyard from the poor people: and if there are any who do not credit my story, they may go and see the Lough of Cork, for there it is to be seen to this day; the road to Kinsale passes at one side of it; and when its waters are low and clear, the tops of towers and stately buildings may be plainly viewed in the bottom by those who have good eyesight, without the help of spectacles.

Origin of the Arms of the Island

'Quocunque Jeceris Stabit' – MOTTO

THE NATIVES say that many centuries before the Christian era the Island was inhabited by Fairies, and that all business was carried on in a supernatural manner. They affirm that a blue mist continually hung over the land, and prevented mariners who passed in ships that way, from even suspecting that there was an Island so near at hand, till a few fishermen, by stress of weather, were stranded on the shore. As they were preparing to kindle a fire on the beach, they were astounded by a fearful noise issuing from the dark cloud which concealed the Island from their view. When the first spark of fire fell into their tinder box, the fog began to move up the side of the mountain, closely followed by a revolving object, closely resembling three legs of men joined together at the upper part of the thighs, and spread out so as to resemble the spokes of a wheel. Hence the Arms of the Island.

Byard's Leap

AT NEWMARKET, near Market Rasen in Lincolnshire, there once lived a witch who was a great trouble to the farmers in the neighbourhood. They bore it for a long time, until one of them made up his mind to stand it no longer. So he went to the wise man and asked him what he was to do to get rid of her.

The wise man said, 'Turn all your horses out of the farmyard, and drive them to the pond. And when they are drinking throw a stone into the water, and take notice of the horse which is the first to lift up its head. You must mount on his back, and in the night you must call at the hut where the witch lives and ask her to get up behind you and ride. But you must take a dagger with you, and keep it sticking out, so that when the witch leaps upon the horse she may cut her arm.'

So the farmer did as the wise man had told him, and took all his horses to the pond. Now it happened that the first horse to lift up its head when the farmer threw a stone into the water was a blind one called Byard. So the farmer leaped on Byard's back, and the same night he rode straight to the hut where the witch dwelt, and knocked at her door.

'Mother,' said the farmer, 'I have come to take thee for a ride, so get up behind me.'

So the witch, whose finger nails were very sharp and long, tried to leap up behind the farmer. In doing so she tried to catch hold of Byard with her finger nails, but she fell back twice, and each time that she fell back Byard leaped seven yards forward. At the third leap the witch clung fast to Byard behind, but she grazed her arm against the dagger which the farmer wore by his side. As soon as her arm began to bleed she lost all her power as a witch, and the country was no more troubled with her.

Byard's footprints are still to be seen in the place where he leaped three times. Whoever farms the land where they are is told to keep them clean and never to plough them up. And so they are carefully preserved to this day.

KINGS AND
HEROES

Kings and Heroes

The prodigious legendary heroes of the Celts – among them Cuchulain and Fionn and Arthur – were not only celebrated by great poets and prose masters in the Middle Ages but also remembered in oral tradition, and the stirring tales that were told about them constitute the primary matter of this category. To them we must add tales about noble but altogether less prepossessing medieval figures both Celtic and Saxon.

According to eleventh-century Irish sources, Fionn mac Cumhaill lived in the third century. He was leader of the Fianna or 'war-band', a company of warrior-huntsmen caught up in a series of heroic and romantic escapades in Leinster and Munster not altogether dissimilar to the more sophisticated Knights of the Round Table.

When, in 1762, James Macpherson published *Fingal* (Fionn), *an ancient epic poem in six books*, claiming it to be a translation from Gaelic of a newly-discovered poem by Fionn's own son, the legendary Ossian (Oisín), he caused a sensation. But sceptics, including Dr Johnson, suspected the unrepentant Macpherson of literary fraud and an enquiry conducted after his death revealed that *Fingal* consisted of a brew of original Gaelic poems and verse written by Macpherson himself. What is important to the folklorist, however, is that Macpherson's authentic Gaelic sources show Fionn to have been remembered through the centuries not only in Ireland but also in Scotland.

This section begins with two tales about Fionn and members of his Fianna, one from Ireland and one from Scotland. *Fionn in Search of his Youth* is an allegorical tale. The way in which the Fianna are magically deceived and upstaged by the personifications of Strength and Death and Youth is altogether reminiscent of the Norse myth that recounts Thor's visit to the court of

Utgard Loki in which he and his companions are outdone by Fire, Thought and Old Age.

This tale was recorded on an Ediphone cylinder in about 1930 by Peig Sayers, author of *An Old Woman's Reflections* and one of the remarkable and attractive group of Blasket Island storytellers and writers that also included Tomás Ó Criomhthain (*The Islandman*) and Maurice O'Sullivan (*Twenty Years A-Growing*). No less than 375 tales were collected from Peig Sayers and Seósamn Ó Daleigh has left this attractive account of her narrating: 'Great artist and wise woman that she was, Peig would at once switch from gravity to gaiety, for she was a light-hearted woman, and her changes of mood and face were like the changes of running water. As she talked her hands would be working too; a little slap of the palms to cap a phrase, a flash of the thumb over her shoulder to mark a mystery, a hand hushed to mouth for mischief or whispered secrecy!' *Fionn in Search of his Youth* is translated here by Sean O'Sullivan, father of Irish folklore in this century and archivist of the Irish Folklore Commission from its inception in 1935. He reports that the manuscript collection of the Commission has no less than thirty-three versions of this tale.

John Francis Campbell of Islay (1822-1885) is one of the most important figures in the history of British folklore. A busy man who was successively government secretary to the Lighthouse Commission and the Coal Commission and author of books on thermography and travel, he trained and sent out a team of educated Gaelic speakers to record tales told by the people – in Richard Dorson's words, the 'fishermen, farm servants, sawyers, drovers, labourers, stable boy, crofters, shoemakers, carters, stalkers, tinkers, gardeners, shepherds, tailors, a pauper, and a blind fiddler' – of the Highlands and Islands. In this way, Campbell assembled no less than 791 tales, of which he printed eighty-six in his four-volume *Popular Tales of the West Highlands* (1860-62).

Campbell is admired today not only for the magnificent stories he collected but also for his administrative skill, scrupulous directives to his collectors and quality of thought. *Popular Tales* is all the more absorbing because Campbell, who was often in the field himself, sets the scene, describing tellers and their recitations. Here, for example, he portrays a retelling of the 'Lay of Diarmaid':

> One woman was industriously weaving in a corner, another was carding wool, and a girl was spinning dexterously with a distaff made of a rough forked birch-branch, and a spindle which was little better than a splinter of fir. In a warm nook behind the fire sat a girl with one of those strange foreign faces which are occasionally to be seen in the Western Isles, and which are often supposed by their neighbours to mark the descendants of the Spanish crews of the wrecked Armada . . . Old men and young lads, newly returned from the eastern fishing, sat about on benches fixed to the wall, and smoked and listened; and MacDonald sat on a low stool in the midst, and chanted forth his lays amidst suitable remarks and ejaculations of praise and sympathy. One of the poems was the 'Lay of Diarmaid' . . . 'Och! och! – aw! is not that sad?' said the women when Diarmaid was expiring.

Diarmaid and Grainne, collected for Campbell by Hector Mac-Lean, a schoolmaster said to dabble in black magic, is only one of several Scottish and Irish versions of this superb story. Diarmaid was Fionn's nephew and his tragic involvement with Grainne is a direct consequence of the love spot he acquired in the last tale. The nobility of tone, alternation of verse and prose, and dramatic intensity with which Fionn's dilemma over whether or not to give Diarmaid life-saving water is presented, give this tale a grandeur far beyond the normal range of folk-tale.

By comparison, the English tale of the Armed Knight of Wandlebury, *Knight to Knight*, is plain fare. Indeed, there are no Saxon king-tales or hero-tales to bear comparison with the best of their Celtic counterparts. Osbert's challenge to the Armed Knight and the ensuing events are first described by the thirteenth-century historian Gervase of Tilbury in his *Otia*

Imperialia in what amounts to an early example of the ghost story. The idea that a spectre cannot survive daylight is a common one in European folklore. Sybil Marshall's robust retelling is in line with her declared intention in the introduction to *Everyman's Book of English Folk-Tales:*

> to recount the tales chosen . . . as they would have been told by a practised raconteur of folk origin, with extraneous detail or vivid turn of phrase added on the spur of the moment to enhance suspense or exaggerate character; in fact, to put new and attractive flesh on the age-old bones of the story without in any way changing the basic structure.

In his *History of the Kings of Britain*, Geoffrey of Monmouth tells us that 'Arthur himself, our renowned King, was mortally wounded and was carried off to the Isle of Avalon', and medieval romancers followed Geoffrey in translating the dying king over the water. But an alternative folk tradition has persisted that Arthur is nearer at hand, asleep with his knights in a great cave, until the day when he will return and drive out the enemies of the Welsh and repossess Britain. In the words of the contemporary Anglo-Welsh poet R. S. Thomas:

> *We are not English* . . . Ni bydd diwedd
> Byth ar sŵn y delyn aur.
> *Though the strings are broken, and time sets*
> *The barbed wire in their place,*
> *The tune endures; on the cracked screen*
> *Of life our shadows are large still*
> *In history's fierce afterglow.**

The idea of the sleeping warrior is a well-known one and there are other Arthurian versions associated with Sewing Shields in Northumberland and Richmond in Yorkshire ('Potter Thompson'), while Irish and Continental European variants have as their sleeping hero Fionn mac Cumhaill, Charlemagne and Barbarossa.

---

*Lines from 'Border Blues', *Poetry for Supper*, 1958. The Welsh words translate: there will never be an end to the sound of the golden harp.

The present version of this tale, which begins with a recognition of the divining properties of hazel, comes from Elijah Waring's *Recollections and Anecdotes of Edward Williams*. It is reprinted and discussed with other Arthurian cave legends by Sir John Rhys (see p.11) in his *Celtic Folklore*, a synthesis of source material and interpretation so packed out with psychological, philological and historical speculation that one of Rhys's obituarists noted: 'As a scholar, Rhys combined with great industry and learning a singularly active, reconstructive imagination. Where a more cautious man would have decided that the data were insufficient he often preferred to suggest a series of alternative theories . . .'

Fionn in Search of his Youth

ONE FINE DAY, Fionn mac Cumhaill and fourteen of his men were hunting on the top of Muisire Mountain. They had spent the whole day since sunrise there but met no game.

Late in the evening, Fionn spoke, ''Tis as well for us to face for home, men. We're catching nothing, and it will be late when we, hungry and thirsty, reach home.'

'Upon my soul. We're hungry and thirsty as it is,' said Conán.

They turned on their heels and went down the mountainside, but if they did, they weren't far down when a dark black fog fell on them. They lost their way and didn't know whether to go east or west. Finally they had to sit down where they were.

'I'm afraid, men, that we're astray for the evening,' said Fionn. 'I never yet liked a fog of this kind.'

After they had sat for a while talking and arguing, whatever look Diarmaid gave around, he saw a beautiful nice lime-white house behind them.

114

'Come along, men, to this house over there,' said he. 'Maybe we'll get something to eat and drink there.'

They all agreed and made their way to the house. When they entered, there was nobody before them but a wizened old man who was lying in a bent position at the edge of the hearth and a sheep which was tied along by the wall. They sat down. The old man raised his head and welcomed Fionn and his men heartily.

'By my soul,' said Diarmaid to himself. ''Tisn't very likely that our thirst or hunger will be eased in this hovel.'

After awhile, the old man called loudly to a young woman who was below in a room telling her to come up and get food ready for Fionn and his men. Then there walked up the floor from below, a fine strapping handsome young woman, and it didn't take her long to get food and drink ready for them. She pulled a long ample table out into the middle of the floor, spread a tablecloth on it, and laid out the dinner for the Fianna. She seated Fionn at the head of the table and set every man's meal in front of him. No sooner had each of them put the first bite of food into his mouth than the sheep which was tied along the wall stretched and broke the hard hempen tying that was holding her and rushed towards the table. She upset it by lifting one end of it and not a scrap of food was left that wasn't thrown to the floor in front of the Fianna.

'The devil take you,' cried Conán. 'Look at the mess you have made of our dinner, and we badly in need of it.'

'Get up, Conán, and tie the sheep,' said Fionn.

Conán, looking very angry at the loss of his dinner, got up against his will and walked to the sheep. He caught her by the top of the head and tried to drag her toward the wall. But if he broke his heart in the attempt, he couldn't tie her up. He stood there looking at her.

'By heavens,' said he. 'As great a warrior and hero as I am, here's this sheep today, and I can't tie her. Maybe someone else can?'

'Get up, Diarmaid, and tie the sheep,' said Fionn.

Diarmaid stood up and tried, but if he did, he failed to tie her.

Each of the fourteen men made an attempt, but it was no use.

'My shame on ye,' said the old man. 'To say that as great as your valour has ever been, ye can't tie an animal as small as a sheep to the side of the wall with a bit of rope.'

He got up from the edge of the hearth and hobbled down the floor. As he went, six pintsful of ashes fell from the backside of his trousers, because he had been so long lying on the hearth. He took hold of the sheep by the scruff of the head, pulled her easily in to the wall, and tied her up. When the Fianna saw him tie the sheep, they were seized with fear and trembling, seeing that he could do it after themselves had failed, brave and all though they were. The old man returned to his place by the fire.

'Come up here and get some food ready for Fionn and his men,' he called to the young woman.

She came up from the room again, and whatever knack or magic she had, she wasn't long preparing new food to set before them.

'Start eating now, men; ye'll have no more trouble,' said the old man. 'This dinner will quench your thirst and hunger.'

When they had eaten and were feeling happy with their stomachs full, they drew their chairs back from the table. Whatever peering around Fionn had – he was always restless – he looked toward the room and saw the young woman sitting on a chair there. He got a great desire to talk to her for a while. He went down to the room to her.

'Fionn mac Cumhaill,' said she, 'you had me once and you won't have me again.'

He had to turn on his heel and go back to his chair. Diarmaid then went down to her, but he got the same answer; so did each of the rest of the Fianna. Oisín was the last to try, but she said the same thing to him. She took him by the hand and led him up the floor till she stood in front of the Fianna.

'Fionn mac Cumhaill,' said she, 'ye were ever famous for strength and agility and prowess, and still each of you failed to tie the sheep. This sheep is not of the usual kind. She is Strength. And that old man over there is Death. As strong as the sheep was, the old man was able to overcome her. Death will overcome ye in the same way, strong and all as ye are. I myself am a planet sent by God, and it is God who has placed this hovel here for ye. I am Youth. Each of you had me once but never will again. And now, I will give each of you whatever gift he asks me for.'

Fionn was the first to speak, and he asked that he might lose the smell of clay, which he had had ever since he sinned with a woman who was dead.

Diarmaid said that what he wanted was a love spot on his body, so that every young woman who saw it would fall in love with him.

Oscar asked for a thong which would never break for his flail.

Conán asked for the power of killing hundreds in battle, while he himself would be invulnerable.

On hearing this, Diarmaid spoke.

'Alas!' said he. 'If Conán is given the power of killing hundreds, for heaven's sake, don't let him know how to use it. He's a very strong, but a very vicious, man, and if he loses his temper, he won't leave one of the Fianna alive.'

And that left Conán as he was ever afterward. He never knew how to use this power that he had, except once at the Battle of Ventry, when he looked at the enemy through his fingers and slew every one of them.

Each of the Fianna in turn asked for what he wanted. I don't know what some of them asked for, but Oisín asked for the grace of God. They say that he went to the Land of Youth and remained there until Saint Patrick came to Ireland, so that he would get the proper faith and knowledge of God and extreme unction when he died. He got them too, for when he returned to Ireland, Saint Patrick himself baptized him and anointed him before he died.

Diarmaid and Grainne

FIONN was going to marry Grainne, the daughter of the King of Carmag in Eirinn. The nobles and great gentles of the Feinne were gathered to the wedding. A great feast was made, and the feast lasted seven days and seven nights; and when the feast was past, their own feast was made for the hounds. Diarmaid was a truly fine man, and there was *ball seirc*, a love spot on his face, and he used to keep his cap always down on the beauty spot; for any woman that might chance to see the *ball seirc*, she would be in love with him. The dogs fell out roughly, and the heroes of the Feinne went to drive them from each other, and when Diarmaid was driving the dogs apart, he gave a lift to the cap, and Grainne saw the *ball seirc* and she was in heavy love for Diarmaid.

She told it to Diarmaid, and she said to him, 'Thou shalt run away with me.'

'I will not do that,' said Diarmaid.

'I am laying it on thee as a wish; and as spells that thou go with me.'

'I will not go with thee; I will not take thee in softness, and I will not take thee in hardness; I will not take thee without, and I will not take thee within; I will not take thee on horseback, and I will not take thee on foot,' said he; and he went away in displeasure, and he went to a place apart, and he put up a house there, and he took his dwelling in it.

On a morning that there was, who cried out in the door but Grainne, 'Art thou within, Diarmaid?'

'I am.'

'Come out and go with me now.'

'Did I not say to thee already that I would not take thee on thy feet, and that I would not take thee on a horse, that I would not take thee without, and that I would not take thee within, and that I would not have anything to do with thee.'

She was between the two sides of the door, on a buck goat. 'I am not without, I am not within, I am not on foot, and I am not on a horse; and thou must go with me,' said she.

'There is no place to which we may go that Fionn will not find us out when he puts his hand under his tooth of knowledge, and he will kill me for going with thee!'

'We will go to Carraig and there are so many Carraigs that he will not know in which we may be.'

They went to Carraig an Daimh.*

Fionn took great wrath when he perceived that his wife had gone away, and he went to search for her. They went over to Ceantire, and no stop went on their foot, nor stay on their step, till they reached Carraig an Daimh in Ceantire, near to Cille Charmaig. Diarmaid was a good carpenter, and he used to be at making dishes, and at fishing, and Grainne used to be going about selling the dishes, and they had beds apart.

On a day that there was there came a great sprawling old man [by] the way, who was called Ciofach Mac a Ghoill, and he sat, and he was playing at *dinnsirean*.† Grainne took a liking for the old carl, and they laid a scheme together that they would kill

---

* The stag's crag.
† Either wedges or dice.

Diarmaid. Diarmaid was working at dishes. The old man laid
hands on him, and he turned against the old man, and they
went into each other's grips. The old man was pretty strong, but
at last Diarmaid put him under. She caught hold of the
gearrasgian, knife, and she put it into the thigh of Diarmaid.
Diarmaid left them, and he was going from hole to hole, and he
was but just alive, and he was gone under hair and under beard.
He came the way of the Carraig and a fish with him, and he
asked leave to roast it. He got a cogie of water in which he might
dip his fingers, while he was roasting it. Now there would be the
taste of honey on anything which Diarmaid might touch with his
finger, and he was dipping his fingers into the cogie. Grainne
took a morsel out of the fish, and she perceived the taste of
honey upon it. To attack Diarmaid went Ciofach, and they were
in each other's grips for a turn of a while, but at last Diarmaid
killed Ciofach, and away he went, and he fled, and he went over
Loch a Chaisteil.

When Grainne saw that Ciofach was dead she followed
Diarmaid, and about the break of day, she came to the strand,
and there was a heron screaming. Diarmaid was up in the face of
the mountain, and said Grainne:

> '*It is early the heron cries,*
> *On the heap above Sliabh gaoil,*
> *Oh Diarmaid O Duibhne to whom love I gave,*
> *What is the cause of the heron's cry?*

> '*Oh Grainne, daughter of Carmaig of Steeds,*
> *That never took a step aright,*
> *It seems that before she gave the cry*
> *Her foot had stuck to a frozen slab.*

'Wouldst thou eat bread and flesh, Diarmaid?'
'Needful were I of it if I had it.'
'Here I will give it to thee; where is a knife will cut it?'
'Search the sheath in which thou didst put it last,' said
Diarmaid.

The knife was in Diarmaid ever since she had put it into him, and he would not take it out. Grainne drew out the knife, and that was the greatest shame that she ever took, drawing the knife out of Diarmaid.

Fear was on Diarmaid that the Feinne would find them out, and they went on forwards to Gleann Eilg.*

They went up the side of a burn that was there, and took their dwelling there, and they had beds apart.

Diarmaid was making dishes, and the shavings which he was making were going down with the burn to the strand.

The Fiantan were hunting along the foot of the strand, and they were on the track of a venomous boar that was discomfiting them. Fionn took notice of the shavings at the foot of the burn.

'These,' said he, 'are the shavings of Diarmaid.'

'They are not; he is not alive,' said they.

'Indeed,' said Fionn, 'they are. We will shout Foghaid! a hunting cry, and in any one place in which he may be, he is sworn to it that he must answer.'

Diarmaid heard the Foghaid.

'That is the Foghaid of the Fiantan; I must answer.'

> *'Answer not the cry, oh Diarmaid;*
> *It is but a lying cry'.*

Diarmaid answered the shout, and he went down to the strand. It was set before Diarmaid to hunt the boar. Diarmaid roused the boar from Bein Eidin to Bein Tuirc.†

> *While drawing down the long mountain,*
> *The brute was bringing Diarmaid to straits.*
> *His tempered blades were twisted*
> *Like withered rushy plaits.*

Diarmaid gave a draw at the slasher that Lon Mac Liobhain‡

* Glen Elg, opposite the narrows between Skye and the mainland.
† Two mountains.
‡ This sword-maker is known by this name in the Isle of Man, and is there called the dark smith of Drontheim.

made, and he put it in under the armpit and he killed the boar.

This was no revenge for Fionn yet over Diarmaid. There was a mole on the sole of the foot of Diarmaid, and if one of the bristles should go into it, it would bring his death.

Said Fionn –

> 'Oh Diarmaid, measure the boar,
> How many feet from his snout to his heel?'

Diarmaid measured the boar.

'Sixteen feet of measure true.'

'Measure the boar against the hair.'

He measured the boar against the hair, one of the bristles went into the mole and he fell.

Fionn took sorrow for him when he fell. 'What would make thee better, Diarmaid?'

'If I could get a draught of water from the palms of Fionn I would be better.'

Fionn went for the water, and when he thought on Grainne he would spill the water, and when he would think of Diarmaid, he would take sorrow, and he would take it with him; but Diarmaid was dead before Fionn returned.

They walked up the side of the burn till they came to where Grainne was; they went in; they saw two beds, and they understood that Diarmaid was guiltless. The Feinne were exceedingly sorrowful about what had befallen. They burned

> Grainne, daughter of Carmaig of steeds
> That never took a step aright,
> In a faggot of grey oak.

Knight to Knight

IT HAD to be a night when the full moon was shining down upon the hills, and showing up the shape of the ancient fort – a level place surrounded by entrenchments of ditch and wall, in the still-remaining outline of which there was only one gap, where the entrance must have been. Then, if a knight dared put on his harness, take lance in hand and ride through the gate on to the level place, he would be sure of a worthy adversary for a joust. Once inside the entrance, he had to call loudly, 'Knight to knight, come forth to fight!' and immediately there would stand before him another mounted knight, in full panoply of armour like himself. Then the charge would take place, and one or the other be dismounted; but the challenging knight had to enter the enclosure alone, or his ghostly adversary would not appear – though companions might remain outside the entrenchments, and watch the charge.

Well, that's what the people said – but there were few knights in and around Cambridge in the Middle Ages willing to put the story to the test.

The Gogmagog hills were eerie places, and the ancient Wandlebury fort up on the summit filled even the bravest with superstitious dread, for were not the old gods buried up there? Good Christians as they were, they crossed themselves in fear at the thought of disturbing Gog and Magog from their pagan slumbers, and gave the place a wide berth, specially at night. Honour for valour was what most knights yearned for, but as everybody knows, there are some things it is better not to meddle with.

However, some proud spirits simply cannot withstand a challenge, especially if it touches a well-earned reputation for courage. There came a-visiting to Cambridge a much renowned knight called Osbert, whose father, Hugh, had also won much honour in his time. Sir Osbert was a great power amongst his noble peers, redoubtable in arms, and chivalrous; indeed, according to all accounts, he was possessed of all knightly virtues to a greater degree than most.

It was winter time when Osbert came to Cambridge, and his hosts made much of him. When supper in the great hall was finished, the family of his noble host, with their famous guest, drew up to the roaring fire, surrounded by an outer circle of the lord's retainers who were for the most part local folk. Then, as always, the talk began to flow as tongues were loosed by comfort and good ale, and old tales began to be told. There were stories of the great deeds of the family in times past; of courage in battle and courtesy in love; there were sad tales of domestic tragedy, and ghostly tales that caused the men to cross themselves devoutly lest like dread happenings should ever come their way.

Then the servants and retainers began to take up the thread, and recount to their master and his honourable friend some of the stories they knew, especially those concerned with their own particular corner of England. And so it was, listening to one of the folk, that Sir Osbert heard the story of the Armed Knight of Wandlebury. It appeared that no one present had ever seen the apparition, or indeed ever attempted to make trial of the truth of it. Such a challenge was, however, too much for the valour of Sir

Osbert to withstand. Calling at once for his squire, he gave orders for his armour to be brought, and his horse to be saddled. The squire was bidden to prepare himself to accompany his master to the top of the Gogmagogs, where the truth of the old legend should be forthwith put to the test.

Amid great excitement the squire armed his knight, and out into the moonlight they sallied, with the host's entire household gathered to see them off. Their horses' hooves struck sparks from the cobbles as they rode away into the frosty night, the jingling of their horses' trappings fading gently in the distance as they went towards the hills.

Once arrived at the ancient fort, Sir Osbert commanded his squire to stand, and wait outside the perimeter of the fort. Then couching his lance at the ready, he urged his own steed through the entrance and out into the moonlit, levelled space. Bringing his horse to a standstill, he looked all around him. There was nothing to be seen but the rime glinting in the moonlight on the frosty bents of grass. Raising his head to send his voice as far afield as possible, he called aloud his challenge, 'Knight to knight, come forth to fight!'

Immediately there appeared in front of him another knight, armed from head to foot, and mounted on a splendid horse. Sir Osbert had no time to take in his opponent's knightly trappings, for the stranger had wheeled his horse, lowered his lance, raised his shield and was already preparing to charge. Sir Osbert hastily collected his wits, and did the same. Across the intervening space the two horses thundered, meeting with the shock of combined weight and speed that sounded far through the moonlit fields. The ghostly knight missed his mark, but the point of Sir Osbert's lance landed fair and square on his adversary's breast, and the next moment the strange knight had been unhorsed, and was lying on the grass. Sir Osbert, rejoicing in his astounding good fortune, urged his horse towards the riderless steed of his adversary; for by all the rules of chivalry, the winner of such a contest was entitled to the horse, and the armour, of his defeated foe.

But the unhorsed warrior sprang to his feet in an instant, and levelling his lance over his shoulder, he hurled it like a javelin at Sir Osbert. His aim was good and true, and the spear took the valiant challenger in the fleshy part of his thigh. Such a wound was as nought, however, to the victor of many such jousts on previous occasions. He barely felt the pain, and regarded his hurt as little more than mere temporary inconvenience. He caught the riderless horse, but when he looked for its master, he looked in vain. The other knight had disappeared into thin air, and the level enclosure lay open to the moon, again as bare as it had been before Osbert had issued his ritual challenge.

So he rode out of the enclosure, and gave the reins of his prize to his squire; and so they returned to their lodging in the lord's castle.

As they clattered into the courtyard, Sir Osbert's host, the family and all the household tumbled out to meet them. They were amazed at the tale, and delighted at the victory of their guest. That he was telling nothing but the truth they could see, for his squire was leading a horse such as few of them had ever seen before – a magnificent creature it was, tall, spirited and utterly beautiful, fierce of eye and proud of neck, with long, silky, jet-black mane and tail. The saddle and the rest of its trappings were likewise black, and very rich and fine. It was, indeed, a worthy prize.

By this time, there were others besides the lord's household gathered to see what was to be seen, for the noise had roused the neighbours, who had come flocking out when news of the knight's nocturnal adventure reached their ears. All joined in unstinted praise of the illustrious stranger's courage, and all rejoiced in his victory; and every eye was upon him as his squire began to untie his points and unarm him. As the squire bent to undo the straps of his lord's greaves, he cried out in alarm, for the metal greave round his calf was filled with clotted blood. It was only then that the hero disclosed the wound in his thigh, from whence the blood had flowed. The host's family were deeply concerned, and hurried him in to have the wound bathed and dressed, though the knight himself still scorned it as being of no consequence.

Out in the courtyard, attention was still focused on the wonderful horse. Ghost though its rider might have been, there could be no doubt about the reality of this wonderful piece of horseflesh. Neverthless, it seemed wise to keep the creature well tethered, and to set a watch on it all night.

Just as the dawn began to break, however, the horse began to become very restive, rolling its eyes, laying back its ears, and straining against its tether. At the first cockcrow it began curvetting and prancing; at the second it began to paw the earth, snorting and whinnying; and at the third it plunged and strained until its tether snapped, and before any man present could leap forward to hold it, it had kicked up its heels and galloped away to freedom, disappearing from view in the direction of the Gogmagog Hills.

In vain did the Baron Osbert and his men search for it next day; in vain did his host send out men to scour the countryside for the precious spoils of the victory, and in vain did all the folk in villages around keep open eyes for a glimpse of its hide or hair, in the hope of handsome reward. The beautiful horse and its fiery eye and jetblack mane and tail was never seen again. Nor, indeed, was its rider.

Sir Osbert's wound presently healed, so that he could return to his own home, but he was to have a perpetual reminder of his strange though valorous encounter. Each year, on the anniversary of his fight with the ghostly knight, the wound in his thigh burst open, and the blood flowed down once more to clot inside his greave. Then, as always, he made light of it, except perhaps for the chance it gave him to recount the strange adventure that had befallen him on a lonely green hilltop one frosty winter night in England. It may be that the memory filled him with homesickness for a sight of those gentle green fields, for by this time he was fighting the infidels far away and under burning skies. There, he did many other deeds to add to his fame and glory and there, at last, he died. His honour and reputation for valour lived on after him, until Gervase of Tilbury wrote down the tale of his Gogmagog adventure – in the early years of the thirteenth century. But the folk in and around Cambridge went on talking – of the ghostly knight of Wandlebury (and more particularly of his magnificent horse) until a century ago, thereabouts. Then the figure of the giant cut on the hills finally became obscured, and the memory of the ghostly horse was fused with that of Lord Godolphin's famous Arabian stallion which was certainly buried up there some time during the eighteenth century.

And that, as the folk of those parts still say – '*that* is how tales get about!'

The Sleeping Warriors

A WELSHMAN walking over London Bridge, with a neat hazel staff in his hand, was accosted by an Englishman, who asked him whence he came.

'I am from my own country,' answered the Welshman, in a churlish tone.

'Do not take it amiss, my friend,' said the Englishman; 'if you will only answer my questions, and take my advice, it will be of greater benefit to you than you imagine. That stick in your hand grew on a spot under which are hid vast treasures of gold and silver; and if you remember the place, and can conduct me to it, I will put you in possession of those treasures.'

The Welshman soon understood that the stranger was what he called a cunning man, or conjurer, and for some time hesitated, not willing to go with him among devils, from whom this magician must have derived his knowledge; but he was at length persuaded to accompany him into Wales; and going to Craig-y-Dinas,* the Welshman pointed out the spot whence he

* Rock of the Fortress.

had cut the stick. It was from the stock or root of a large old hazel: this they dug up, and under it found a broad flat stone. This was found to close up the entrance into a very large cavern, down into which they both went. In the middle of the passage hung a bell, and the conjurer earnestly cautioned the Welshman not to touch it. They reached the lower part of the cave, which was very wide, and there saw many thousands of warriors lying down fast asleep in a large circle, their heads outwards, every one clad in bright armour, with their swords, shields, and other weapons lying by them, ready to be laid hold on in an instant, whenever the bell should ring and awake them. All the arms were so highly polished and bright, that they illumined the cavern, as with the light of ten thousand flames of fire. They saw amongst the warriors one greatly distinguished from the rest by his arms, shield, battle-axe, and a crown of gold set with the most precious stones, lying by his side.

In the midst of this circle of warriors they saw two very large heaps, one of gold, the other of silver. The magician told the Welshman that he might take as much as he could carry away of either the one or the other, but that he was not to take from both the heaps. The Welshman loaded himself with gold: the conjurer took none, saying that he did not want it, that gold was of no use but to those who wanted knowledge, and that his contempt of gold had enabled him to acquire that superior knowledge and wisdom which he possessed. In their way out he cautioned the Welshman again not to touch the bell, but if unfortunately he should do so, it might be of the most fatal consequence to him, as one or more of the warriors would awake, lift up his head, and ask *if it was day*.

'Should this happen,' said the cunning man, 'you must, without hesitation, answer *No, sleep thou on;* on hearing which he will again lay down his head and sleep.'

In their way up, however, the Welshman, overloaded with gold, was not able to pass the bell without touching it – it rang – one of the warriors raised up his head, and asked, 'Is it day?'

'No,' answered the Welshman promptly, 'it is not, sleep thou on;' so they got out of the cave, laid down the stone over its entrance, and replaced the hazel tree.

The cunning man, before he parted from his companion, advised him to be economical in the use of his treasure; observing that he had, with prudence, enough for life: but that if by unforeseen accidents he should be again reduced to poverty, he might repair to the cave for more; repeating the caution, not to touch the bell if possible, but if he should, to give the proper answer, *that it was not day*, as promptly as possible. He also told him that the distinguished person they had seen was Arthur, and the others his warriors; and they lay there asleep with their arms ready at hand for the dawn of that day when the *Black Eagle* and the *Golden Eagle* should go to war, the loud clamour of which would make the earth tremble so much, that the bell would ring loudly, and the warriors awake, take up their arms, and destroy all the enemies of the Cymry, who afterwards should repossess the Island of Britain, re-establish their own king and govern-ment at Caerlleon, and be governed with justice, and blessed with peace so long as the world endures.

The time came when the Welshman's treasure was all spent: he went to the cave, and as before over-loaded himself. In his way out he touched the bell: it rang: a warrior lifted up his head, asking if it was day, but the Welshman, who had covetously overloaded himself, being quite out of breath with labouring under his burden, and withal struck with terror, was not able to give the necessary answer; whereupon some of the warriors got up, took the gold away from him, and beat him dreadfully. They afterwards threw him out, and drew the stone after them over the mouth of the cave. The Welshman never recovered the effects of that beating, but remained almost a cripple as long as he lived, and very poor. He often returned with some of his friends to Craig-y-Dinas; but they could never afterwards find the spot, though they dug over, seemingly, every inch of the hill.

ABULOUS

BEASTS

Fabulous Beasts

All over Britain there are monuments and mementoes, paint-
ings, pew-ends and place names, stories and snatches of song
associated with dragons. The Muckle Mester Stoor Worm, the
Laidly Worm and Knucker and the Serpent of Henham: the
names themselves are potent and, if belief in the dragon as such
is long since dead, he still lives in folk-tales and is cherished in
more than seventy villages as a source of local pride.

There is nothing safe or wholesome about British dragons.
Like all European dragons, beginning with those despatched by
Sigurd and Beowulf, and unlike their oriental counterparts who
are often benevolent and protective, they are dangerous and
incendiary and often evil. In her illuminating *British Dragons*
(1980), Jacqueline Simpson argues that dragon stories have
served three functions: to provide the hero with a worthy
opponent, to explain a coat of arms or a crest with a dramatic
story, and to offer explanations of material objects, place names
and topographical features.

There is probably no more entertaining dragon tale in Britain
than the ballad of *The Dragon of Wantley*. Unlike the cosmic
Muckle Mester Stoor Worm (see p.86), this dragon and his
opponent, More of More Hall, are presented as farcical music-
hall turns. In fact, Henry Carey based a successful burlesque
opera, first performed in 1737, on the legend. The wit is both of
language and situation. There are many vivid, unexpected and
sometime earthy turns of phrase, while More of More Hall has
recourse to hiding himself at the bottom of a well and shouting
'Boh!' at the dragon, and dressing himself up in hideous spiked
armour that makes him look like a mock-monster himself.
Indeed, the unedifying way in which More finally kills the
dragon is scarcely becoming to a 'furious knight'!

The ballad of *The Dragon of Wantley* first appears in the 1699 edition of *Wit and Mirth: Or, Pills to Purge Melancholy* and was reprinted by Thomas Percy in his *Reliques of Ancient English Poetry* (1765).

Bishop Percy noted that the poem was a political satire about a Yorkshire lawsuit over the payment of tithes – a contest between the draconic Sir Francis Wortley who held the tithes and an attorney (More) representing the neighbourhood. Jacqueline Simpson writes: '. . . seeing how many parallels the poem has with traditional tales elsewhere, it is obvious that whoever wrote it had a sound knowledge of dragon legends and did not invent his plot out of the blue; more likely, there already was a legend either at Wantley or nearby, which a clever writer versified with additional touches which alluded satirically to the lawsuit'.

There are almost as many black dog tales in Britain as there are tales about dragons – tales about the demon dog (sometimes called the Barguest) with saucer eyes, dogs that are ghosts of human beings, and huge prowling shaggy hounds like Shuck (Norfolk), Hooter (Warwickshire) and Skriker (Lancashire).

The Black Dog of the Wild Forest was one of the many tales collected from the Welsh gypsies in the 1890s by John Sampson and printed by Francis Hindes Groome (1810-1889) in his *Gypsy Folk-Tales* (1899). Both men are significant figures in the history of folklore. Sampson was master of both English and Welsh Rómani and Groome designated him 'the Rómani Grimm', praising his ability to 'take down a story in the very words, the very accents even, of its teller'. Sampson himself said:

> On the slopes of Cader I have laboured for days together taking down these things in a sort of phrenzy. No work could be more exhausting. To note every accent, to follow the story, and to keep the wandering wits of my Rómani raconteur to the point, all helped to make it trying work . . .

After first meeting gypsies during his Suffolk childhood, Groome married a gypsy girl called Esmerelda Lock, and devoted his life to the study of gypsy tales and traditions. He won wide popular recognition with his portrait of gypsy life, *In Gypsy Tents* (1880), wrote a novel of gypsy life, *Kriegspiel* (1896), and with Sampson established the Gypsy Lore Society. Arguing against Andrew Lang and Edwin Sidney Hartland who held that folk-tales with similar motifs were nonetheless of independent growth, but in line with Joseph Jacobs, Groome first advanced the diffusionist theory that gypsies carried oriental tales with them from Asia to Europe.

The Spirit Horse was collected by Thomas Crofton Croker (see p.9) who was told by a boy who guided him through the mountains from Kenmare to Killarney in 1825: 'Old people used to say that the Phookas (animal spirits) were very numerous in the times long ago: they were wicked-minded, black-looking, bad things, that would come in the form of wild colts with chains hanging about them. The Phookas did great hurt to benighted travellers.' It seems clear, however, that hard-drinking Morty Sullivan's spirit horse is also something of a spirits horse!

Two elements in the tale may require elucidation. The light from the fire which for mile after mile moves ahead of Morty is often referred to as the *ignis fatuus*, and many tales are told to account for it. But no matter whether the source of light is, as here, an old woman, or Will o' the Wisp or Jack-a-Lantern or some malicious boggart, its purpose is invariably to mislead some mortal and give him or her a terrible fright.

At the end of the tale, Morty Sullivan swears an oath 'by the hand of O'Sullivan'. This is an allusion to the family tag

> *Nulla manus*
> *Tam liberalis,*
> *Atque generalis,*
> *Atque universalis,*
> *Quam Sullivanus.*

Reluctantly setting aside fabulous cats, white rabbits and snakes, I take the bull as the last representative in this category. The heroine of *The Black Bull of Norroway* is a third and youngest daughter; she loses her protector by breaking a taboo and crossing her feet when she has been enjoined not to move; she is caught up in a long quest; she climbs a glass hill; she works as a servant: these and other well-known motifs make for an unusually rich and impressive tale. It was reworked by Andrew Lang, Joseph Jacobs and Walter de la Mare but first recorded in the version printed here by Robert Chambers (1802-71) in his *Popular Rhymes of Scotland*.

Encouraged and supplied with material by Sir Walter Scott, Chambers published his pioneering work in urban folklore, *Traditions of Edinburgh* (1824) when he was only twenty-two. But despite the rapid growth of the science of folklore, Chambers did not change his own methods but viewed folklore as the collection of antiquities (that is to say, customs, historical anecdotes, short biographies, Christian traditions, legends, superstitions etc.) and saw himself as the descendant of the great seventeenth and eighteenth-century antiquaries John Aubrey and John Stow, Dr Borlase and Dr William Stukeley. His last and greatest work, effectively the last work in a long tradition, was *The Book of Days* (1863-64).

The Dragon of Wantley

Old stories tell, how Hercules
    A dragon slew at Lerna,
With seven heads, and fourteen eyes,
    To see and well discern-a:
But he had a club, this dragon to drub,
    Or he had ne'er done it, I warrant ye;
But More of More Hall, with nothing at all,
    He slew the dragon of Wantley.

This dragon had two furious wings,
    Each one upon each shoulder;
With a sting in his tail, as long as a flail,
    Which made him bolder and bolder.
He had long claws, and in his jaws
    Four and forty teeth of iron;
With a hide as tough as any buff,
    Which did him round environ.

Fabulous Beasts

Have you not heard how the Trojan horse
    Held seventy men in his belly?
This dragon was not quite so big,
    But very near, I tell ye.
Devoured he poor children three,
    That could not with him grapple;
And at one sup he ate them up,
    As one would eat an apple.

All sorts of cattle this dragon did eat,
    Some say he ate up trees,
And that the forest sure he would
    Devour up by degrees;
For houses and churches were to him geese and turkies;
    He ate all, and left none behind,
But some stones, dear Jack, which he could not crack
    Which on the hills you will find.

In Yorkshire, near fair Rotherham,
    The place I know it well;
Some two or three miles, or thereabouts,
    I vow I cannot tell;
But there is a hedge, just on the hill's edge,
    And Matthew's house hard by it;
There and then was this dragon's den,
    You could not chuse but spy it.

Some say, this dragon was a witch;
    Some say, he was a devil,
For from his nose a smoke arose,
    And with it burning snivel,
Which he cast off, when he did cough,
    In a well that he did stand by;
Which made it look just like a brook
    Running with burning brandy.

Fabulous Beasts

Hard by a furious knight there dwelt,
    Of whom all towns did ring,
For he could wrestle, play at quarter-staff, kick, cuff and huff,
    Call son of a whore, do anything more;
By the tail and the mane, with his hands twain,
    He swung a horse till he was dead;
And that which is stranger, he for very anger
    Ate him all up but his head.

These children, as I told, being eat,
    Men, women, girls and boys,
Sighing and sobbing, came to his lodging,
    And made a hideous noise:
'Oh save us all, More of More Hall,
    Thou peerless knight of these woods;
Do but slay this dragon, who won't leave us a rag on,
    We'll give thee all our goods.'

'Tut, tut,' quoth he, 'no goods I want;
    But I want, I want, in sooth,
A fair maid of sixteen, that's brisk and keen,
    With smiles about the mouth;
Hair black as sloe, skin white as snow,
    With blushes her cheeks adorning;
To anoint me o'er night, e'er I go to fight,
    And to dress me in the morning.'

This being done, he did engage
    To hew the dragon down;
But first he went, new armour to
    Bespeak at Sheffield town;
With spikes all about, not within but without,
    Of steel so sharp and strong;
Both behind and before, arms, legs, and all o'er,
    Some five or six inches long.

Fabulous Beasts

Had you but seen him in this dress,
    How fierce he looked and how big,
You would have thought him for to be
    Some Egyptian porcupig.
He frighted all, cats, dogs and all,
    Each cow, each horse and each hog;
For fear they did flee, for they took him to be
    Some strange, outlandish hedgehog.

To see this fight, all people then
    Got up on trees and houses,
On churches some, and chimneys too,
    But these put on their trousers,
Not to spoil their hose. As soon as he rose,
    To make him strong and mighty,
He drank by the tale six pots of ale,
    And a quart of aqua-vitae.

It is not strength that always wins,
    For wit doth strength excell;
Which made our cunning champion
    Creep down into a well,
Where he did think this dragon would drink,
    And so he did in truth;
And as he stooped low, he rose up and cried 'Boh!'
    And hit him in the mouth.

'Oh' quoth the dragon, 'pox take thee, come out,
    Thou disturbst me in my drink.'
And then he turned, and shat at him –
    Good lack! How he did stink!
'Beshrew thy soul, thy body's foul,
    Thy dung smells not like balsam;
Thou son of a whore, thou stinkest so sore,
    Sure thy diet is unwholsome.'

Fabulous Beasts

Our politic knight, on the other side,
　　Crept out upon the brink,
And gave the dragon such a douse
　　He knew not what to think.
'By cock,' quoth he, 'say you so, do you see?'
　　And then at him he let fly
With hand and foot, and so they went to't,
　　And the word was 'Hey, boys, hey!'

'Your words,' quoth the dragon, 'I don't understand.'
　　Then to it they fell at all
Like two boars so fierce, if I may
　　Compare great things with small.
Two days and a night, with this dragon did fight
　　Our champion on this ground;
Though their strength it was great, their skill it was neat,
　　They never had one wound.

At length the hard earth began to quake,
　　The dragon gave him a knock,
Which made him to reel, and straightaway he thought
　　To lift him as high as a rock,
And thence let him fall. But More of More Hall
　　Like a valiant son of Mars,
As he came like a lout, so he turned him about,
　　And hit him a kick on the arse.

'Oh,' quoth the dragon, with a deep sigh,
　　And turned six times together,
Sobbing and tearing, cursing and swearing,
　　Out of his throat of leather;
'More of More Hall! Oh thou rascal!
　　Would I had seen thee never!
With the thing at thy foot, thou has prick'd my arse-gut,
　　And I'm quite undone for ever.

Fabulous Beasts

'Murder, murder!' the dragon cried,
  'Alack, alack for grief!
Had you but missed that place, you could
  Have done me no mischief.'
Then his head he shaked, trembled and quaked,
  And down he laid and cried;
First on one knee, then on back tumbled he,
  So groaned, kicked, shat, and died.

The Black Dog of the Wild Forest

THERE was a king and queen in the north of Ireland, and they had one son. The son had to be devoured when he came of age by the Black Dog of the Wild Forest, and his father was very fond of his son. When he came close to the time when he had to be devoured, his father took him a shorter journey every day; and one day his father saddled the best horse as he had in his stable, and gave him as much money as he liked to take with him. He galloped away as hard as ever he could till he got benighted. He rode some hundreds and hundreds of miles, and he could see a small little light a little distance off him, maybe a hundred miles off him to the best of his knowledge in the dark, and he makes for this little light. And who was living there but an old witch.

'Well, come in, my king's son,' she said, 'from the North of Ireland. I know you aren't very well.'

And so when he comes in, she puts him in the ess-hole under the fire. He hadn't been in there but twenty minutes, but in comes the Black Dog of the Wild Forest, spitting fire yards away out of his mouth, th' owd lady and her little dog named Hear-all after him. But they beat him.

'Now,' she says, 'my king's son, please to get up. You can have your tea now. We have beat him.'

So he gets up, has his tea with her, and gives a lot of money to the old lady, which says they have got a sister living from her three hundred miles. 'And if you can get there, ten to one she will give you her advice to get safe. I will give you my favours, the bread out of my mouth, that is Hear-all, the dog. I will give you that dog with you.'

He gallops on, gallops on, till he gets benighted. He looks behind him on the way he was going; his horse was getting very tired; and he could see the Black Dog of the Wild Forest after him. And he gallops on till he comes to t'other sister's house.

'Well, come in,' she says, 'my king's son from the North of Ireland. I know you aren't very well.'

She puts him down into the ess-hole again, sir; and she had a little dog named Spring-all. If they fought hard the first night they fought fifteen times harder with Hear-all and Spring-all and th' owd lady herself.

'Well,' she said, 'my king's son, I will do the best as ever I can for you. I will give you Spring-all, and I will give you the rod. Don't forget what I tell you to do with this rod. You follow this ball of worsted. Now it will take you right straight to a river. You will see the Black Dog of the Wild Forest, and s'ever you get to this river, you hit this rod in the water, and a fine bridge will jump up. And when you get to t'other side, just hit the water, and the bridge will fall in again, and the Black Dog of the Wild Forest cannot get you.'

He got into another wild forest over the water, and he got romping and moping about the forest by himself till he got very wild. He got moping about, and he found he got to a castle. That was the king's castle as he got over there to. He got to this castle, and the gentleman put him on to a job at this castle.

So he says to him, 'Jack, are you ony good a-shooting?'

'Yes, sir,' he says, 'I can shoot a little bit. I can shoot a long way further.'

'Well, will you go out today, Jack, and we will have a shot or two in the forest?'

They killed several birds and wild varmints in the forest. So him being sweet upon a daughter at this big hall, her and Jack got very great together. Jack tuck her down to the river to show her what he could do with his rod, him being laughing and joking with her. The king wanted a bridge made over the river, and he said there was no one as could do it.

'My dear,' says Jack, 'I could do it,' he says.

'With what?' she says.

'With my rod.'

He touched the water with his rod, and up springs as nice a bridge as ever you have seen up out of the water. Him being laughing and joking with this young girl, he come away and forgot the bridge standing. He comes home. Next day following he goes off again shooting with the king again, and the Black Dog of the Wild Forest comes to the king's house.

He says to th' owd lady herself, 'Whatever you do tomorrow, Jack will be going out shooting again, and you get Jack to leave his two little dogs, as I am going to devour Jack. And whatever you do, you fasten 'em down in the cellar tomorrow, and I will follow Jack to the forest where he is going shooting. And if Jack kills me, he will bring me back on the top of his horse on the front of him; and you will say to him, "O Jack, what ever are you going to do with that?" "I am going to make a fire of it," he will say. And he will burn me, and when he burns me he will burn me to dust. And you get a small bit of stick – Jack will go away and leave me after – and you go and rake my dust about, and you will find a lucky-bone. And when Jack goes to his bed, you drop this lucky-bone in Jack's ear, he will never rise no more, and you can take and bury him.'

Now th' owd lady was against Jack a lot for being there. So the Black Dog of the Wild Forest told th' owd lady the way to kill Jack. 'So see as when Jack brings me back and burns me, you look in my dust, and you will find a lucky-bone, and you drop it when Jack goes to bed, drop it into his ear, and Jack will never rise from his bed no more, he will be dead. Take Jack and bury him.'

147

Jack goes to the forest a-shooting, and the Black Dog of the Wild Forest follows him, and Jack begin to cry. Now if the fire came from his mouth the first time, it came a hundred times more, and Jack begin to cry.

'Oh dear!' he cried, 'where is my little Hear-all and Spring-all?'

He had no sooner said the words, five minutes but scarcely, comes up the two little dogs, and they's a very terrible fight. But Jack masters him and kills him. He brings home the Black Dog of the Wild Forest on the front of his horse; he brings him back, Jack, on the front of his horse; and the king says, 'What ever are you going to do with that?'

'I'm going to burn him.'

After he burns him, he burns him to dust.

The Black Dog of the Wild Forest says to th' owd lady, 'When Jack burns me to dust, you get a little stick and rake my dust about, and you will find a lucky-bone. You drop that lucky-bone in Jack's ear when he goes to bed, and Jack will never waken no more, and then you can take and bury him, and after that Jack is buried there will be no more said about him.'

Well, th' owd woman did do so, sir. When Jack went to bed, she got this lucky-bone and did as the Black Dog of the Wild Forest told her. She did drop it in Jack's ear, and Jack was dead. They take Jack off to bury him. Jack been buried three days, and the parson wondered what these two little dogs was moping about the grave all the time. He couldn't get them away.

'I think we'll rise Jack again,' he says.

And s'ever they rise him, off opened the lid of the coffin, and little Hear-all jumped to the side of his head, and he licked the lucky bone out of his ear. And up Jack jumped alive.

Jack says, 'Who ever put me here?'

'It was the king as had you buried here, Jack.'

Jack made his way home to his own father and mother. Going on the road Jack was riding bounded on the back of his horse's back. Hear-all says to him, 'Jack,' he says, 'come down, cut my head off.'

'Oh dear, no! Hear-all. I couldn't do that for the kindness you have done for me.'

'If you don't do it, Jack, I shall devour you.'

He comes down off his horse's back, and he kills little Hear-all. He cuts his head off, and well off timed he goes crying about Hear-all, for what he done. Goes on a little further. Spring-all says to him, 'Jack, you have got to come down and serve me the same.'

'Oh dear, no!' he says, 'Spring-all, I shall take it all to heart.'

'Well,' he says, 'if you don't come down, Jack,' he says, 'I will devour you.'

Jack comes down, and he cuts his head off, and he goes on the road, crying very much to hisself about his two little dogs. So going on this road as he was crying, he turned his head round at the back of his horse, looking behind him, and he sees two of the handsomest young ladies coming as ever he saw in his life.

'What are you crying for?' said these ladies to him.

'I am crying,' he said, 'about two little dogs, two faithful dogs, what I had.'

'What was the name of your little dogs?'

'One was named Hear-all, and the t'other was named Spring-all.'

'Would you know them two dogs if you would see them again?'

'Oh dear, yes!' says Jack. 'Oh dear, yes!' says Jack.

'Well, I am Hear-all, and this is Spring-all.'

Away Jack goes home to his father and mother, and lives very happy there all the days of his life.

The Spirit Horse

THE HISTORY of Morty Sullivan ought to be a warning to all young men to stay at home, and to live decently and soberly if they can, and not to go roving about the world. Morty, when he had just turned of fourteen, ran away from his father and mother, who were a mighty respectable old couple, and many and many a tear they shed on his account. It is said they both died heart-broken for his loss: all they ever learned about him was that he went on board of a ship bound to America.

Thirty years after the old couple had been laid peacefully in their graves, there came a stranger to Beerhaven inquiring after them – it was their son Morty; and, to speak the truth of him, his heart did seem full of sorrow when he heard that his parents were dead and gone; – but what else could he expect to hear? Repentance generally comes when it is too late.

Morty Sullivan, however, as an atonement for his sins, was recommended to perform a pilgrimage to the blessed chapel of Saint Gobnate, which is in a wild place called Ballyvourney.

This he readily undertook; and willing to lose no time,

commenced his journey the same afternoon. Morty had not proceeded many miles before the evening came on: there was no moon, and the starlight was obscured by a thick fog, which ascended from the valleys. His way was through a mountainous country, with many cross-paths and byways, so that it was difficult for a stranger like Morty to travel without a guide. He was anxious to reach his destination, and exerted himself to do so; but the fog grew thicker and thicker, and at last he became doubtful if the track he was in led to Saint Gobnate's chapel. Seeing therefore a light, which he imagined not be far off, he went towards it, and when he thought himself close to it the light suddenly seemed at a great distance, twinkling dimly through the fog. Though Morty felt some surprise at this, he was not disheartened, for he thought that it was a light which the blessed Saint Gobnate had sent to guide his feet through the mountains to her chapel.

Thus did he travel for many a mile, continually, as he believed, approaching the light, which would suddenly start off to a great distance. At length he came so close as to perceive that the light came from a fire; seated beside which he plainly saw an old woman; then, indeed, his faith was a little shaken, and much did he wonder that both the fire and the old woman should travel before him so many weary miles, and over such uneven roads.

'In the pious names of Saint Gobnate, and of her preceptor Saint Abban,' said Morty, 'how can that burning fire move on so fast before me, and who can that old woman be sitting beside the moving fire?'

These words had no sooner passed Morty's lips than he found himself, without taking another step, close to this wonderful fire, beside which the old woman was sitting munching her supper. With every wag of the old woman's jaw her eyes would roll fiercely upon Morty, as if she was angry at being disturbed; and he saw with more astonishment than ever that her eyes were neither black, nor blue, nor grey, nor hazel, like the human eye, but of a wild red colour, like the eye of a ferret. If before he wondered at the fire, much greater was his wonder at the old woman's appearance; and stout-hearted as he was, he could not but look upon her with fear – judging, and judging rightly, that it was for no good purpose her supping in so unfrequented a place, and at so late an hour, for it was near midnight. She said not one word, but munched and munched away, while Morty looked at her in silence. 'What's your name?' at last demanded the old hag, a sulphureous puff coming out of her mouth, her nostrils distending, and her eyes growing redder than ever, when she had finished her question.

Plucking up all his courage, 'Morty Sullivan,' replied he, 'at your service;' meaning the latter words only in civility.

'*Ubbubbo!*' said the old woman, 'we'll soon see that;' and the red fire of her eyes turned into a pale green colour. Bold and fearless as Morty was, yet much did he tremble at hearing this dreadful exclamation, he would have fallen down on his knees and prayed to Saint Gobnate, or any other saint, for he was not particular; but he was so petrified with horror that he could not move in the slightest way, much less go down on his knees.

'Take hold of my hand, Morty,' said the old woman: 'I'll give you a horse to ride that will soon carry you to your journey's end.' So saying, she led the way, the fire going before them – it is beyond mortal knowledge to say how, but on it went, shooting out bright tongues of flame, and flickering fiercely.

Presently they came to a natural cavern in the side of the mountain, and the old hag called aloud in a most discordant voice for her horse! In a moment a jet-black steed started from its gloomy stable, the rocky floor of which rung with a sepulchral echo to the clanging hoofs.

'Mount, Morty, mount!' cried she, seizing him with supernatural strength, and forcing him upon the back of the horse. Morty finding human power of no avail, muttered, 'Oh that I had spurs!' and tried to grasp the horse's mane; but he caught at a shadow, which nevertheless bore him up and bounded forward with him, now springing down a fearful precipice, now clearing the rugged bed of a torrent, and rushing like the dark midnight storm through the mountains.

The following morning Morty Sullivan was discovered by some pilgrims (who came that way after taking their rounds at Gougane Barra) lying on the flat of his back, under a steep cliff, down which he had been flung by the Phooka. Morty was severely bruised by the fall, and he is said to have sworn on the spot, by the hand of O'Sullivan (and that is no small oath), never again to take a full quart bottle of whiskey with him on a pilgrimage.

The Black Bull of Norroway

In Norroway, langsyne, there lived a certain lady, and she had three dochters. The auldest o' them said to her mither: 'Mither, bake me a bannock, and roast me a collop, for I'm gaun awa' to spotch my fortune.'

Her mither did sae; and the dochter gaed awa' to an auld witch washerwife and telled her purpose. The auld wife bade her stay that day, and gang and look out o' her backdoor, and see what she could see. She saw nocht the first day. The second day she did the same, and saw nocht. On the third day she looked again, and saw a coach-and-six coming alang the road. She ran in and telled the auld wife what she saw. 'Aweel,' quo' the auld wife, 'yon's for you.' Sae they took her into the coach, and galloped aff.

The second dochter next says to her mither: 'Mither, bake me a bannock, and roast me a collop, for I'm gaun awa' to spotch my fortune.'

Her mither did sae; and awa she gaed to the auld wife, as her sister had dune. On the third day she looked out o' the backdoor, and saw a coach-and-four coming alang the road. 'Aweel,' quo' the auld wife, 'yon's for you.' Sae they took her in, and aff they set.

The third dochter says to her mither: 'Mither, bake me a bannock, and roast me a collop, for I'm gaun awa' to spotch my fortune.'

Her mither did sae, and awa' she gaed to the auld witch wife. She bade her look out o' her backdoor, and see what she could see. She did sae; and when she came back, said she saw nocht. The second day she did the same, and saw nocht. The third day she looked again, and on coming back, said to the auld wife she saw nocht but a muckle Black Bull coming crooning alang the road. 'Aweel,' quo' the auld wife, 'yon's for you.' On hearing this she was next to distracted wi' grief and terror; but she was lifted up and set on his back, and awa' they went.

Aye they travelled, and on they travelled, till the lady grew faint wi' hunger. 'Eat out o' my right lug,'* says the Black Bull, 'and drink out o' my left lug, and set by your leavings.' Sae she did as he said, and was wonderfully refreshed. And lang they gaed, and sair they rade, till they came in sight o' a very big and bonny castle.

'Yonder we maun be this night,' quo' the bull; 'for my auld† brither lives yonder;' and presently they were at the place. They lifted her aff his back, and took her in, and sent him away to a park for the night.

In the morning, when they brought the bull hame, they took the lady into a fine shining parlour, and gave her a beautiful apple, telling her no to break it till she was in the greatest strait ever mortal was in in the world, and that wad bring her out o't. Again she was lifted on the bull's back, and after she had ridden far, and farer than I can tell, they came in sight o' a far bonnier castle, and far farther awa' than the last.

Says the bull till her: 'Yonder we maun be the night, for my second brither lives yonder;' and they were at the place directly.

*Ear.
†Eldest.

They lifted her down and took her in, and sent the bull to the field for the night.

In the morning they took the lady into a fine and rich room, and gave her the finest pear she had ever seen, bidding her no to break it till she was in the greatest strait ever mortal could be in, and that wad get her out o't. Again she was lifted and set on his back, and awa' they went. And lang they rade, and sair they rade, till they came in sight o' the far biggest castle, and far farthest aff, they had yet seen.

'We maun be yonder the night,' says the bull, 'for my young brither lives yonder;' and they were there directly. They lifted her down, and took her in, and sent the bull to the field for the night. In the morning they took her into a room, the finest of a', and gied her a plum, telling her no to break it till she was in the greatest strait mortal could be in, and that wad get her out o't. Presently they brought hame the bull, set the lady on his back, and awa' they went.

And aye they rade, and on they rade, till they came to a dark and ugsome glen, where they stopped, and the lady lighted down.

Says the bull to her: 'Here ye maun stay till I gang and fight the deil. Ye maun seat yoursel' on that stane, and move neither hand nor fit* till I come back, else I'll never find ye again. And if everything round about ye turns blue, I hae beaten the deil; but should a' things turn red, he'll hae conquered me.'

She set hersel' down on the stane, and by-and-by a' round her turned blue. O'ercome wi' joy, she lifted the ae fit and crossed it owre the ither, sae glad was she that her companion was victorious. The bull returned and sought for, but never could find her.

Lang she sat, and aye she grat, till she wearied. At last she rase and gaed awa', she kendna whaur till.† On she wandered, till she came to a great hill o' glass, that she tried a' she could to climb, but wasna able. Round the bottom o' the hill she gaed,

* Foot.
† She didn't know where to.

sabbing and seeking a passage owre, till at last she came to a smith's house; and the smith promised, if she wad serve him seven years, he wad make her airn shoon, wherewi' she could climb owre the glassy hill.

At seven years' end she got her airn shoon, clamb the glassy hill, and chanced to come to the auld washerwife's habitation. There she was telled of a gallant young knight that had given in some bluidy sarks* to wash, and whaever washed thae sarks was to be his wife. The auld wife had washed till she was tired, and then she set to her dochter, and baith washed, and they washed, and they better washed, in hopes of getting the young knight; but a' they could do, they couldna bring out a stain.

At length they set the stranger damosel to wark; and whenever she began, the stains came out pure and clean, and the auld wife made the knight believe it was her dochter had washed the sarks. So the knight and the eldest dochter were to be married, and the stranger damosel was distracted at the thought of it, for she was deeply in love wi' him.

So she bethought her of her apple, and breaking it, found it filled with gold and precious jewellery, the richest she had ever seen. 'All these,' she said to the eldest dochter, 'I will give you, on condition that you put off your marriage for ae day, and allow me to go into his room alone at night.'

So the lady consented; but meanwhile the auld wife had prepared a sleeping drink, and given it to the knight, wha drank it, and never wakened till next morning. The lee-lang night the damosel sabbed and sang:

> '*Seven lang years I served for thee,*
> *The glassy hill I clamb for thee,*
> *The bluidy shirt I wrang for thee;*
> *And wilt thou no wauken and turn to me?*'

Next day she kentna what to do for grief. She then brak the pear, and fan't filled wi' jewellery far richer than the contents o'

---

* Shirts.

the apple. Wi' thae jewels she bargained for permission to be a second night in the young knight's chamber: but the auld wife gied him anither sleeping drink, and he again sleepit till morning. A' night she kept sighing and singing as before:

'*Seven lang years I served for thee,*' &c.

Still he sleepit, and she nearly lost hope a'thegither. But that day, when he was out at the hunting, somebody asked him what noise and moaning was yon they heard all last night in his bedchamber. He said he heardna ony noise. But they assured him there was sae; and he resolved to keep waking that night to try what he could hear.

That being the third night, and the damosel being between hope and despair, she brak her plum, and it held far the richest jewellery of the three. She bargained as before; and the auld wife, as before, took in the sleeping drink to the young knight's chamber; but he told her he couldna drink it that night without sweetening. And when she gaed awa' for some honey to sweeten it wi', he poured out the drink, and sae made the auld wife think he had drunk it. They a' went to bed again, and the damosel began, as before, singing:

'*Seven lang years I served for thee,*
The glassy hill I clamb for thee,
The bluidy shirt I wrang for thee;
And wilt thou no wauken and turn to me?'

He heard, and turned to her. And she told him a' that had befa'en her, and he told her a' that had happened to him. And he caused the auld washerwife and her dochter to be burnt. And they were married, and he and she are living happy till this day, for aught I ken.

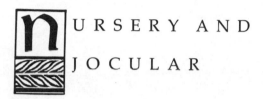

NURSERY AND

JOCULAR

Nursery and Jocular

There is no simple answer to the question of whether tales about fairies and other supernatural beings, and kings and heroes and other legendary figures, were once believed to be true. But with nursery tales and jocular tales, there can be no argument that we enter the world of folk fiction, in which tales are told simply to delight and entertain; the two categories are brought together here for that reason. It must also be true, as Katharine Briggs notes, that 'The Nursery Tales are perhaps those that have the greatest chance of survival among us, for small children will always demand them... People also commonly remember longest what they have heard earliest.'

One of the best-loved nursery tales is *The Story of the Three Bears*. The poet laureate Robert Southey (1774-1843) first printed it in his fourth anonymous collection of essays and prose pieces called *The Doctor* (1837), with a note to the effect that the Doctor had heard the tale from his uncle. For the next sixty years it was assumed that Southey had made up the story himself. And as it passed through the hands of a number of retellers, it began to undergo changes: notably Southey's 'little old woman' was replaced by a little girl, first called Silver-Locks, then Golden Hair and, finally, Goldilocks.

But no sooner had Joseph Jacobs declared in 1890 that 'The Three Bears is the only example I know of where a tale that can definitely be traced to a specific author has become a folk-tale' than he heard of a variant of the tale that he took to be in an older form than Southey's version. When in 1951 there came to light in the Osborne Collection of Early Children's Books a version of the tale told in 1831 by Eleanor Mure, the matter was clinched: Southey, whose poetry and *Common-Place Books* show him always alive to folklore and antiquities, was clearly (as he said he was) retelling an older tale. Nor, of course, is the form of the tale restricted to England: the best known parallel is 'Sneewittchen' or 'Snow White and the Seven Dwarfs' collected by the brothers Grimm.

Like Southey's shapely story, *The Wee Bunnock* hinges on repetition and variation. Picaresque tales are always liable to seem episodic and accidental in a way that soon becomes frustrating, but this tale is redeemed by its racy style and very lively dialogue. It was collected by Robert Chambers (see p.138) from an old man born in Ayrshire. 'It was one of a great store of similar legends,' Chambers noted, 'possessed by his grandmother, and which she related, upon occasion, for the gratification of himself and other youngsters, as she sat spinning by the fireside, with these youngsters clustered around her. This venerable person was born in the year 1704...'

Munachar and Manachar is printed as representative of all those tales that build up step by step like 'The House that Jack Built', 'The Old Woman and her Pig', and the tale collected by Campbell in *Popular Tales of the West Highlands*, 'Moonachug and Meenachug'; and, for better or worse, it has more steps than any of them. It was first collected in Irish by Douglas Hyde and translated by him for inclusion in W. B. Yeats' *Fairy and Folk Tales of the Irish Peasantry*.

A friend of Yeats, Lady Gregory and other participants in the Irish Renaissance, Douglas Hyde had great gifts as a poet, dramatist and, above all, scholar. He is valued by folklorists as a collector, translator and commentator, and his *Beside the Fire* (1890) is generally reckoned to be the book with which the science of folklore became as thorough and well-rounded in Ireland as it already was in England and Scotland. Hyde was partly motivated in his collection of folk-tales by the conviction that it would help to lead to a renewal of interest in Irish language and literature, and so to political independence. He founded the influential Gaelic League, became the first president of the Republic of Eire, and lived until 1949.

One does not have to read many jocular tales, moreover – that is to say, tales about fools and simpletons, numskulls and noodles, punning tales and practical jokes, nonsense stories and Shaggy Dog stories – before thinking one has heard it all before. *The Cow on the Roof* revolves around the well-worked theme of male arrogance and domestic inadequacy, and was collected from a Denbighshire teamsman by T. Gwynn Jones, while *The Three Wise Men of Gotham* is one of the well-known group of tales (others include the attempts to hedge in a cuckoo and to drown an eel) directed against that village in Nottinghamshire. No less than forty-five places in England, including Borrowdale in Westmoreland, Coggeshall (Essex), St Ives (Cornwall) and the whole of the Isle of Wight, are likewise supposed to be inhabited by simpletons and have similar stories told against them.

The first folklorist to give undivided attention to tales about simpletons was the prolific Orcadian William Alexander Clouston (1843-96), and he has left us with an excellent working definition:

> Poor fellow! he follows his instructions only too literally, and with a firm conviction that he is thus doing a very clever thing. But the consequence is almost always ridiculous . . . . His mind is incapable of entertaining more than one idea at a time; but to that he holds fast, with the tenacity of the lobster's claw: he cannot be diverted from it until, by some accident, a fresh idea displaces it; and so on he goes from one blunder to another. His blunders, however, which in the case of an ordinary man would infallibly result in disaster to himself or to others, sometimes lead him to unexpected good fortune.

In *The Book of Noodles*, Clouston reprinted many of the Gothamite tales (first found scattered through eighteenth century chap books and in *Tales of the Men of Gotham* printed in 1840) and traced the origins of the simpleton story to Ancient Greek and early Buddhist sources. His principal work was as an arabist, translating and commenting on such Persian and Arabic romances as *The Book of Sindibad* and *The Romance of Antar*. In his most significant book, *Popular Tales and Fictions, Their Migrations and Transformations*, he tried to show that folk romance, so

163

popular in medieval Europe, originated in India and the Middle East, and shared many characteristics with folk legend.

It would be wrong to leave the jocular genre without so much as a nip of nonsense, and there is none better or briefer than this short tale collected by Sidney Oldall Addy (see p.85):

A number of pynots* fought in a crabtree so fiercely that their beaks struck fire and set the tree ablaze. Then roasted crabs fell to the ground, which children picked up and ate.

* Magpies.

The Story of the Three Bears

ONCE upon a time there were Three Bears, who lived together in a house of their own, in a wood. One of them was a Little, Small, Wee Bear; and one was a Middle-sized Bear, and the other was a Great, Huge Bear. They had each a pot for their porridge, a little pot for the Little, Small, Wee Bear; and a middle-sized pot for the Middle Bear, and a great pot for the Great, Huge Bear. And they had each a chair to sit in; a little chair for the Little, Small, Wee Bear; and a middle-sized chair for the Middle Bear; and a great chair for the Great, Huge Bear. And they had each a bed to sleep in; a little bed for the Little, Small, Wee Bear; and a middle-sized bed for the Middle Bear; and a great bed for the Great, Huge Bear.

One day, after they had made the porridge for their breakfast, and poured it into their porridge-pots, they walked out into the wood while the porridge was cooling, that they might not burn their mouths, by beginning too soon to eat it. And while they were walking, a little old Woman came to the house. She could not have been a good, honest old Woman; for first she looked in at the window, and then she peeped in at the keyhole; and seeing nobody in the house, she lifted the latch. The door was not fastened, because the Bears were good Bears, who did nobody any harm, and never suspected that any body would harm them. So the little old Woman opened the door, and went in; and well pleased she was when she saw the porridge on the table. If she had been a good little old Woman, she would have waited till the Bears came home, and then, perhaps, they would have asked her to breakfast; for they were good Bears – a little rough or so, as the manner of Bears is, but for all that very good natured and hospitable. But she was an impudent, bad old Woman, and set about helping herself.

So first she tasted the porridge of the Great, Huge Bear, and that was too hot for her; and she said a bad word about that. And then she tasted the porridge of the Middle Bear, and that was too cold for her; and she said a bad word about that, too. And then she went to the porridge of the Little, Small, Wee bear, and tasted that; and that was neither too hot, nor too cold, but just right; and she liked it so well, that she ate it all up: but the naughty old Woman said a bad word about the little porridge-pot, because it did not hold enough for her.

Then the little old Woman sate down in the chair of the Great Huge Bear, and that was too hard for her. And then she sate down in the chair of the Middle Bear, and that was too soft for her. And then she sate down in the chair of the Little, Small, Wee Bear, and that was neither too hard, nor too soft, but just right. So she seated herself in it, and there she sate till the bottom of the chair came out, and down came hers, plump upon the ground. And the naughty old Woman said a wicked word about that too.

Then the little old Woman went up stairs into the bed-chamber in which the three Bears slept. And first she lay down upon the bed of the Great, Huge Bear; but that was too high at the head for her. And next she lay down upon the bed of the Middle Bear; and that was too high at the foot for her. And then she lay down upon the bed of the Little, Small, Wee Bear; and that was neither too high at the head, nor at the foot, but just right. So she covered herself up comfortably, and lay there till she fell fast asleep.

By this time the Three Bears thought their porridge would be cool enough; so they came home to breakfast. Now the little old Woman had left the spoon of the Great, Huge Bear, standing in his porridge.

'SOMEBODY HAS BEEN AT MY PORRIDGE!'

said the Great, Huge Bear, in his great, rough, gruff voice. And when the Middle Bear looked at his, he saw that the spoon was standing in it too. They were wooden spoons; if they had been silver ones, the naughty old Woman would have put them in her pocket.

'SOMEBODY HAS BEEN AT MY PORRIDGE!'

said the Middle Bear, in his middle voice.

Then the Little, Small, Wee Bear, looked at his, and there was the spoon in the porridge-pot, but the porridge was all gone.

'SOMEBODY HAS BEEN AT MY PORRIDGE, AND HAS EATEN IT ALL UP!'

said the Little, Small, Wee Bear, in his little, small, wee voice.

Upon this the Three Bears, seeing that some one had entered their house, and eaten up the Little, Small, Wee Bear's breakfast, began to look about them. Now the little old Woman had not put the hard cushion straight when she rose from the chair of the Great, Huge Bear.

'SOMEBODY HAS BEEN SITTING IN MY CHAIR!'

said the Great, Huge Bear, in his great, rough, gruff voice.

And the little old Woman had squatted down the soft cushion of the Middle Bear.

'SOMEBODY HAS BEEN SITTING IN MY CHAIR!'

said the Middle Bear, in his middle voice.

And you know what the little old Woman had done to the third chair.

'SOMEBODY HAS BEEN SITTING IN MY CHAIR, AND HAS SATE THE BOTTOM
OF IT OUT!'

said the Little, Small, Wee Bear, in his little, small, wee voice.

Then the Three Bears thought it necessary that they should make farther search; so they went up stairs into their bed-chamber. Now the little old Woman had pulled the pillow of the Great, Huge Bear, out of its place.

'SOMEBODY HAS BEEN LYING IN MY BED!'

said the Great, Huge Bear, in his great, rough, gruff voice.

And the little old Woman had pulled the bolster of the Middle Bear out of its place.

'SOMEBODY HAS BEEN LYING IN MY BED!'

said the Middle Bear, in his middle voice.

And when the Little, Small, Wee Bear, came to look at his bed, there was the bolster in its place; and the pillow in its place under the bolster; and upon the pillow was the little old Woman's ugly, dirty head, – which was not in its place, for she had no business there.

'SOMEBODY HAS BEEN LYING IN MY BED, – AND HERE SHE IS!'

said the Little, Small, Wee Bear, in his little, small, wee voice.

The little old Woman had heard in her sleep the great, rough, gruff voice, of the Great, Huge Bear; but she was so fast asleep that it was no more to her than the roaring of wind, or the rumbling of thunder. And she had heard the middle voice of the Middle Bear, but it was only as if she had heard some one speaking in a dream. But when she heard the little, small, wee voice, of the Little, Small, Wee Bear, it was so sharp, and so shrill, that it awakened her at once. Up she started; and when she saw the Three Bears on one side of the bed, she tumbled herself out at the other, and ran to the window. Now the window was open, because the Bears, like good, tidy Bears, as they were, always opened their bed-chamber window when they got up in the morning. Out the little old Woman jumped;

and whether she broke her neck in the fall; or ran into the wood and was lost there; or found her way out of the wood, and was taken up by the constable and sent to the House of Correction for a vagrant as she was, I cannot tell. But the Three Bears never saw anything more of her.

The Wee Bunnock

'GRANNIE, grannie, come tell us the story o' the wee bunnock.'

'Hout, bairns, ye've heard it a hunner times afore. I needna tell it owre again.'

'Ah, but, grannie, it's sic a fine ane. Ye maun tell't. Just ance.'

'Weel, weel, bairns, if ye'll a' promise to be guid, I'll tell ye't again.

> Some tell about their sweethearts, how they tirled them to the winnock,*
> But I'll tell you a bonny tale about a guid aitmeal bunnock.

There lived an auld man and an auld wife at the side o' a burn. They had twa kye, five hens and a cock, a cat and twa kittlins. The auld man lookit after the kye, and the auld wife span on the tow-rock. The kittlins aft grippit at the auld wife's spindle, as it tussled owre the hearth-stane. 'Sho, sho,' she wad say, 'gae wa';' and so it tussled about.

Ae day, after parritch time[†], she thought she wad hae a

* Tapped at the window to bring them out.
† Porridge-time, i.e. breakfast.

bunnock. Sae she bakit twa aitmeal bunnocks, and set them to the fire to harden. After a while, the auld man came in, and sat down aside the fire, and takes ane o' the bunnocks, and snappit it through the middle. When the tither ane sees this, it rins aff as fast as it could, and the auld wife after't, wi' the spindle in the tae hand and the tow-rock in the tither. But the wee bunnock wan awa', and out o' sight, and ran till it came to a guid muckle thack house,* and ben it ran boldly to the fireside; and there were three tailors sitting on a muckle table. When they saw the wee bunnock come ben, they jumpit up, and gat in ahint the goodwife, that was cardin' tow ayont the fire.

'Hout,' quo' she, 'be na fleyt,† it's but a wee bunnock. Grip it, and I'll gie ye a soup milk till't.'

Up she gets wi' the towcards, and the tailor wi' the goose, and the twa prentices, the ane wi' the muckle shears, and the tither wi' the lawbrod; but it jinkit‡ them, and ran round about the fire; and ane o' the prentices, thinking to snap it wi' the shears, fell i' the ase-pit. The tailor cuist the goose, and the goodwife the tow-cards; but a' wadna do. The bunnock wan awa', and ran till it came to a wee house at the roadside; and in it rins, and there was a weaver sittin' on the loom, and the wife winnin' a clue o' yarn.

'Tibby,' quo' he, 'what's tat?'

'Oh,' quo' she, 'it's a wee bunnock.'

'It's weel come,' quo' he, 'for our sowens§ were but thin the day. Grip it, my woman; grip it.'

'Ay,' quo' she; 'what recks! That's a clever bunnock. Kep,** Willie; kep, man.'

'Hout,' quo' Willie, 'cast the clue at it.'

But the bunnock whipit round about, and but the floor, and aff it gaed, and owre the knowe,†† like a new-tarred sheep or a daft

---

* Large thatched house.
† Don't be frightened.
‡ Eluded.
§ Thin soup.
** Intercept.
††Knoll.

yell cow.* And forrit it runs to the niest house, and ben to the fireside; and there was the goodwife kirnin'.

'Come awa', wee bunnock,' quo' she; 'I'se hae ream[†] and bread the day.'

But the wee bunnock whipit round about the kirn, and the wife after 't, and i' the hurry she had near-hand coupit the kirn.[‡] And afore she got it set right again, the wee bunnock was aff, and down the brae to the mill; and in it ran.

The miller was siftin' meal i' the trough; but, looking up: 'Ay,' quo' he, 'it's a sign o' plenty when ye're rinnin' about, and naebody to look after ye. But I like a bunnock and cheese. Come your wa's ben, and I'll gie ye a night's quarters.'

But the bunnock wadna trust itsel' wi' the miller and his cheese. Sae it turned and ran its wa's out; but the miller didna fash his head wi't.[§]

So it toddled awa', and ran till it came to the smithy; and in it rins, and up to the studdy.[**] The smith was making horsenails. Quo' he: 'I like a bicker o' guid yill[††] and a weel-toastit bunnock. Come your wa's in by here.'

But the bunnock was frightened when it heard about the yill, and turned and aff as hard as it could, and the smith after't, and cuist the hammer. But it whirlt awa', and out o' sight in a crack,[‡‡] and ran till it came to a farmhouse wi' a guid muckle peat-stack at the end o't. Ben it rins to the fireside. The goodman was clovin'[§§] lint, and the goodwife hecklin'.

'Oh Janet,' quo' he, 'there's a wee bunnock; I'se hae the hauf o't.'

'Weel, John, I'se hae the tither hauf. Hit it owre the back wi' the clove.'

---

* Cow which has ceased to yield milk.
† Cream.
‡ Overturned the churn.
§ Trouble himself
** Anvil.
†† A stoup of good ale
‡‡ Out of sight in a moment.
§§ Separating lint from the stalk by means of a certain iron implement.

But the bunnock playt *jink-about*. 'Hout, tout,' quo' the wife, and gart the heckle flee at it. But it was owre clever for her.

And aff and up the burn it ran to the niest house, and whirlt its wa's ben to the fireside. The goodwife was stirrin' the sowens, and the goodman plettin' sprit-binnings for the kye.*

'Ho, Jock,' quo' the goodwife, 'come here. Thou's aye crying about a wee bunnock. Here's ane. Come in, haste ye, and I'll help thee to grip it.'

'Ay, mither, whaur is't?'

'See there. Rin owre o' that side.'

But the bunnock ran in ahint the goodman's chair. Jock fell amang the sprits. The good-man cuist a binning, and the goodwife the spurtle. But it was owre clever for Jock and her baith. It was aff and out o' sight in a crack, and through among the whins,† and down the road to the niest house, and in, and ben to the fireside. The folk were just sittin' down to their sowens, and the goodwife scartin' the pat.

'Losh,' quo' she, 'there's a wee bunnock come in to warm itsel' at our fireside.'

'Steek the door,' quo' the goodman, 'and we'll try to get a grip o't.'

When the bunnock heard that, it ran but the house, and they after 't wi' their spunes, and the goodman cuist his bunnat. But it whirlt awa', and ran, and better ran, till it came to another house; and when it gaed ben, the folk were just gaun to their beds. The goodman was castin' aff his breeks, and the goodwife rakin' the fire.

'What's tat?' quo' he.

'Oh,' quo' she, 'it's a wee bunnock.'

Quo' he, 'I could eat the hauf o't, for a' the brose I hae suppit.'

'Grip it,' quo' the wife, 'and I'll hae a bit too.'

'Cast your breeks at it – kep – kep!'

The goodman cuist the breeks, and had near-hand smoor't it. But it warsl't out, and ran, and the goodman after't, wanting the

* Plaiting straw ropes for the cattle.
† Furze.

breeks; and there was a clean chase owre the craft park, and up the wunyerd, and in amang the whins; and the goodman lost it, and had to come his wa's trottin' hame hauf-nakit. But now it was grown dark, and the wee bunnock couldna see; but it gaed into the side o' a muckle whin bush, and into a tod's hole. The tod had gotten nae meat for twa days.

'Oh welcome, welcome,' quo' the tod, and snappit it in twa i' the middle. And that was the end o' the wee bunnock.

> *Now, be ye lords or commoners*
> *Ye needna laugh nor sneer,*
> *For ye'll be a' i' the tod's hole*
> *In less than a hunner year.*

Munachar and Manachar

THERE once lived a Munachar and a Manachar, a long time ago, and it is a long time since it was, and if they were alive then they would not be alive now. They went out together to pick raspberries, and as many as Munachar used to pick Manachar used to eat. Munachar said he must go look for a rod to make a gad* to hang Manachar, who ate his raspberries every one; and he came to the rod.

'God save you,' said the rod.

'God and Mary save you.'

'How far are you going?'

'Going looking for a rod, a rod to make a gad, a gad to hang Manachar, who ate my raspberries every one.'

'You will not get me,' said the rod, 'until you get an axe to cut me.' He came to the axe. 'God save you,' said the axe.

'God and Mary save you.'

'How far are you going?'

'Going looking for an axe, an axe to cut a rod, a rod to make a

* A withy band.

175

gad, a gad to hang Manachar, who ate my raspberries every one.'

'You will not get me' said the axe, 'until you get a flag to edge me.'

He came to the flag. 'God save you,' says the flag.

'God and Mary save you.'

'How far are you going?'

'Going looking for an axe, axe to cut a rod, a rod to make a gad, a gad to hang Manachar, who ate my raspberries every one.'

'You will not get me,' says the flag, 'till you get water to wet me.'

He came to the water. 'God save you,' says the water.

'God and Mary save you.'

'How far are you going?'

'Going looking for water, water to wet flag to edge axe, axe to cut a rod, a rod to make a gad, a gad to hang Manachar, who ate my raspberries every one.'

'You will not get me,' said the water, 'until you get a deer who will swim me.'

He came to the deer. 'God save you,' says the deer.

'God and Mary save you.'

'How far are you going?'

'Going looking for a deer, deer to swim water, water to wet flag, flag to edge axe, axe to cut a rod, a rod to make a gad, a gad to hang Manachar, who ate my raspberries every one.'

'You will not get me,' said the deer, 'until you get a hound who will hunt me.'

He came to the hound. 'God save you,' says the hound.

'God and Mary save you.'

'How far are you going?'

'Going looking for a hound, hound to hunt deer, deer to swim water, water to wet flag, flag to edge axe, axe to cut a rod, a rod to make a gad, a gad to hang Manachar, who ate my raspberries every one.'

'You will not get me,' said the hound, 'until you get a bit of butter to put in my claw.'

He came to the butter. 'God save you,' says the butter.

'God and Mary save you.'

'How far are you going?'

'Going looking for butter, butter to go in claw of hound, hound to hunt deer, deer to swim water, water to wet flag, flag to edge axe, axe to cut a rod, a rod to make a gad, a gad to hang Manachar, who ate my raspberries every one.'

'You will not get me,' said the butter, 'until you get a cat who shall scrape me.'

He came to the cat. 'God save you,' said the cat.

'God and Mary save you.'

'How far are you going?'

'Going looking for a cat, cat to scrape butter, butter to go in claw of hound, hound to hunt deer, deer to swim water, water to wet flag, flag to edge axe, axe to cut a rod, a rod to make a gad, gad to hang Manachar, who ate my raspberries every one.'

'You will not get me,' said the cat, 'until you will get milk which you will give me.'

He came to the cow. 'God save you,' said the cow.

'God and Mary save you.'

'How far are you going?'

'Going looking for a cow, cow to give me milk, milk I will give to the cat, cat to scrape butter, butter to go in claw of hound, hound to hunt deer, deer to swim water, water to wet flag, flag to edge axe, axe to cut a rod, a rod to make a gad, a gad to hang Manachar, who ate my raspberries every one.'

'You will not get any milk from me,' said the cow, 'until you bring me a whisp of straw from those threshers yonder.'

He came to the threshers. 'God save you,' said the threshers.

'God and Mary save ye.'

'How far are you going?'

'Going looking for a whisp of straw from ye to give to the cow, the cow to give me milk, milk I will give to the cat, cat to scrape butter, butter to go in claw of hound, hound to hunt deer, deer to swim water, water to wet flag, flag to edge axe, axe to cut a rod, a rod to make a gad, a gad to hang Manachar, who ate my raspberries every one.'

'You will not get any whisp of straw from us,' said the threshers, 'until you bring us the makings of a cake from the miller over yonder.'

He came to the miller. 'God save you.'

'God and Mary save you.'

'How far are you going?'

'Going looking for the makings of a cake, which I will give to the threshers, the threshers to give me a whisp of straw, the whisp of straw I will give to the cow, the cow to give me milk, milk I will give to the cat, cat to scrape butter, butter to go in claw of hound, hound to hunt deer, deer to swim water, water to wet flag, flag to edge axe, axe to cut a rod, a rod to make a gad, a gad to hang Manachar, who ate my raspberries every one.'

'You will not get any makings of a cake from me,' said the miller, 'till you bring me the full of that sieve of water from the river over there.'

He took the sieve in his hand and went over to the river, but as often as ever he would stoop and fill it with water, the moment he raised it the water would run out of it again, and sure, if he had been there from that day till this, he never could have filled it.

A crow went flying by him, over his head. 'Daub! daub!' said the crow.

'My soul to God, then,' said Munachar, 'but it's the good advice you have,' and he took the red clay and the daub that was by the brink, and he rubbed it to the bottom of the sieve, until all the holes were filled, and then the sieve held the water, and he brought the water to the miller, and the miller gave him the makings of a cake, and he gave the makings of the cake to the threshers, and the threshers gave him a whisp of straw, and he gave the whisp of straw to the cow, and the cow gave him milk, the milk he gave to the cat, the cat scraped the butter, the butter went into the claw of the hound, the hound hunted the deer, the deer swam the water, the water wet the flag, the flag sharpened the axe, the axe cut the rod, and the rod made a gad, and when he had it ready – I'll go bail that Manachar was far enough away from him.

The Cow on the Roof

SIÔN DAFYDD always grumbled that his wife could do nothing properly in the house. Neither a meal nor anything else ever pleased him. At last his wife got tired with his grumbling, and one day told him she would go to weed turnips and that he should stay to take care of the baby and the house, to make dinner, and some other things which she used to do. Siôn easily agreed, so that she might have an example.

In starting to the field, the wife said: 'Now, you take care of the baby, feed the hens, feed the pig, turn out the cow to graze, sweep the floor, and make the porridge ready for dinner.'

'Don't you bother about all that,' said Siôn, 'you see to the turnips.'

The wife went to the field, Siôn to the house. The baby awoke. For a long time, Siôn rocked the cradle, and tried to sing to the child, which seemed to make the poor thing worse. Siôn then remembered the pig, which was squeaking very loudly. He went to get some buttermilk to make food for it. He spilt the milk on the kitchen floor. The pig heard the sound of the bucket, and made such noise that Siôn could not stand it.

'You wait a bit, you rascal!' he said to himself, but he meant the pig, 'you shall go out to find food for yourself!'

So he opened the door to turn out the pig. Out went the pig like a shot, right between Siôn's legs, throwing him into the dunghill. By the time he got up and tried to scrape a little of the dirt off his clothes, the pig was out of sight. Siôn went into the house. There the pig had gone to lap up the milk from the floor, and had besides, overthrown another pot of milk and was busy with that.

'You rascal!' shouted Siôn, and catching hold of an axe, he struck the pig a blow on the head. The poor pig wobbled like a man in drink, then fell by the door and parted with this life.

By this time it was getting late, and Siôn thought of the porridge, but the cow had to be turned out to graze, and he had quite forgotten the hens, poor souls. The field where the cow had to gather its daily bread, as it were, was some distance from the yard, and if Siôn went to take it there, the porridge would never be ready in time. At that moment, Siôn happened to notice that there was some fine grass growing on the roof of the house. There was a rise at the back of the house, and the roof reached almost to the ground. Siôn thought the grass on the roof would be a good meal for a cow, and in order to be able to make the porridge as well, he took a rope, tied it round the cow's neck, ran up the roof and dropped the other end of the rope through the chimney. Then he went to the porridge. So that he might have his two hands free, he tied the end of the rope round his ankle. In grazing on the roof the cow, without thinking, as it were, came to the top and slipped over suddenly. Siôn felt himself being pulled up by the leg, and into the chimney he went, feet first. Somehow, his legs went one on each side of the iron bar from which the kettle was hung over the fire, and there he stuck.

Just at that moment, the wife came back from the turnip field, and was horrified to see the cow dangling in the air. She ran to the door and fell across the dead pig, and without seeing anything else, picked up the axe and ran to cut the rope and save the poor cow. Then she ran into the house, and the first thing she saw there was Siôn, standing on his head in the porridge.

The Three Wise Men of Gotham

THERE were two men of Gotham, and one of them was going to the market at Nottingham to buy sheep, and the other was coming from the market, and both met on Nottingham bridge.

'Well met!' said the one to the other. 'Whither are you a-going?' said he that came from Nottingham.

'Marry,' said he that was going thither. 'I am going to the market to buy sheep.'

'Buy sheep!' said the other. 'And which way will you bring them home?'

'Marry,' said the other, 'I will bring them over this bridge.'

'By Robin Hood,' said he that came from Nottingham, 'but thou shalt not.'

'By Maid Marian,' said he that was going thither, 'but I will.'

'Thou shalt not,' said the one.

'I will,' said the other.

Then they beat their staves against the ground, one against the other, as if there had been a hundred sheep betwixt them.

'Hold them there,' said the one.

'Beware of the leaping over the bridge of my sheep,' said the other.

'They shall all come this way,' said one.

'But they shall not,' said the other. And as they were in contention, another wise man that belonged to Gotham came from the market, with a sack of meal upon his horse; and seeing and hearing his neighbours at strife about sheep, and none betwixt them, said he, 'Ah, fools, will you never learn wit? Then help me,' said he that had the meal, 'and lay this sack upon my shoulder.'

They did so, and he went to the one side of the bridge and unloosed the mouth of the sack, and did shake out all the meal into the river. Then said he, 'How much meal is there in the sack, neighbours?'

'Marry,' answered they, 'none.'

'Now, by my faith,' answered this wise man, 'even so much wit is there in your two heads to strive for the thing which you have not.'

Now which was the wisest of these three persons, I leave you to judge.

GHOSTS

Ghosts

Although there never has been accord over what happens to a person when he dies, every culture and religious belief has shared the view that the deceased needs 'a decent burial', and far more customs and superstitions surround burial than any other stage in our passage through this world. When Ancient Greeks placed a penny on the dead man's tongue to pay the ferryman Charon, when the Anglo-Saxons and Norsemen buried men in ships complete with grave goods, when many people (including the Celts) held wakes in honour of the departed, when the Church of England recently held a full-scale funeral for an unknown sailor who went down four hundred years ago in the *Mary Rose*, in differing degrees they were all motivated by a mixture of piety and fear. In piety, they were trying to give the deceased rest and maybe arrange for his transfer from this world to the next; in fear, they were trying to protect themselves against the possibility of his return.

The conviction that a dead person can return as a living ghost is pronounced in Britain today; many people say they have seen ghosts and most profess belief in them. This has naturally led to a great body of ghost stories – well-rounded tales that do not simply tell how a ghost appeared but also explain why it appeared and what happened as a result of its appearance. It may be helpful to think of ghosts as, in Katharine Briggs' words, 'divided into those of people who have done wrong and of people who have suffered it' and, of course, the reasons for haunting range from the vengeful and vindictive to the benign.

Whatever is concealed has intrinsic power, so if a person hides anything at all during his lifetime, and more especially money, it may prevent his spirit from resting. This is the superstition underlying *The Ghosts and the Game of Football* which was included by Patrick Kennedy (1801-187?) in his *Legendary Fictions of the Irish Celts* (1866). This was an important book in the history of Irish folklore, for Kennedy was concerned not only with fairy tales, as were Crofton Croker and Keightley, but was the first to reprint tales of enchantment, ghost stories, heroic legends and legends of saints. His versions are lively *recollections* of tales he heard in *English* as a boy in County Wexford – two black marks in the eyes of folklorists who are nonetheless impressed by the professional way in which he described his sources and pointed to parallel stories.

The Bewitched Sixareen, collected on Yell in Shetland and reprinted by Ernest Marwick in *The Folklore of Orkney and Shetland*, is untidy and intriguing. The tale is based on the actual loss of a Yell fishing boat at Lammastide in 1811 or 1812 but in the course of time several conflicting traditions seem to have become attached to it. The 'pretty young woman' in love with Andrew Grott, who later appears to Tarrel in the form of a 'flain bullock', is clearly an agent of the Devil and one expects the tale to end with her demise. But in the second part her role is taken over by the black dog accompanying the crew of spirits who is 'damned for time to come' and is presumably the Devil himself. This, then, is a tale of people who have had wrong done to them, unable to rest until they have vented their sense of injustice and right and wrong have got their just deserts. Ernest Marwick draws particular attention to 'the interesting series of questions put by Francis Smollett to the ghosts – obviously some ancient formula of recognition, if so it can be called'.

It seems entirely proper to include a tale, *The Great Giant of Henllys*, first printed in *The Athenaeum* (anonymously in 1847) for this leading weekly review of literature, science and the arts published many folkloric contributions throughout the nineteenth century. On 22 August 1846, indeed, the following letter from William John Thoms appeared under the caption FOLK-LORE:

Your pages have so often given evidence of the interest which you take in what we in England designate as Popular Antiquities or Popular Literature, (though by-the-bye it is more a Lore than a Literature, and would be most aptly described by a good Saxon compound, Folk-Lore, – *The Lore of the People*) that I am not without hopes of enlisting your aid in garnering the few ears which are remaining, scattered over that field from which our forefathers might have gathered a goodly crop.

It is that bracketed aside that was momentous: here is the first use of a new word for the science that was replacing Popular Antiquities – *Folk-Lore*.

The Great Giant of Henllys, one of several British folk-tales that tell how an evil person changes shape after his death and returns as an animal or a demon, is valuable for its description of an eighteenth century Christian exorcism. The idea of being able to reduce the size of the spirit and to imprison it as a fly in a tobacco box has a number of European analogues, including the magnificent Icelandic tale of 'The Wizards of the Vestmanna Isles' in which a Sending in the shape of a fly is plugged inside a marrowbone.

Croglin Grange is the most complete tale of a vampire (a reanimated corpse) in the British Isles. In some respects Augustus Hare's retelling is too literary and absurdly genteel. The first words of someone who has just been bitten in the throat by a vampire are unlikely to be 'What has happened is most extraordinary and I am very much hurt'! Yet Hare's portrayal of a characterful and sensible English girl (just the sort who would not normally believe in such things) and of a placid English summer evening, serve as a marvellous foil for the vampire. The family's stoic return to sinister Croglin Grange signals a rapid increase in tension and overall this is one of the most terrifying of all British folk-tales. Vampire belief is said to be strongest in China, Greece and Eastern Europe, and there the customary method of laying a vampire is to pierce its heart with a stake; the use of fire appears to be peculiar to this tale.

Augustus Hare (1834-1903) was a literary dandy – an indiscreet, snobbish, nasal bachelor who was also a great raconteur and a very good watercolourist. He wrote countless guide books, and ghosted 'massive memoirs of worthy ladies', while his three volumes of autobiography give an entertaining and outspoken picture of aristocratic and middle-class life, at home and abroad, in mid-Victorian England.

The Somerset 'liddlin' of *The Men in the Turnip Field* is one of many very brief ghost tales. The shortest of all is said to be:

He woke up frightened and reached for the matches and the matches were put in his hand.

They are tales which need to be printed with a good deal of white space around them. *The Men in the Turnip Field* was collected from her own brother by Ruth Tongue, one of England's leading twentieth-century folklorists and editor with Katharine Briggs of *Folktales of England* (1965).

Radio and television militate against the survival of folk-tales and during the second part of the twentieth century the collection of tales has largely been restricted to a few remote communities. So the publication in 1963 and 1964 of *Tales from the Fens* and *More Tales from the Fens* by an old Norfolk fenman, W. H. Barrett, was a surprise and a delight. The fifty-seven tales in those two books are not only irrepressible pieces of story-telling but constitute a collection with a distinctive identity shaped by the marshland of Norfolk and Cambridgeshire, the tales of an inward-looking community with its own history and traditions.

Lamplighter's Dream is a ghost story about a haunted object. It presents us with two worlds, the world of Lamplighter, impoverished and exacting and squelching, and the world of the Romans brutally imposing their will on the fen tigers. The portrayal of the crucifixion is graphic and all the more terrible for the routine manner in which it is carried out and the idiomatic half-humorous way ('the poor chap tried to sit up', 'some quick work on the other one' and, of the crucifixion nails, 'just the very things to hang the hams on') in which it is described.

Lamplighter may be exaggerating in his allusion to the stigmata but this should not conceal the fact that the tale may well have had its origin in an attempt to explain the causes of a birthmark and that the tale as a whole arises from a potent belief in the supernatural.

The Ghosts and the Game of Football

THERE was once a poor widow woman's son that was going to look for service, and one winter's evening he came to a strong farmer's house, and this house was very near an old castle.

'God save all here,' says he, when he got inside the door.

'God save you kindly,' says the farmer. 'Come to the fire.'

'Could you give me a night's lodging?' says the boy.

'That we will, and welcome, if you will only sleep in a comfortable room in the old castle above there; and you must have a fire and candlelight, and whatever you like to drink; and if you're alive in the morning I'll give you ten guineas.'

'Sure I'll be 'live enough if you send no one to kill me.'

'I'll send no one to kill you, you may depend. The place is haunted ever since my father died, and three or four people that slept in the same room were found dead next morning. If you can banish the spirits I'll give you a good farm and my daughter, so that you like one another well enough to be married.'

'Never say't twice. I've a middling safe conscience, and don't fear any evil spirit that ever smelled of brimstone.'

Well and good, the boy got his supper, and then they went up

192

with him to the old castle, and showed him into a large kitchen, with a roaring fire in the grate, and a table, with a bottle and glass, and tumbler on it, and the kettle ready on the hob. They bade him goodnight and God speed, and went off as if they didn't think their heels were half swift enough.

'Well,' says he to himself, 'if there's any danger, this prayer-book will be usefuller than either the glass or tumbler.' So he kneeled down and read a good many prayers, and then sat by the fire, and waited to see what would happen. In about a quarter of an hour, he heard something bumping along the floor overhead till it came to a hole in the ceiling. There it stopped, and cried out, 'I'll fall, I'll fall.'

'Fall away,' says Jack, and down came a pair of legs on the kitchen floor. They walked to one end of the room, and there they stood, and Jack's hair had like to stand upright on his head along with them. Then another crackling and whacking came to the hole, and the same words passed between the thing above and Jack, and down came a man's body, and went and stood upon the legs. Then comes the head and shoulders, till the whole man, with buckles in his shoes and knee-breeches, and a big flapped waistcoat and a three-cocked hat, was standing in one corner of the room. Not to take up your time for nothing, two more men, more old-fashioned dressed than the first, were soon standing in two other corners. Jack was a little cowed at first; but found his courage growing stronger every moment, and what would you have of it, the three old gentlemen began to kick a *puckeen** as fast as they could, the man in the three-cocked hat playing again' the other two.

'Fair play is bonny play,' says Jack, as bold as he could; but the terror was on him, and the words came out as if he was frightened in his sleep; 'so I'll help *you*, sir.'

Well and good, he joined the sport, and kicked away till his shirt was ringing wet, savin' your presence, and the ball flying from one end of the room to the other like thunder, and still not a word was exchanged. At last the day began to break, and poor

* Football.

Jack was dead beat, and he thought, by the way the three ghosts began to look at himself and themselves, that they wished him to speak.

So, says he, 'Gentlemen, as the sport is nearly over, and I done my best to please you, would you tell a body what is the reason of yous coming here night after night, and how could I give you rest, if it is rest you want?'

'Them is the wisest words', says the ghost with the three cocked hat, 'you ever said in your life. Some of those that came before you found courage enough to take a part in our game, but no one had *misnach** enough to speak to us. I am the father of the good man of next house, that man in the left corner is *my* father, and the man on my right is my grandfather. From father to son we were too fond of money. We lent it at ten times the honest interest it was worth; we never paid a debt we could get over, and almost starved our tenants and labourers.

'Here,' says he, lugging a large drawer out of the wall; 'here is the gold and notes that we put together, and we were not honestly entitled to the one-half of it; and here,' says he, opening another drawer, 'are bills and memorandums that'll show who were wronged, and who are entitled to get a great deal paid back to them. Tell my son to saddle two of his best horses for himself and yourself, and keep riding day and night, till every man and woman we ever wronged be rightified. When that is done, come here again some night; and if you don't hear or see anything, we'll be at rest, and you may marry my granddaughter as soon as you please.'

Just as he said these words, Jack could see the wall through his body, and when he winked to clear his sight, the kitchen was as empty as a noggin turned upside down. At the very moment the farmer and his daughter lifted the latch, and both fell on their knees when they saw Jack alive. He soon told them everything that happened, and for three days and nights did the farmer and himself ride about, till there wasn't a single wronged person left without being paid to the last farthing.

* Courage.

The next night Jack spent in the kitchen he fell asleep before he was after sitting a quarter of an hour at the fire, and in his sleep he thought he saw three white birds flying up to heaven from the steeple of the next church.

Jack got the daughter for his wife, and they lived comfortably in the old castle; and if ever he was tempted to hoard up gold, or keep for a minute a guinea or a shilling from the man that earned it through the nose, he bethought him of the ghosts and the game of football.

The Bewitched Sixareen*

A LOT O' YEARS gone by, there was a young pretty woman that lived in Herra, Yell. She was supposed to be able to do anything she wished to do. And there was a young man that came to a shop near by her. She fell in love wi' him, but he didna' fall in love wi' her. She would have given all the world to have gotten him, but he keepid a stand-off o' her . . .

Time passed, nearly a year, and then summer cam'.

There were sixareens then-a-days that went to sea from the place where the girl lived. Wan night a sixareen cam' back wi' a man badly ill aboard. They couldna go to sea without him, but the young man that was at the shop volunteered to take his place. And his name was Andrew Grott.

The skipper that was aboard o' this boat was named Tarrel . . . This Tarrel was a very very wise man, but he was very old. The sixareen gud† wi' a beautiful day, and when it was that she came through a voe . . . there were three awful waves that rose; and yet the sun was shinin'.

* Six-oared fishing boat. † Went.

Andrew Grott wisno used wi' the sea, and he said to this skipper, 'I' the name o' the Loard, what a mountain o' seas is that?'

Tarrel says, 'My boy,' he says, 'pay no attention to that', he says, 'while I'm aboard. This is not real seas; this seas is from the Wicked One.'

And Andrew Grott says, 'We'll never live in that sea, and I'm terribly frightened!'

And Tarrel says, 'You needna be frightened,' he says, 'while I'm with you. But,' he says, 'if you ever are off again, and meet a thing like that, pity be on you if I'm not with you.'

The first sea cam', and the boat shivered, and they thowt she was going to sink. The second sea was still greater, and halfleens waterlogged her. And the third sea was so terrible that it looked as if she wad go to the bottom, a mountain above her. And when Tarrel saw this, he sprang from the steering and telled another one to steer. And he took a huggie-staff* that they had in this sixareen for luck and a big fish, and he strak[†] the water. And he said, 'Either in the name o' God or the name o' the Devil, whatever this is that appears,' he says, 'we'll get through it.'

And as he strak the water, the sea aised, and he saw alongside o' the boat a thing like a flain[‡] bullock. This thing put its feet in over the boat and said, 'Give me oot Andrew Grott.'

But Tarrel says, 'No, you'll never get oot Andrew Grott, for,' he says, 'if Andrew Grott is pitten oot we'll all be pitten oot; we'll all perish together. But,' he says, 'never will du[§] get this ship destroyed while God is stronger as the Devil.'

Then the sea aised, and they gud to the fishing grunds. They were a week away, and they made a beautiful fishing. When they cam' back, they heard that the man that Andrew Grott had taken the place o' was all right again. And they heard that the young woman, that was in love with Andrew, had been going to

* Gaff.
[†] Struck.
[‡] Flayed.
[§] You.

jump over her yard dyke at the very time that the bullock put its feet in the boat. There was a stone that rolled oot o' the dyke, and she fell, and this stone fell on her and broke her leg. So she was lying in bed wi' her leg spelkéd*.

All gaed weel eftir that, and some years passed, and Tarrel had ceased fae going to the sea. Another man was skipper o' the boat. And two years eftir the same thing occurred again, and Andrew Grott took some man's place in the boat. The young woman was still in love wi' Andrew Grott, but she couldna get him. It was a beautiful day and they went to sea . . . And nobody knew anything concerning them until the boats cam' home at the weekend. None had seen this boat coming to the grund where they fished. That was the boat Andrew Grott was in. And she never came. And it was thowt that she was casten away by this same girl that tried to cast her away when Tarrel was in her, and that cam' in the form of a flain bullock.

Time passed on – and this girl lived in the same place.

And winter cam'. And the boat's crew o' men that had been casten away cam' to the township. Everyone that went out saw them: some saw them at the scroos† in the yard, and some saw them aroond the hooses. In this district, from Hallowmas till coming up eftir Christmas, all the people were frightened to go oot.

There was a man that lived in Nort Grummon in this place that was supposed to be the strongest man that was ever in Yell. He was John Smollett. And this John Smollett wad be a man probably about forty or forty-two. Him and his two sisters and his aged father all lived together in a hoose. And then-a-time the hooses wisno like what they are now. They had lambs into the hooses at the back o' the restin'-chairs. These people had four lambs in.

They were‡ made a supper, away about 11 o'clock at night. And one o' the sisters lifted the big kettle o' soup, and she was

---

* In splints.
† Stacks.
‡ Had.

going to dish it up, when one o' the lambs jumped oot over it; and she was frightened it would get burned in the soup, and she had to hang the kettle back on the crook again. She said til her brither John, 'Will you go oot, and go in the yard and fetch some hay to this lambs, to eat till we get wir supper.'

He was supposed to rise fae where he was sittin'; and he put his feet into clogs, and he went out. He seemed to be out no time until he cam' in the door; and he opened the door very quickly. And as he opened the door very quickly, he dropped down inta the door, a-soond* wi' fright. And his father, Francis Smollett, was a very old man, probably eighty or eighty-two. He knew what had happened to John his son. And he sprang up, old as he was, and went to where John was lying: where his sister was trying to get him oot a-soond[†]. And he pulled the warm clogs off o' his son's feet, and he put them on. And he went right out to the stack o' hay, where his son was supposed to go.

When he cam' out to this stack o' hay, here was this boat's crew of men standing anunder the stack o' hay . . . And he came out and he saw them, and he knew that this was what had frightened John . . . And he came out, and he said to the men. 'Speak, either in the name o' God or in the name o' the Wicked One!'

There was no answer.

He asked them two or three times, but got no answer.

It was five men and a black dog that was standin' at the haystack. So he said to them, he says, 'I'll mak' you speak. Is it ebban or flowan?'

And one o' them lifted up his face, and he says, 'Thou knowest,' he says, 'it's flowan.'

Francis says, 'Is the meun[‡] wannan or growan?'

He says, 'Thou knowest, she's wannan.'

Francis says, 'Is the crow black or white?'

He says, 'Thou knowest, she's black.'

* Insensible.
[†] Bring him round.
[‡] Moon.

Then Francis says, 'And what's the name o' this black een?*'

They says, 'He's damned for time to come. We're all eternally happy, but he's damned. And owing to this we can't get rest; and we can't get rest until we've told the tale that we had to tell.'

And then one o' them said: 'We were casten away by that young woman that was in love wi' Andrew Grott. We met the same three seas when we went out as what Tarrel met. But the skipper didna have the common sense to do what Tarrel did; and the third een engulfed us and we were all lost. And we've gone aboot the eart', and we've neither been in heaven nor no place. And why we werena there is that we had to come back to the world to tell this tale. For the world contains black and it contains white; and the two cannot exist tagidder; and they must be separated.'

And then the een that was speaking – he was been the skipper – he said some rhyme:

> *'Jesus, the name high over all,*
> *At Hell, or Earth, or Sea,*
> *Angels and men before him fall,*
> *And Devils fear and flee.'*

Then the black dog fetched a bark and they saw the flames coming oot o' his jaws, and away he went right over the banks.[†] And the other five went from Francis singin' a hyme.[‡]

They gaed doon towards the banks; and then it was the same as if there had been a beautiful light around them. They disappeared, just down through the ground, and were no more seen on eart'; and they were no more heard o'; and they never tormented the place evermore; and they were gone to their eternal rest – him damned for evermore, and them to eternal happiness for evermore.

---

* One.
† High cliffs.
‡ Hymn.

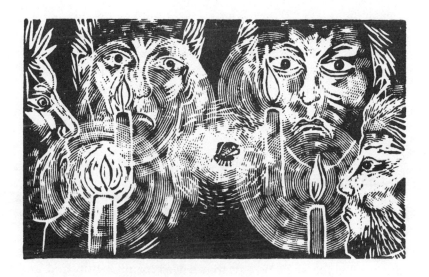

The Great Giant of Henllys

SOME TIME in the eighteenth century there lived on the banks of the Wye a man so rich, wicked and tyrannous that he was called *The Great Giant of Henllys*. All the countryside rejoiced when he died, but they did not rejoice long, for he came again in a form so terrible that no one dared to be out of doors after dark, and even the horses and cattle huddled round the farms. At length it was determined that he must be laid, and three clergymen went at dead of night to the church of Henllys to exorcise him. They drew a circle before the altar and took their stand within it. Each man had a lighted candle in his hand, and together they began their prayers.

Suddenly a terrific monster appeared in the church and came roaring up towards them, but when it came to the circle it stopped as if it had hit against a stone wall. They went on with their prayers, but so terrible were the roarings and so close did the monster come that one man's heart failed him, and the candle that he held went out. But they continued with their exorcism.

201

Then the giant reappeared as a roaring lion, and then as a raging bull; then it seemed as if a wave of the sea was flooding the church, and then as if the west wall was falling down. The second man wavered in his faith, and the second candle went out. Still the third went on, though his candle was faint. At last the Great Giant appeared in his mortal form, and they questioned him, and asked why he had come in such dreadful shapes.

'I was bad as a man,' he said, 'and I am worse now as a devil.' And he vanished in a flash of fire.

Then their candles all burned up again and they prayed steadily, and the Great Giant appeared in smaller and smaller forms, until at last he was only a fly, and they conjured him into a tobacco box and threw him into Llynwyn Pool, to lie there for ninety-nine years. Some say that it was for nine hundred and ninety-nine; but at any rate they are very careful not to disturb the tobacco box when they are dredging Llynwyn Pool.

Croglin Grange

FISHER may sound a very plebeian name, but this family is of very ancient lineage, and for many hundreds of years they have possessed a very curious old place in Cumberland, which bears the weird name of Croglin Grange. The great characteristic of the house is that never at any period of its very long existence has it been more than one story high, but it has a terrace from which large grounds sweep away towards the church in the hollow, and a fine distant view.

When, in lapse of years, the Fishers outgrew Croglin Grange in family and fortune, they were wise enough not to destroy the long-standing characteristic of the place by adding another story to the house, but they went away to the south, to reside at Thorncombe near Guildford, and they let Croglin Grange.

They were extremely fortunate in their tenants, two brothers and a sister. They heard their praises from all quarters. To their poorer neighbours they were all that is most kind and beneficent, and their neighbours of a higher class spoke of them as a most welcome addition to the little society of the neighbourhood. On their part the tenants were greatly delighted with their new residence. The arrangement of the house, which would have been a trial to many, was not so to them. In every respect Croglin Grange was exactly suited to them.

The winter was spent most happily by the new inmates of Croglin Grange, who shared in all the little social pleasures of the district, and made themselves very popular. In the following summer, there was one day which was dreadfully, annihilatingly hot. The brothers lay under the trees with their books, for it was too hot for any active occupation. The sister sat in the verandah and worked, or tried to work, for, in the intense sultriness of that summer day, work was next to impossible. They dined early, and after dinner they still sat out in the verandah, enjoying the cool air which came with evening, and they watched the sun set, and the moon rise over the belt of trees which separated the grounds from the churchyard, seeing it mount the heavens till the whole lawn was bathed in silver light, across which the long shadows from the shrubbery fell as if embossed, so vivid and distinct were they.

When they separated for the night, all retiring to their rooms on the ground-floor (for, as I said, there was no upstairs in that house), the sister felt that the heat was still so great that she could not sleep, and having fastened her window, she did not close the shutters – in that very quiet place it was not necessary – and, propped against the pillows, she still watched the wonderful, the marvellous beauty of that summer night. Gradually she became aware of two lights, two lights which flickered in and out in the belt of trees which separated the lawn from the churchyard, and as her gaze became fixed upon them, she saw them emerge, fixed in a dark substance, a definite ghastly *something*, which seemed every moment to become nearer, increasing in size and substance as it approached. Every now and then it was lost for a moment in the long shadows which stretched across the lawn from the trees, and then it emerged larger than ever, and still coming on – on. As she watched it, the most uncontrollable horror seized her. She longed to get away, but the door was close to the window and the door was locked on the inside, and while she was unlocking it, she must be for an instant nearer to *it*. She longed to scream, but her voice seemed paralysed, her tongue glued to the roof of her mouth.

Suddenly, she never could explain why afterwards, the terrible object seemed to turn to one side, seemed to be going round the house, not to be coming to her at all, and immediately she jumped out of bed and rushed to the door, but as she was unlocking it, she heard scratch, scratch, scratch upon the window, and saw a hideous brown face with flaming eyes glaring in at her. She rushed back to the bed, but the creature continued to scratch, scratch, scratch upon the window. She felt a sort of mental comfort in the knowledge that the window was securely fastened on the inside. Suddenly the scratching sound ceased, and a kind of pecking sound took its place. Then, in her agony, she became aware that the creature was unpicking the lead! The noise continued, and a diamond pane of glass fell into the room. Then a long bony finger of the creature came in and turned the handle of the window, and the window opened, and the creature came in; and it came across the room, and her terror was so great that she could not scream, and it came up to the bed and it twisted its long bony fingers into her hair, and it dragged her head over the side of the bed, and – it bit her violently in the throat.

As it bit her, her voice was released, and she screamed with all her might and main. Her brothers rushed out of their rooms, but the door was locked on the inside. A moment was lost while they got a poker and broke it open. Then the creature had already escaped through the window, and the sister, bleeding violently from a wound in the throat, was lying unconscious over the side of the bed. One brother pursued the creature, which fled before him through the moonlight with gigantic strides, and eventually seemed to disappear over the wall into the churchyard. Then he rejoined his brother by the sister's bedside. She was dreadfully hurt and her wound was a very definite one, but she was of strong disposition, not given either to romance or superstition, and when she came to herself she said, 'What has happened is

205

most extraordinary and I am very much hurt. It seems inexplicable, but of course there *is* an explanation, and we must wait for it. It will turn out that a lunatic has escaped from some asylum and found his way here.' The wound healed and she appeared to get well, but the doctor who was sent for to her would not believe that she could bear so terrible a shock so easily, and insisted that she much have change, mental and physical; so her brothers took her to Switzerland.

Being a sensible girl, when she went abroad, she threw herself at once into the interests of the country she was in. She dried plants, she made sketches, she went up mountains, and, as autumn came on, she was the person who urged that they should return to Croglin Grange. 'We have taken it,' she said, 'for seven years, and we have only been there one; and we shall always find it difficult to let a house which is only one story high, so we had better return there; lunatics do not escape every day.' As she urged it, her brothers wished nothing better, and the family returned to Cumberland. From there being no upstairs in the house, it was impossible to make any great change in their arrangements. The sister occupied the same room, but it is unnecessary to say she always closed her shutters, which, however, as in many old houses, always left one top pane of the window uncovered. The brothers moved, and occupied a room together exactly opposite that of their sister, and they always kept loaded pistols in their room.

The winter passed most peacefully and happily. In the following March the sister was suddenly awakened by a sound she remembered only too well – scratch, scratch, scratch upon the window, and looking up, she saw, climbed up to the topmost pane of the window, the same hideous brown shrivelled face, with glaring eyes, looking in at her. This time she screamed as loud as she could. Her brothers rushed out of their room with pistols, and out of the front door. The creature was already scudding away across the lawn. One of the brothers fired and hit it in the leg, but still with the other leg it continued to make way, scrambled over the wall into the churchyard, and seemed to disappear into a vault which belonged to a family long extinct.

The next day the brothers summoned all the tenants of Croglin Grange, and in their presence the vault was opened. A horrible scene revealed itself. The vault was full of coffins; they had been broken open, and their contents, horribly mangled and distorted, were scattered over the floor. One coffin alone remained intact. Of that the lid had been lifted, but still lay loose upon the coffin. They raised it, and there, brown, withered, shrivelled, mummified, but quite entire, was the same hideous figure which had looked in at the windows of Croglin Grange, with the marks of a recent pistol-shot in the leg; and they did the only thing that can lay a vampire – they burnt it.

The Men in the Turnip Field

THERE was two fellows out working in a field, hoeing turnips they was, and the one he stop and he lean on his hoe, and he mop his vace and he say, 'Yur – I don't believe in these yur ghosteses!'

And t'other man he say, 'Don't 'ee?'

And he VANISHED!

Lamplighter's Dream*

I HADN'T been married very long when I fell out of work. There were a lot like me wandering over the Fens looking for a job and it was a real godsend to us when the drainage commissioners decided to cut a new drain on the outskirts of Hockwold. It meant a long shack[†] before starting work, though, and another one when the day's work was over, but I didn't mind that.

One day, as I was digging out the peat, my spade struck something that I reckoned was a piece of bog oak, but when I dug it out I found it was a bit of timber about four foot long and six inches wide. It had been hewn by an axe, I knew, because the marks were still showing, and near each end were two big iron spikes. The heads of the spikes hadn't been driven into the wood – they stood out nearly three inches – but the points had been driven right through and then bent over, so it looked as though something had been nailed to the wood hundreds of years ago.

* W. H. Barrett heard this story in 1900 from old 'Lamplighter' Miller, who used to light the lamps in a small chapel in Hockwold Fen.
† Walk.

209

None of the other chaps working with me wanted the wood so I carried it home thinking I'd saw it up to make a few logs for the fire. I hadn't a shed so I stood the piece of wood up to dry by the hearth, but that didn't please my old woman. You see, she was expecting a baby and a lot of little things upset her, and she said that that bit of black wood gave her the creeps; and do you know, it even looked a bit queer to me as it stood there with the firelight playing on it. So I made up my mind to saw it up as soon as it was dry enough: but it took quite a while to dry out and in the meantime the wife went to her mother's for a bit of a change.

Well, our peat fire was kept burning night and day, so when I got home from work all I had to do was to give it a poke up, put on some more peat and it would soon be blazing away. One night, after I'd done all that and had finished my tea, I sat down to enjoy a good warm and it wasn't long before I fell fast asleep in my chair. And while I was asleep I had a dream which I can still remember as clearly as anything, and I'll tell you what it was.

I dreamed that I was back again where I'd been working that day, but instead of the lonely fen, there were a lot of houses and people coming out of them and crowding on to the river bank. There were a lot of soldiers, too, moving about, wearing brass hats which were shining in the sunlight. Two of the soldiers were digging a deep hole and, close by, a huge man, who was nearly naked except for a leather apron, was busy making a cross out of two pieces of rough hewn wood. As I watched all this, two soldiers came along dragging a man dressed only in a bit of sheepskin and with his hands and feet tied together. The soldiers threw him on the ground and then stood waiting as if they expected someone to come along. And so they did, because presently a man in a red cloak rode up on horseback and told all those people on the bank that one of the local folk had been caught stealing corn from the storehouse and, to stop others from doing the same thing, he'd ordered him to be whipped and then hung on a cross.

Then he gave the sign to the soldiers and they dragged the chap to his feet and made him bend over a fallen tree trunk while they tied his wrists to stakes driven into the ground. Then the chap with the leather apron came up with a whip made of leather thongs, and at the end of each thong there was a bit of brass. The soldiers tore the sheepskin off the thief and someone banged on a gong to drown the man's screams as that whip ripped open his flesh till I could see his bare ribs. When all this was over the soldiers threw jars of water over the man to bring him to his senses again, which took some time; so, while they waited, Leather Apron tested the cross as it lay flat on the ground by walking up and down on it. Then, after putting his hammer and nails handy on the ground, he and the soldiers picked up the thief and put him on the cross. As the first spike was driven into his hand the poor chap tried to sit up, but some quick work on the other one soon stretched him out again. Then the soldiers broke his legs with a couple of heavy blows from the hammer, nailed his two feet to the wood and with a single spike then lowered the butt end of the cross into the hole they'd dug, ramming the soil back to make it stand firm.

As soon as the cross was set upright, all the folk on the bank started throwing clods of earth at the man till they got tired; then they sat down and cakes and wine were brought along and sold to them. They all seemed to be enjoying themselves, making fun of the dying man and throwing wine on to his body; even the children joined in. Then, as the sun was beginning to go down, they all moved off towards their houses, shouting out that they'd be back in a twelvemonth to see what the corn thief's bones looked like after they'd been well weathered.

Just before it got properly dark a crowd of men, women, and children came along, whipped on their way, in a cloud of dust, by soldiers on horseback. When they got near the cross they were all made to get into a circle and the man in the red cloak shouted to them at the top of his voice:

'You lot of thieves and robbers will stay here till your fellow thief is dead, and that won't be till tomorrow's sunrise. As you watch him die I hope it'll be a lesson to you, so you know who your masters are.'

211

Then he and some of the soldiers rode off, leaving about a dozen behind to keep order. They lit torches so that the circle of people could see the man on the cross, and some jars of wine were brought along for the guards. I saw one of the women in the circle suddenly stretch out her arm and drop something into one of the jars, and then, after another round of drinks, those soldiers suddenly dropped their spears and swords and fell flat on the ground, twisting about as if they were in agony. The men in the crowd picked up the swords and after one of them had put an end to the miseries of the chap on the cross, all the others crept along to the soldiers' quarters and killed the lot of them. Then, just before daylight, they went round the houses, killing as they went, and those that didn't die outright were finished off by the women. Then the houses were set on fire, and the men, women and children all rushed off across the fen to hide up in a big wood on the other side. Just before I woke up all I could see was the man hanging on the cross on the top of the river bank. It was a loud crashing noise that woke me up and broke my dream, and I found that that piece of timber had dried out and warped in the heat of the fire, so it had toppled over; and as I looked at it, I wondered and wondered about that dream.

Well, next day, when I got back from work, I found that my wife was home again and that her mother had come with her. Before I could sit down to my tea, the old girl started:

'If you don't want a baby with a lot of birthmarks on it then you'd better get rid of that bit of wood, for it's properly got on my girl's nerves and you don't want to upset her at a time like this.'

So I picked up the piece of timber and pushed it into the fire as far as it would go, and watched it burn until all that was left of it was white ash and two red hot spikes. When these had cooled down a bit I picked them out of the fire, sharpened the ends and drove them into the ceiling beam.

'Just the very thing to hang the hams on when we kill the pig,' I said.

About three weeks afterwards our foreman, who'd spent most of his working life digging dykes and drains in the Fens, came along to me with a hammer head and a few iron spikes in his hand.

'Look', he said, 'what one of the chaps has just dug up. I reckon they're Roman; some old carpenter must have lost them hundreds of years ago. We find a lot of things like these round about here, and I've heard the old chaps say that, a good many years ago, this part of the Fens was full of Romans and this place where we're digging was given its name by them, though why they called it Cross Bank beats me. Have you any ideas about it, Lamplighter?'

'Maybe the name was given because a lot of crosses stood here at one time,' I said.

'What do you mean?' asked the foreman. 'Do you mean that this part of the fen was a churchyard once?'

'No, I don't mean that,' I said. 'But as you go to chapel the same as I do, you often sing that hymn "When I survey the wondrous Cross", so you ought to know what those Romans used to do to those that fell foul of them, and I wouldn't be at all surprised if some of our ancestors weren't crucified right where we're standing and that's how the place came to be called Cross Bank, because of the crosses that stood here. And I can tell you something else. I dug up a length of oak some time ago and took it home for firewood. It had two nails on it, just like those you've got there, and was about the size of a cross's arms. Well, time it was drying out beside the hearth, my old woman complained that it haunted her, and said that if I didn't get rid of it she'd really start worrying, and worrying about that evil bit of wood was the last thing she wanted to do. How she knew that the wood was evil beats me, all I know is that when our baby was born last week it had a red spot, as large as a sixpenny piece, on the palms of its hands and the soles of its feet.'

ABLES AND

ANIMAL TALES

Fables and Animal Tales

We may or may not remember such maxims as 'Little liberties are great offences' and 'Misfortune tries the sincerity of friends' but, from the time we first heard them, probably as young children, we are unlikely to have forgotten such vivid metaphorical tales as 'The Hare and the Tortoise', 'The Frogs Asking for a King' and 'The Fox and Mr Crane'. All of them come from the great collection of fables (a form defined by Joseph Jacobs as 'a short humorous allegorical tale, in which animals act in such a way as to illustrate a simple moral truth or inculcate a wise maxim') attributed to Aesop but actually written by many hands during the sixth century BC.

Aesop's *Fables*, the cornerstone of the fable tradition in the west, were first translated into English by Caxton and in 1481 he also translated and printed the medieval satirical fables known collectively as *Roman de Renart* or *Reynard the Fox*. (Chaucer's story of Chanticleer and Pertelote in *The Canterbury Tales* is a fable of this kind.) These are the ultimate sources of many of the fables collected from oral tradition during the nineteenth century, a time when the fable was also resuscitated in England as a literary form, as it had been by Jean de la Fontaine in seventeenth-century France, by writers such as Charles Kingsley and Lewis Carroll, Rudyard Kipling and Beatrix Potter.

In Scotland, John Francis Campbell (see p.110) found a delightful cache of fables. Of *The Fox and the Geese*, he wrote:

The wild goose in the Highland has her true character; she is one of the most wary and sagacious of birds, and a Gaelic proverb says: *Sealgair thu mar a mharbhas thu Gèadh a's Corr' a's Crotach* – Sportsman thou, when killest thou goose, and heron, and curlew?

Rory, nowadays quite a popular Christian name in Scotland, is an anglicisation of the Gaelic *ruadh*, 'the red-brown haired one'.

How the Wolf Lost his Tail is also taken from *Popular Tales of the West Highlands* (1860-62). This fable bears a close resemblance to 'Why the Bear is Stumpy-tailed', included by Campbell's friend and mentor George Webbe Dasent in his *Popular Tales from the Norse* (1859), but was collected from a source in Sutherland that knew nothing of that book. Doubtless the tale had been carried from Scandinavia to Scotland at some earlier time and embodies a memory of the days when wolves ran free on both sides of the North Sea. But what remains difficult to explain is why country-men should come to tell a tale that is inaccurate: wolves do not have stumpy tails.

While the primary purpose of this book is to represent the field work of the nineteenth- and early twentieth-century folklorists, it also attempts to show the way in which folk-tales have been appropriated and retold in the name of art, entertainment or edification. *The Fox and the Geese*, undoubtedly modelled on James Orchard Halliwell's 'The Three Little Pigs', forms part of *A Treasury of Pleasure Books for Young People* by Joseph Cundall, evidently a man not averse to tinkering with his sources: it was he who changed the heroine of Southey's 'The Story of the Three Bears' from a little old woman to a young girl. Despite the poem's Victorian gentility and sometimes intrusive moralising ('Because she preferred her own silly way,/And would not to her own mother attend') the tale is well told and the description of the fair is particularly lively.

Two Women or Twelve Men, collected in County Waterford in 1934, perpetuates as longstanding an idea as that in 'The Cow on the Roof' (see p.180). Sean O'Sullivan says that 'The jocose reason given for the loquaciousness of the fair sex is that a woman's tongue is attached to the throat by only its middle part, while a man's tongue is attached by both sides. Thus a woman's tongue can wag more freely.'

The Long-Lived Ancestors, collected by P. H. Emerson in Angle-sey (see p.83), is in a sense an aetiological tale: it explains to us why certain beasts are the oldest in the world. Stately and formulaic, it offers exceptionally vivid portraits of stag, salmon, blackbird and frog, and its musical invocation of place names is an integral part of the story.

The Fox and the Wild Goose

ONE DAY the fox succeeded in catching a fine fat goose asleep by the side of a loch, he held her by the wing, and making a joke of her cackling, hissing and fears, he said:

'Now, if you had me in your mouth as I have you, tell me what you would do?'

'Why,' said the goose, 'that is an easy question. I would fold my hands, shut my eyes, say a grace, and then eat you.'

'Just what I mean to do,' said Rory, and folding his hands, and looking very demure, he said a pious grace with his eyes shut.

But while he did this the goose had spread her wings, and she was now half way over the loch; so the fox was left to lick his lips for supper.

'I will make a rule of this,' he said in disgust, 'never in all my life to say a grace again till after I feel the meat warm in my belly.'

How the Wolf Lost his Tail

ONE DAY the wolf and the fox were out together, and they stole a dish of crowdie. Now the wolf was the biggest beast of the two, and he had a long tail like a greyhound, and great teeth.

The fox was afraid of him, and did not dare to say a word when the wolf ate the most of the crowdie, and left only a little at the bottom of the dish for him, but he determined to punish him for it; so the next night when they were out together the fox said:

'I smell a very nice cheese, and (pointing to the moonshine on the ice) there it is too.'

'And how will you get it?' said the wolf.

'Well, stop you here till I see if the farmer is asleep, and if you keep your tail on it, nobody will see you or know that it is there. Keep it steady. I may be some time coming back.'

So the wolf lay down and laid his tail on the moonshine in the ice, and kept it for an hour till it was fast. Then the fox, who had been watching him, ran in to the farmer and said: 'The wolf is there; he will eat up the children – the wolf! the wolf!'

Then the farmer and his wife came out with sticks to kill the wolf, but the wolf ran off leaving his tail behind him, and that's why the wolf is stumpy tailed to this day, though the fox has a long brush.

The Fox and the Geese

There was once a goose at the point of death,
  So she called her daughters near,
And desired them all with her latest breath,
  Her last dying word to hear.

'There's a Mr Fox', said she, 'that I know,
  Who lives in a covert near by,
To our race he has proved a deadly foe,
  So beware of his treachery.

'Build houses, ere long, of stone or of bricks,
  And get tiles for your roofs, I pray;
For I know of old Mr Reynard's tricks,
  And I fear he may come any day.'

Thus saying, she died, and her daughters fair,
  Gobble, Goosey, and Ganderee,
Agreed together, that they would beware
  Of Mr Fox, their enemy.

But Gobble, the youngest, I grieve to say,
   Soon came to a very bad end,
Because she preferred her own silly way,
   And would not to her mother attend.

For she made, with some boards, an open nest,
   For a roof took the lid of a box;
Then quietly laid herself down to rest,
   And thought she was safe from the fox.

But Reynard, in taking an evening run,
   Soon scented the goose near the pond;
Thought he, 'Now I'll have some supper and fun,
   For of both I am really fond.'

Then on to the box he sprang in a trice,
   And roused Mrs Gobble from bed;
She only had time to hiss once or twice
   Ere he snapped off her lily-white head.

Her sisters at home felt anxious and low
   When poor Gobble did not appear,
And Goosey, determined her fate to know,
   Went and sought all the field far and near.

At last she descried poor Gobble's head,
   And some feathers not far apart,
So she told Ganderee she had found her dead,
   And they both felt quite sad at heart.

Now Goosey was pretty, but liked her own way,
   Like Gobble and some other birds.
"'Tis no matter', said she, 'if I only obey
   A part of my mother's last words.'

So her house she soon built of nice red brick,
  But she only thatched it with straw;
And she thought that however the fox might kick,
  He could not get e'en a paw.

So she went to sleep, and at dead of night
  She heard at the door a low scratch;
And presently Reynard, with all his might,
  Attempted to jump on the thatch.

But he tumbled back, and against the wall
  Grazed his nose in a fearful way,
Then, almost mad with the pain of his fall,
  He barked and ran slowly away.

So Goosey laughed, and felt quite o'erjoyed
  To have thus escaped from all harm;
But had she known how the fox was employed,
  She would have felt dreadful alarm.

For Gobble had been his last dainty meat,
  So hungry he really did feel,
And resolved in his mind to accomplish this feat,
  And have this young goose for his meal.

So he slyly lighted a bundle of straws,
  And he made no more noise than a mouse,
The lifted himself up on his hind paws,
  And quickly set fire to the house.

'Twas soon in a blaze, and goosey awoke,
  With fright almost ready to die,
And, nearly smothered with heat and with smoke,
  Up the chimney was forced to fly.

225

The fox was rejoiced to witness her flight
  And, heedless of all her sad groans,
He chased her until he saw her alight,
  Then ate her up all but her bones.

Poor Ganderee's heart was ready to break
  When the sad news reached her ear.
''Twas that villain the fox,' said good Mr Drake,
  Who lived in a pond very near.

'Now listen to me, I pray you,' he said,
  'And roof your new house with some tiles,
Or you, like your sisters, will soon be dead,
  A prey to your enemy's wiles.'

So she took the advice of her mother and friend,
  And made her house very secure,
Then she said, 'Now, whatever may be my end,
  The fox cannot catch me, I'm sure.'

He called at her door the very next day,
  And loudly and long did he knock,
But she said to him, 'Leave my house, I pray,
  For the door I will not unlock;

'For you've killed my sisters I know full well,
  And you wish that I too were dead.'
'Oh dear,' said the fox, 'I really can't tell
  Who put such a thought in your head:

'For I've always liked geese more than other birds
  And you of your race I've loved best.'
But the goose ne'er heeded his flattering words,
  So hungry he went to his rest.

Next week she beheld him again appear,
   'Let me in very quick,' he cried,
'For the news I've to tell you'll be charmed to hear
   And 'tis rude to keep me outside.'

But the goose only opened one window-pane,
   And popped out her pretty red bill,
Said she, 'Your fair words are all in vain.
   But talk to me here if you will.'

'Tomorrow', he cried, 'there will be a fair,
   All the birds and the beasts will go;
So allow me, I pray, to escort you there,
   For you will be quite charmed, I know.'

'Many thanks for your news,' said Ganderee,
   'But I had rather not go with you;
I care not for any gay sight to see.'
   So the window she closed and withdrew.

In the morning, howe'er, her mind she changed,
   And she thought she would go to the fair;
So her numerous feathers she nicely arranged,
   And cleaned her red bill with much care.

She went, I believe, before it was light
   For of Reynard she felt much fear;
So quickly she thought she would see each sight,
   And return ere he should appear.

When the goose arrived she began to laugh
   At the wondrous creatures she saw;
There were dancing bears, and a tall giraffe,
   And a beautiful red macaw.

227

A monkey was weighing out apples and roots,
   An ostrich, too, sold by retail;
There were bees and butterflies tasting the fruits,
   And a pig drinking out of a pail.

Ganderee went into an elephant's shop,
   And quickly she bought a new churn;
For as it grew late, she feared to stop,
   As in safety she wished to return.

Ere, however, she got about half the way,
   She saw approaching her foe,
And now she hissed with fear and dismay,
   For she knew not which way to go.

But at last of a capital plan she bethought
   Of a place where she safely might hide;
She got into the churn that she just had bought,
   And then fastened the lid inside.

The churn was placed on the brow of the hill,
   And with Ganderee's weight down it rolled,
Passing the fox, who stood perfectly still,
   Quite alarmed, though he was very bold.

For the goose's wings flapped strangely about,
   And the noise was fearful to hear;
And so bruised she felt she was glad to get out,
   When she thought the coast was clear.

So safely she reaches her own home at noon,
   And the fox ne'er saw her that day;
But after the fair he came very soon,
   And cried out in a terrible way —

'Quick, quick, let me in! Oh, for once be kind,
   For the huntsman's horn I hear;
Oh, hide me in any snug place you can find,
   For the hunters and hounds draw near.'

So the goose looked out in order to see
   Whether Reynard was only in jest;
Then, knowing that he in her power would be,
   She opened the door to her guest.

'I'll hide you,' she said, 'in my nice new churn.'
   'That will do very well,' said he;
'And thank you for doing me this good turn;
   Most friendly and kind Ganderee.'

Then into the churn the fox quickly got;
   But, ere the goose put on the top,
A kettle she brought of water quite hot,
   And poured in every drop.

Then the fox cried, 'Oh! I burn, I burn,
   And I feel in a pitiful plight.'
   But the goose held fast the lid of the churn,
   So Reynard he died that night.

MORAL

Mankind have an enemy whom they well know,
   Who tempts them in every way;
But they too at length shall o'ercome this foe,
   If wisdom's right law they obey.

Two Women or Twelve Men

THERE was a fox that had three young ones, and when the time came to teach them how to fend for themselves, the old fox took them to a house. There was great talk going on inside the house. He asked the first two young ones if they could tell him who was in the house. They couldn't. Then he tried the third.

'Who is inside?' asked the old fox.

'Either two women or twelve men,' said the young one.

'You'll do well in the world,' said the old fox.

The Long-Lived Ancestors

THE EAGLE of Gwernabwy had been long married to his female, and had by her many children: she died, and he continued a long time a widower: but at length he proposed a marriage with the Owl of Cwm Cwmlwyd; but afraid of her being young, so as to have children by her, and thereby degrade his own family, he first of all went to enquire about her age amongst the aged of the world. Accordingly he applied to the Stag of Rhedynfre, whom he found lying close to the trunk of an old oak, and requested to know the Owl's age.

'I have seen,' said the Stag, 'this oak an acorn, which is now fallen to the ground through age, without either bark or leaves, and never suffered any hurt or strain except from my rubbing myself against it once a day, after getting up on my legs; but I never remember to have seen the Owl you mention younger or older than she seems to be at this day. But there is one older than I am, and that is the Salmon of Glynllifon.'

The Eagle then applied to the Salmon for the age of the Owl. The Salmon answered, 'I am as many years old as there are scales upon my skin, and particles of spawn within my belly; yet never saw I the Owl you mention but the same in appearance. But there is one older than I am, and that is the Blackbird of Cilgwri.'

The Eagle next repaired to the Blackbird of Cilgwri, whom he found perched upon a small stone, and enquired of him the Owl's age.

'Dost thou see this stone upon which I sit,' said the Blackbird, 'which is now no bigger than what a man can carry in his hand? I have seen this very stone of such weight as to be a sufficient load for a hundred oxen to draw, which has suffered neither rubbing nor wearing, save that I rub my bill on it once every evening, and touch the tips of my wings on it every morning, when I expand them to fly; yet I have not seen the Owl either older or younger than she appears to be at this day. But there is one older than I am, and that is the Frog of Mochno Bog, and if he does not know her age, there is not a creature living that does know it.'

The Eagle went last of all to the Frog and desired to know the Owl's age. He answered, 'I never ate anything but the dust from the spot which I inhabit, and that very sparingly, and dost thou see these great hills that surround and overawe this bog where I lie? They are formed only of the excrements from my body since I have inhabited this place, yet I never remember to have seen the Owl but an old hag, making that hideous noise, Too, hoo, hoo! always frightening the children in the neighbourhood.'

So the Eagle of Gwernabwy, the Stag of Rhedynfre, the Salmon of Glynllifon, the Blackbird of Cilgwri, the Frog of Mochno Bog, and the Owl of Cwm Cawlwyd are the oldest creatures in the whole world!

GIANTS AND
STRONG MEN

Giants and Strong Men

On the whole, the giants in British folklore are a bad lot. They are self-interested and destructive and sometimes ravenous. But as in the mythology of Northern Europe, there are a few exceptions, giants who are benevolent. The tales in this section nicely illustrate the range of giants one may expect to meet in the British Isles.

The magnificent tale of *The Son of the King of Erin and the Giant of Loch Léin* portrays a giant who is primarily a magician, and can only be defeated by magic. He forfeits estates and bullocks to the king's son only to ensure that he is snared into a head-contest – the kind of situation experienced by Oedipus in his confrontation with the Sphinx and by the enterprising Scheherezade in the *Arabian Nights*. But by the time the king's son has to give himself up after a year and a day, he has gained access (like the hero of *Sir Gawain and the Green Knight*) to protective magic, and once he has performed the three labours with the help of the giant's daughter, the giant's power is immediately broken. There is something unusually satisfying about the resolution of the tale: the situation is highly dramatic, Yellow Lily's magical 'trick' could scarcely be more pointed, and the words of the king of Denmark are shrewd and dignified; it is only the king's daughter who cannot have been too happy about the outcome.

This myth-tale was collected by Jeremiah Curtin in the west of Ireland in 1887, and published by him in *Myths and Folk-Lore of Ireland* (1889). Curtin, an American from Wisconsin who could read seventy languages, came to Ireland expressly in search of myth-tales of the kind that Campbell of Islay had found in the Western Highlands, convinced that he had the best chance of finding them amongst 'the old people for whom Gaelic is the everyday speech'. He was right and, with the help of an interpreter (Curtin could read but not converse in Gaelic), he collected an important and stirring body of twenty long tales of giants and kings, including several about Fionn mac Cumhaill (see p.109) and one about Cuchulainn. Curtin went on to publish two further collections of Irish folk-tales and, in the history of Irish folklore, stands somewhere between Kennedy, whose tales were recollected and in English, and the new professionalism of Douglas Hyde.

'We soon arrived', writes Abraham Elder in *Tales and Legends of the Isle of Wight* (1839)

at Black Gang Chine, which corresponds well to its gloomy name. The land on each side of the glen, standing 400 feet above the neighbouring ocean, is composed of a dark and almost black clay, with layers of yellow sand-stone cutting across it at different heights. But from the whole surface continually crumbling away, the two sides of the chine appeared like huge heaps of black earth supported by a course of stone, which look almost as if they had been placed there for that purpose. Not a tree or a shrub, scarcely a tuft of grass, was growing there. A little rill of red irony-looking water runs along the bottom of the glen, till it comes nearly to the sea, and then falls in a narrow thread of water, about seventy feet perpendicular, into a dismal hollow of dark mouldering clay.

Such is the setting and perhaps also the cause of the lurid legend of *The Giant of Chale*, and this giant is an ogre, a hideous man-eating monster. The anonymous and presumably early nineteenth-century author manages a splendidly gruesome evocation of the giant's lair but is not so strong as a storyteller; his sylvan aside goes on for rather too long. Abraham Elder notes that the holy man in the tale was said to be Walter de Langstrell, the hermit of St Katherine, who lived during the reign of Edward II. As we should expect of a story with a Christian hero, it is the power of the cross that destroys the ogre and desolates his lair.

There remain two kinds of giant, and they both appear in the tale of *Tom Hickathrift*. The hero of that name is a shambling, amiable, overgrown human who, when only ten years old, 'was already eight feet high, and his hand like a shoulder of mutton'. He is none too quick in the uptake but his enormous strength more than compensates for his dull wits. Like the Giant of Grabbist in Somerset and one or two other friendly giants in British folklore, he exercises this strength against wrongdoers, first four thieves and then a 'monstrous giant' controlling the marshland between King's Lynn and Wisbech. This second giant, with a roar in his mouth and a club in his hand, destructive without ulterior motive, is of course common to many tales and we will meet him again in *The History of Jack and the Bean-Stalk*. It seems likely that this tale has a historical origin, probably medieval, for there are various traditions associating Tom with the Tilney villages near King's Lynn. The oldest surviving version appears in a chap-book printed between 1660 and 1690. In that version, the death of the giant is followed by the episodes with the footballers, the thieves and the tinker. In retelling the tale for Joseph Jacobs to include in his *More English Fairy Tales*, Alfred Nutt rearranged the order so as to make Tom's killing of the giant the climax of the tale.

The tale of *The Blacksmith and the Horseman*, rich in wit and generous in spirit, is a further illustration of human physical strength. Recorded in the Dingle Peninsula of County Kerry in 1944, it is included by Sean O'Sullivan in his *Folktales of Ireland*, and he notes, 'The blacksmith held a unique place in Irish social life in earlier times. His magical and curative powers derived from the metal he used for this craft. His curse was feared by all. Many stories are told in Ireland to also illustrate his physical strength.'

The History of Jack and the Bean-Stalk is one of the best loved of English folk-tales. Jack's meeting with the 'infirm looking woman' introduces an element of magic and gives Jack's adventures powerful motivation; his encounters with the giant and his wife are convincingly hazardous; there is a constant undercurrent of affection between Jack and his mother; while the bean-stalk itself perpetuates the ancient idea that it is possible to ascend from one world to another. The concept of a tree that embraced and linked all creation occurs in both European and Asian mythologies, and the natural ancestor of Jack's homely bean-stalk, so appropriate to a folk-tale, is the mighty world ash tree of Norse mythology, Yggdrasill.

While there is evidence that this tale was known early in the eighteenth century, the two earliest surviving versions both date only from 1807. The one reprinted here, identified by the Opies as 'the source for all substantial retellings of the story', was edited by William Godwin for Benjamin Tabart.

The Son of the King of Erin and
the Giant of Loch Léin

ON A TIME there lived a king and a queen in Erin, and they had an only son. They were very careful and fond of this son; whatever he asked for was granted, and what he wanted he had.

When grown to be almost a young man the son went away one day to the hills to hunt. He could find no game – saw nothing all day. Towards evening he sat down on a hillside to rest, but soon stood up again and started to go home empty-handed. Then he heard a whistle behind him, and turning, saw a giant hurrying down the hill.

The giant came to him, took his hand, and said: 'Can you play cards?'

'I can indeed,' said the king's son.

'Well, if you can,' said the giant, 'we'll have a game here on this hillside.'

So the two sat down, and the giant had out a pack of cards in a twinkling. 'What shall we play for?' asked the giant.

'For two estates,' answered the king's son.

They played: the young man won, and went home the better for two estates. He was very glad, and hurried to tell his father the luck he had.

Next day he went to the same place, and didn't wait long till the giant came again.

'Welcome, king's son,' said the giant. 'What shall we play for today?'

'I'll leave that to yourself,' answered the young man.

'Well,' said the giant, 'I have five hundred bullocks with golden horns and silver hoofs, and I'll play them against as many cattle belonging to you.'

'Agreed,' said the king's son.

They played. The giant lost again. He had the cattle brought to the place; and the king's son went home with five hundred bullocks. The king his father was outside watching, and was more delighted than the day before when he saw the drove of beautiful cattle with horns of gold and hoofs of silver.

When the bullocks were driven in, the king sent for the old blind sage (Sean dall Glic), to know what he would say of the young man's luck.

'My advice,' said the old blind sage, 'is not to let your son go the way of the giant again, for if he plays with him a third time he'll rue it.'

But nothing could keep the king's son from playing the third time. Away he went, in spite of every advice and warning, and sat on the same hillside.

He waited long, but no one came. At last he rose to go home. That moment he heard a whistle behind him, and turning, saw the giant coming.

'Well, will you play with me today?' asked the giant.

'I would,' said the king's son, 'but I have nothing to bet.'

'You have indeed.'

'I have not,' said the king's son.

'Haven't you your head?' asked the Giant of Loch Léin, for it was he that was in it.

'I have,' answered the king's son.

'So have I my head,' said the giant; 'and we'll play for each other's heads.'

This third time the giant won the game; and the king's son was to give himself up in a year and a day to the giant in his castle.

The young man went home sad and weary. The king and queen were outside watching, and when they saw him approaching, they knew great trouble was on him. When he came to where they were, he wouldn't speak, but went straight into the castle, and wouldn't eat or drink.

He was sad and lamenting for a good while, till at last he disappeared one day, the king and queen knew not whither. After that they didn't hear of him – didn't know was he dead or alive.

The young man after he left home was walking along over the kingdom for a long time. One day he saw no house, big or little, till after dark he came in front of a hill, and at the foot of the hill saw a small light. He went to the light, found a small house, and inside an old woman sitting at a warm fire, and every tooth in her head as long as a staff.

She stood up when he entered, took him by the hand, and said, 'You are welcome to my house, son of the King of Erin.' Then she brought warm water, washed his feet and legs from the knees down, gave him supper, and put him to bed.

When he rose next morning he found breakfast ready for him. The old woman said: 'You were with me last night; you'll be with my sister tonight, and what she tells you to do, do, or your head'll be in danger. Now take the gift I give you. Here is a ball of thread: do you throw it in front of you before you start, and all day the ball will be rolling ahead of you, and you'll be following behind winding the thread into another ball.'

He obeyed the old woman, threw the ball down, and followed. All the day he was going up hill and down, across valleys and open places, keeping the ball in sight and winding the thread as he went, till evening, when he saw a hill in front, and a small light at the foot of it.

He went to the light and found a house, which he entered. There was no one inside but an old woman with teeth as long as a crutch.

'Oh! then you are welcome to my house, King's son of Erin,' said she. 'You were with my sister last night; you are with me tonight; and it's glad I am to see you.'

She gave him meat and drink and a good bed to lie on.

When he rose next morning breakfast was there before him, and when he had eaten and was ready for the journey, the old woman gave him a ball of thread, saying: 'You were with my younger sister the night before last; you were with me last night; and you'll be with my elder sister tonight. You must do what she tells you, or you'll lose your head. You must throw this ball before you, and follow the clew till evening.'

He threw down the ball: it rolled on, showing the way up and down mountains and hills, across valleys and braes. All day he wound the ball; unceasingly it went till nightfall, when he came to a light, found a little house, and went in. Inside was an old woman, the eldest sister, who said: 'You are welcome, and glad am I to see you, king's son.'

She treated him as well as the other two had done. After he had eaten breakfast next morning, she said:

'I know well the journey you are on. You have lost your head to the Giant of Loch Léin, and you are going to give yourself up. This giant has a great castle. Around the castle are seven hundred iron spikes, and on every spike of them but one is the head of a king, a queen, or a king's son. The seven hundredth spike is empty, and nothing can save your head from that spike if you don't take my advice.

'Here is a ball for you: walk behind it till you come to a lake near the giant's castle. When you come to that lake at midday the ball will be unwound.

'The giant has three young daughters, and they come at noon every day of the year to bathe in the lake. You must watch them well, for each will have a lily on her breast – one a blue, another a

242

white, and the third a yellow lily. You mustn't let your eyes off the one with the yellow lily. Watch her well: when she undresses to go into the water, see where she puts her clothes; when the three are out in the lake swimming, do you slip away with the clothes of Yellow Lily.

'When the sisters come out from bathing, and find that the one with the yellow lily has lost her clothes, the other two will laugh and make game of her, and she will crouch down crying on the shore, with nothing to cover her, and say, "How can I go home now, and everybody making sport of me? Whoever took my clothes, if he'll give them back to me, I'll save him from the danger he is in, if I have the power." '

The king's son followed the ball till nearly noon, when it stopped at a lake not far from the giant's castle. Then he hid behind a rock at the water's edge, and waited.

At midday the three sisters came to the lake, and, leaving their clothes on the strand, went into the water. When all three were in the lake swimming and playing with great pleasure and sport, the king's son slipped out and took the clothes of the sister with the yellow lily.

After they had bathed in the lake to their hearts' content, the three sisters came out. When the two with the blue and the white lilies saw their sister on the shore and her clothes gone, they began to laugh and make sport of her. Then, cowering and crouching down, she began to cry and lament, saying: 'How can I go home now, with my own sisters laughing at me? If I stir from this, everybody will see me and make sport of me.'

The sisters went home and left her there. When they were gone, and she was alone in the water crying and sobbing, all at once she came to herself and called out: 'Whoever took my clothes, I'll forgive him if he brings them to me now, and I'll save him from the danger he is in if I can.'

When he heard this, the king's son put the clothes out to her, and stayed behind himself till she told him to come forth.

Then she said: 'I know well where you are going. My father, the Giant of Loch Léin, has a soft bed waiting for you, – a deep tank of water for your death. But don't be uneasy; go into the water, and wait till I come to save you. Be at that castle above before my father. When he comes home tonight and asks for you, take no meat from him, but go to rest in the tank when he tells you.'

The giant's daughter left the king's son, who went his way to the castle alone at a fair and easy gait, for he had time enough on his hands and to spare.

When the Giant of Loch Léin came home that night, the first question he asked was, 'Is the son of the King of Erin here?'

'I am,' said the king's son.

'Come,' said the giant, 'and get your evening's meat.'

'I'll take no meat now, for I don't need it,' said the king's son.

'Well, come with me then, and I'll show you your bed.' He went, and the giant put the king's son into the deep tank of water to drown, and being tired himself from hunting all day over the mountains and hills of Erin, he went to sleep.

That minute his youngest daughter came, took the king's son out of the tank, placed plenty to eat and to drink before him, and gave him a good bed to sleep on that night.

The giant's daughter watched till she heard her father stirring before daybreak; then she roused the king's son, and put him in the tank again.

Soon the giant came to the tank and called out: 'Are you here, son of the King of Erin?'

'I am,' said the king's son.

'Well, come out now. There is a great work for you today. I have a stable outside, in which I keep five hundred horses, and that stable has not been cleaned these seven hundred years. My great-grandmother when a girl lost a slumber pin (*bar an suan*) somewhere in that stable, and never could find it. You must have that pin for me when I come home tonight; if you don't, your head will be on the seven hundredth spike tomorrow.'

Then two shovels were brought for him to choose from to clean out the stable, an old and a new one. He chose the new shovel, and went to work.

For every shovelful he threw out, two came in; and soon the

door of the stable was closed on him. When the stabledoor was closed, the giant's daughter called from outside: 'How are you thriving now, king's son?'

'I'm not thriving at all,' said the king's son; 'for as much as I throw out, twice as much comes in, and the door is closed against me.'

'You must make a way for me to come in, and I'll help you,' said she.

'How can I do that?' asked the king's son.

However, she did it. The giant's daughter made her way into the stable, and she wasn't long inside till the stable was cleared, and she saw the *bar an suan*.

'There is the pin over there in the corner,' said she to the king's son, who put it in his bosom to give to the giant.

Now he was happy, and the giant's daughter had good meat and drink put before him.

When the giant himself came home, he asked: 'How did you do your work today?'

'I did it well; I thought nothing of it.'

'Did you find the *bar an suan*?'

'I did indeed; here 'tis for you.'

'Oh! then', said the giant, 'it is either the devil or my daughter that helped you to do that work, for I know you never did it alone.'

'It's neither the Devil nor your daughter, but my own strength that did the work,' said the son of the King of Erin.

'You have done the work; now you must have your meat.'

'I want no meat today; I am well satisfied as I am,' said the king's son.

'Well,' said the giant, 'since you'll have no meat, you must go to sleep in the tank.'

He went into the tank. The giant himself was soon snoring, for he was tired from hunting over Erin all day.

The moment her father was away, Yellow Lily came, took the king's son out of the tank, gave him a good supper and bed, and watched till the giant was stirring before daybreak. Then she roused the king's son and put him in the tank.

'Are you alive in the tank?' asked the giant at daybreak.

'I am,' said the king's son.

'Well, you have a great work before you today. That stable you cleaned yesterday hasn't been thatched these seven hundred years, and if you don't have it thatched for me when I come home tonight, with birds' feathers, and not two feathers of one colour or kind, I'll have your head on the seven hundredth spike tomorrow.

'Here are two whistles, – an old, and a new one; take your choice of them to call the birds.'

The king's son took the new whistle, and set out over the hills and valleys whistling as he went. But no matter how he whistled, not a bird came near him. At last, tired and worn out with travelling and whistling, he sat down on a hillock and began to cry.

That moment Yellow Lily was at his side with a cloth, which she spread out, and there was a grand meal before him. He hadn't finished eating and drinking, before the stable was thatched with birds' feathers, and no two of them of one colour or kind.

When he came home that evening the giant called out: 'Have you the stable thatched for me tonight?'

'I have indeed,' said the king's son; 'and small trouble I had with it.'

'If that's true,' said the giant, 'either the Devil or my daughter helped you.'

'It was my own strength, and not the Devil or your daughter that helped me,' said the king's son.

He spent that night as he had the two nights before.

Next morning, when the giant found him alive in the tank, he said: 'There is great work before you today, which you must do, or your head'll be on the spike tomorrow. Below here, under my castle, is a tree nine hundred feet high, and there isn't a limb on that tree, from the roots up, except one small limb at the very top, where there is a crow's nest. The tree is covered with glass

246

from the ground to the crow's nest. In the nest is one egg. You must have that egg before me here for my supper tonight, or I'll have your head on the seven hundredth spike tomorrow.'

The giant went hunting, and the king's son went down to the tree, tried to shake it, but could not make it stir. Then he tried to climb; but no use, it was all slippery glass. Then he thought, 'Sure I'm done for now; I must lose my head this time.'

He stood there in sadness, when Yellow Lily came, and said: 'How are you thriving in your work?'

'I can do nothing,' said the king's son.

'Well, all that we have done up to this time is nothing to climbing this tree. But first of all let us sit down together and eat, and then we'll talk,' said Yellow Lily.

They sat down, she spread the cloth again, and they had a splendid feast. When the feast was over she took out a knife from her pocket and said:

'Now you must kill me, strip the flesh from my bones, take all the bones apart, and use them as steps for climbing the tree. When you are climbing the tree, they will stick to the glass as if they had grown out of it; but when you are coming down, and have put your foot on each one, they will drop into your hand when you touch them. Be sure and stand on each bone, leave none untouched; if you do, it will stay behind. Put all my flesh into this clean cloth by the side of the spring at the roots of the tree. When you come to the earth, arrange my bones together, put the flesh over them, sprinkle it with water from the spring, and I shall be alive and well before you. But don't forget a bone of me on the tree.'

'How could I kill you', asked the king's son, 'after what you have done for me?'

'If you won't obey, you and I are done for,' said Yellow Lily. 'You must climb the tree, or we are lost; and to climb the tree you must do as I say.'

The king's son obeyed. He killed Yellow Lily, cut the flesh from her body, and unjointed the bones, as she had told him.

As he went up, the king's son put the bones of Yellow

Lily's body against the side of the tree, using them as steps, till he came under the nest and stood on the last bone.

Then he took the crow's egg; and coming down, put his foot on every bone, then took it with him, till he came to the last bone, which was so near the ground that he failed to touch it with his foot.

He now placed all the bones of Yellow Lily in order again at the side of the spring, put the flesh on them, sprinkled it with water from the spring. She rose up before him, and said: 'Didn't I tell you not to leave a bone of my body without stepping on it? Now I am lame for life! You left my little toe on the tree without touching it, and I have but nine toes.'

When the giant came home that night, the first words he had were, 'Have you the crow's egg for my supper?'

'I have,' said the king's son.

'If you have, then either the Devil or my daughter is helping you.'

'It is my own strength that's helping me,' said the king's son.

'Well, whoever it is, I must forgive you now, and your head is your own.'

So the king's son was free to go his own road, and away he went, and never stopped till he came home to his own father and mother, who had a great welcome before him; and why not? for they thought he was dead.

When the son was at home a time, the king called up the old blind sage, and asked, 'What must I do with my son now?'

'If you follow my advice,' said the old blind sage, 'you'll find a wife for him; and then he'll not go roaming away again, and leave you as he did before.'

The king was pleased with the advice, and he sent a message to the King of Lochlin* to ask his daughter in marriage.

The King of Lochlin came with the daughter and a ship full of attendants, and there was to be a grand wedding at the castle of the King of Erin.

*Denmark.

Now, the king's son asked his father to invite the Giant of Loch Léin and Yellow Lily to the wedding. The king sent messages for them to come.

The day before the marriage there was a great feast at the castle. As the feast went on, and all were merry, the Giant of Loch Léin said: 'I never was at a place like this but one man sang a song, a second told a story, and the third played a trick.'

Then the King of Erin sang a song, the King of Lochlin told a story, and when the turn came to the giant, he asked Yellow Lily to take his place.

She threw two grains of wheat in the air, and there came down on the table two pigeons. The cock pigeon pecked at the hen and pushed her off the table. Then the hen called out to him in a human voice, 'You wouldn't do that to me the day I cleaned the stable for you.'

Next time Yellow Lily put two grains of wheat on the table. The cock ate the wheat, pecked the hen, and pushed her off the table to the floor. The hen said: 'You would not do that to me the day I thatched the stable for you with birds' feathers, and not two of one colour or kind.'

The third time Yellow Lily put two more grains of wheat on the table. The cock ate both, and pushed the hen off to the floor. Then the hen called out: 'You wouldn't do that to me the day you killed me and took my bones to make steps up the glass tree nine hundred feet high to get the crow's egg for the supper of the Giant of Loch Léin, and forgot my little toe when you were coming down, and left me lame for life.'

'Well,' said the king's son to the guests at the feast, 'when I was a little younger than I am now, I used to be everywhere in the world sporting and gaming; and once when I was away, I lost the key of a casket that I had. I had a new key made, and after it was brought to me I found the old one. Now, I'll leave it to any one here to tell what am I to do – which of the keys should I keep?'

'My advice to you', said the King of Lochlin, 'is to keep the old key, for it fits the lock better, and you're more used to it.'

Then the king's son stood up and said: 'I thank you, King of Lochlin, for a wise advice and an honest word. This is my bride, the daughter of the Giant of Loch Léin. I'll have her, and no other woman. Your daughter is my father's guest, and no worse, but better, for having come to a wedding in Erin.'

The king's son married Yellow Lily, daughter of the Giant of Loch Léin, the wedding lasted long, and all were happy.

A Legend of Black Gang Chyne

The dwellers in Wight they once did wail,
When they lived in dread of the giant of Chale
The giant of Chale was mighty and big,
And he loved man's flesh better than pig.
He chose those that were tall and heavy,
And slew'd the fat ones in their own gravy.
The children he tied with bonds of wire.
And broiled them alive on a charcoal fire.
He dyed his hands with man's blood red;
He laughed and shook his sides, and said,
'I care not for saint in his lonely cell –
I care not for book, and I care not for bell –
I care not for heaven, I care not for hell –
I live upon man's flesh, and fat me well.'

The saint was praying on his knee
For those that are dead, and those that be;
And as he raised his voice in prayer,
He heard the curses fly through the air.

251

The holy man was struck with dread,
And every hair stood up on his head;
For he knew the time was a fated hour,
When the spirits of earth and sea have power,
And that which is holy quakes and quails,
For the time of the spirit of sin prevails.
The fiendish laughter thrilled through his bones;
And he answered the sound of mirth with groans.

He hailed the voice as it came on the wind,
'What is thy title, what is thy kind?
Who is it scoffs at saint and cell?
Who cares not for book, and cares not for bell?
Who cares not for heaven, and cares not for hell;
But lives upon man's flesh, and fats him well?'

The burly giant rose from his lair,
When he heard the questions ring through the air.
Then he poured a goblet filled with blood,
And he dipped his hands in the gory flood;
He made a sign with his bloody hand,
And drew the figure in the sand.
'I'll make his spirit quake and quail
That questioneth the ogre of Chale.
I dare him to meet me at midnight dread,
When the horned moon is over our head;
For then the lower spirits, and upper,
And those of the earth I've ask'd to supper —
Then the imps that ride on the desolate wind
Shall chant him in thunder my title and kind.'

There was heard, when the blood of the sign had dried,
A whizzing sound on every side;
It sang in the Culver's goblin cave —
It sang at the Needles and over the wave —
It sang on Hecla's frozen strand —

Giants and Strong Men

It sang on the desert's burning sand —
It sang the mountains and clouds aboon —
And the whizzing sound went up to the moon.
The sound went down to the ocean's deep,
And the kelpies were roused from their evening sleep.
And though the night was clear and still,
The wind seemed to whistle round Katherine's Hill;
But the sound came not in the chapel fair,
Because the sign of the cross was there.
The bloody sign was a sign of might
To every being that shuns the light;
Whether made by sprite or child of clay,
The bloody signal they must obey.

The holy man was struck with fear
When the words of the giant rang in his ear;
For the giant was mighty in wizard power,
And Hallowe'en was a dreadful hour.
But the fearfullest time was the midnight dread,
When the horned moon is over one's head.
The saint had been dared to come that night,
Or acknowledge his fear of the giant sprite.
He took him a staff of the mountain ash,
His pilgrim scrip and calabash;
Nor spirit did he hold in scorn,
Distilled from the barleycorn,
To keep himself from catching cold,
For he had grown infirm and old.
At midnight he left his lonely cell
To seek the giant's flowery dell.
In a lovely vale, all down by the sea,
Was the cave of the giant's cruelty.
The valley side was blooming fair,
For every flower blossomed there;
The violet and primrose gay,
And cowslip tall, adorned the way;

253

Nodded to him the blue harebell,
And smiled the yellow daffodil;
The heath its little eye did twinkle,
And stared the humble periwinkle;
Snapdragon opened its yellow mouth,
Sunflower turned his face from the south;
The blown rose smiled, in matron pride,
At the little rosebuds round by her side,
Bespangled with dewdrops all around,
Like a diamond necklace down to the ground;
The foxglove showed its sunburnt face,
And bent and bowed with vulgar grace,
Fluttered a leaf to the moonbeam wan,
Just as a lady flutters her fan;
And every daisy on the hill,
With its yellow face and clean white frill,
Seemed each to giggle and shake its head
As though, if it could, it would have said,
'Twas a comical time and a comical place
To look the giant of Chale in the face.
But though the bank was blooming fair,
The robin redbreast dwelt not there;
For the robin was a friend of man,
And would not eat from an ogre's hand.
Though all things seemed to laugh and jeer,
They could not put the saint in fear;
For he had dared both death and chains,
And a noble spirit ran in his veins.

Sudden there crashed a clap of thunder,
Which filled the saint with awe and wonder;
And just before his footpath way
A cavern yawned in the mountain clay.
The cavern it was not paved with stones,
But strewed around with dead men's bones.

Giants and Strong Men

On a throne of skulls the giant sat,
And his lamps were fed with dead men's fat.
The sea was studded with goblin sails,
And snakes and adders danced on their tails.
The bats fly high, the bats fly low,
The owlets hoot, and the ravens crow;
The dragons they rattle their scaly wings;
The scorpions show their poison stings:
For the spirits appeared in every shape –
One took the form of a long-legged ape;
And one was like a large black cat;
And one like a boar, and one like a rat;
One grinned in the form of a dusky bear,
Another was like a spotted hare;
Another was like a bloated toad,
That spat his venom on the road;
They laughed, and they grinned, and they jeered to see
The saint come to join their revelry.
The owlet he hooted his laugh in the air,
And in laughter growled the dusky bear.
'Twas a horrible thing to hear and see
These beasts how they mimicked humanity.

On a table, in lieu of a loaf of bread,
Was a bodiless but living head;
Its sightless eyeballs it roll'd about,
And its bloodless tongue it lolled out.
The giant has called for his favourite dish
Of reptiles alive, and loathsome fish.
The soup it was brought in earthenware pails –
The mermen who carried them hopped on their tails;
The leeches crept in and the leeches crept out,
The blind worms and lizards wriggled about.

As the demons raised their cups on high,
There arose a shout, a yell, a cry –

255

'Here's a curse on the living, a curse on the dead!
But here's a health to the head – the head!
Old man, there's a fire of charcoal and peat:
Do you wish to be roasted? or will you eat?
Here's a boiling lake – you stand on the brink –
Do you wish to be stewed down? or will you drink?'
The saint was filled with such dismay,
He could not speak, and he could not pray.
The carrion vulture was over his head,
And under his feet were the bones of the dead:
And human skeletons round were lain,
And one of them turned, as it were, in pain.
But when the sign of the cross he made,
His courage came; he spoke, and said –
'I bless the living, I bless the dead;
A curse upon thee, and I curse the head.
I curse the hill, and I curse the strand –
I curse the ground whereon I stand.
Nor flowers nor fruit this earth shall bear;
But all shall be dark, and waste, and bare!
Nor shall the ground give footing dry
To beasts that walk, or birds that fly;
But a poisonous stream shall run to the sea,
Bitter to taste, and bloody to see!
And the earth it shall crumble and crumble away,
And crumble on till the judgment day.'

He spoke, and a mist came over his eye –
He saw not the land, and he saw not the sky.
But when the mist had rolled away,
The earth looked black, and the rocks looked gray;
At his feet there flowed a blood-stained rill,
And bleak and lonely stood the hill.

Tom Hickathrift

BEFORE the days of William the Conqueror there dwelt a man in the marsh of the Isle of Ely whose name was Thomas Hickathrift, a poor day labourer, but so stout that he could do two days' work in one. His one son he called by his own name, Thomas Hickathrift, and he put him to good learning, but the lad was none of the wisest, and indeed seemed to be somewhat soft, so he got no good at all from his teaching.

Tom's father died, and his mother being tender of him, kept him as well as she could. The slothful fellow would do nothing but sit in the chimney-corner, and eat as much at a time as would serve four or five ordinary men. And so much did he grow that when but ten years old he was already eight feet high, and his hand like a shoulder of mutton.

One day his mother went to a rich farmer's house to beg a bottle of straw for herself and Tom. 'Take what you will,' said the farmer, an honest charitable man. So when she got home she told Tom to fetch the straw, but he wouldn't and, beg as she might, he wouldn't till she borrowed him a cart rope. So off he went, and when he came to the farmer's, master and men were all a-thrashing in the barn.

'I'm come for the straw,' said Tom.

'Take as much as thou canst carry,' said the farmer.

So Tom laid down his rope and began to make his bottle.

'Your rope is too short,' said the farmer by way of a joke; but the joke was on Tom's side, for when he had made up his load there was some twenty hundredweight of straw, and though they called him a fool for thinking he could carry the tithe of it, he flung it over his shoulder as if it had been a hundredweight, to the great admiration of master and men.

Tom's strength being thus made known there was no longer any basking by the fire for him; every one would be hiring him to work, and telling him 'twas a shame to live such a lazy life. So Tom seeing them wait on him as they did, went to work first with one, then with another. And one day a woodman desired his help to bring home a tree. Off went Tom and four men besides, and when they came to the tree they began to draw it into the cart with pulleys.

At last Tom, seeing them unable to lift it, 'Stand away, you fools,' said he, and taking the tree, set it on one end and laid it in the cart. 'Now,' said he, 'see what a man can do.'

'Marry, 'tis true,' said they, and the woodman asked what reward he'd take.

'Oh, a stick for my mother's fire,' said Tom; and espying a tree bigger than was in the cart, he laid it on his shoulders and went home with it as fast as the cart and six horses could draw it.

Tom now saw that he had more strength than twenty men, and began to be very merry, taking delight in company, in going to fairs and meetings, in seeing sports and pastimes. And at cudgels, wrestling, or throwing the hammer, not a man could stand against him, so that at last none durst go into the ring to wrestle with him, and his fame was spread more and more in the country.

Far and near he would go to any meetings, as football play or the like. And one day in a part of the country where he was a stranger, and none knew him, he stopped to watch the company at football play; rare sport it was; but Tom spoiled it all, for meeting the ball he took it such a kick that away it flew none could tell whither. They were angry with Tom, as you may fancy, but got nothing by that, as Tom took hold of a big spar, and laid about with a will, so that though the whole countryside was up in arms against him, he cleared his way wherever he came.

It was late in the evening ere he could turn homeward, and on the road there met him four lusty rogues that had been robbing passengers all day. They thought they had a good prize in Tom, who was all alone, and made cocksure of his money.

'Stand and deliver!' said they.

'What should I deliver?' said Tom.

'Your money, sirrah,' said they.

'You shall give me better words for it first,' said Tom.

'Come, come, no more prating; money we want, and money we'll have before you stir.'

'Is it so?' said Tom, 'nay, then come and take it.'

The long and the short of it was that Tom killed two of the rogues and grievously wounded the other two, and took all their money, which was as much as two hundred pounds. And when he came home he made his old mother laugh with the story of how he served the football players and the four thieves.

But you shall see that Tom sometimes met his match. In wandering one day in the forest he met a lusty tinker that had a good staff on his shoulder, and a great dog to carry his bag and tools.

'Whence come you and whither are you going?' said Tom: 'this is no highway.'

'What's that to you?' said the tinker; 'fools must needs be meddling.'

'I'll make you know,' said Tom, 'before you and I part, what it is to me.'

'Well,' said the tinker, 'I'm ready for a bout with any man, and I hear there is one Tom Hickathrift in the country of whom great things are told. I'd fain see him to have a turn with him.'

259

'Ay,' said Tom, 'methinks he might be master with you. Anyhow, I am the man; what have you to say to me?'

'Why, verily, I'm glad we are so happily met.'

'Sure, you do but jest,' said Tom.

'Marry, I'm in earnest,' said the tinker. 'A match?' ''Tis done.' 'Let me first get a twig,' said Tom. 'Ay,' said the tinker, 'hang him that would fight a man unarmed.'

So Tom took a gate-rail for his staff, and at it they fell, the tinker at Tom, and Tom at the tinker, like two giants they laid on at each other. The tinker had a leathern coat on, and at every blow Tom gave the tinker his coat roared again, yet the tinker did not give way one inch. At last Tom gave him a blow on the side of his head which felled him.

'Now, tinker, where are you?' said Tom.

But the tinker, being a nimble fellow, leapt up again, gave Tom a blow that made him reel again, and followed his blow with one on the other side that made Tom's neck crack again. So Tom flung down his weapon and yielded the tinker the better on it, took him home to his house, where they nursed their bruises, and from that day forth there was no stauncher pair of friends than they two.

Tom's fame was thus spread abroad till at length a brewer at Lynn, wanting a good lusty man to carry his beer to Wisbeach went to hire Tom, and promised him a new suit of clothes from top to toe, and that he should eat and drink of the best, so Tom yielded to be his man and his master told him what way he should go, for you must understand there was a monstrous giant who kept part of the marsh-land, so that none durst go that way.

So Tom went every day to Wisbeach, a good twenty miles by the road. 'Twas a wearisome journey, thought Tom, and he soon found that the way kept by the giant was nearer by half. Now Tom had got more strength than ever, being well kept as he was and drinking so much strong ale as he did. One day, then, as he was going to Wisbeach, without saying anything to his master or any of his fellow servants, he resolved to take the nearest road or to lose his life; as they say, to win horse or lose saddle. Thus resolved, he took the near road, flinging open the gates for his cart and horses to go through. At last the giant spied him, and came up speedily, intending to take his beer for a prize.

He met Tom like a lion as though he would have swallowed him. 'Who gave you authority to come this way?' roared he. 'I'll make you an example for all rogues under the sun. See how many heads hang on yonder tree. Yours shall hang higher than all the rest for a warning.'

But Tom made him answer. 'A fig in your teeth; you shall not find me like one of them, traitorly rogue that you are.'

The giant took these words in high disdain, and ran into his cave to fetch his great club, intending to dash out Tom's brains at the first blow.

Tom knew not what to do for a weapon; his whip would be but little good against a monstrous beast twelve foot in length and six foot about the waist. But whilst the giant went for his club, bethinking him of a very good weapon, he made no more ado, but took his cart, turned it upside down, and took axle-tree and wheel for shield and buckler. And very good weapons they were found!

Out came the giant and began to stare at Tom. 'You are like to do great service with those weapons,' roared he. 'I have here a twig that will beat you and your wheel to the ground.'

Now this twig was as thick as some mileposts are, but Tom was not daunted for all that, though the giant made at him with such force that the wheel cracked again. But Tom gave as good as he got, taking the giant such a weighty blow on the side of the head that he reeled again. 'What,' said Tom, 'are you drunk with my strong beer already?'

So at it they went, Tom laying such huge blows at the giant, down whose face sweat and blood ran together, so that, being fat and foggy and tired with the long fighting, he asked Tom would he let him drink a little?

'Nay, nay,' said Tom, 'my mother did not teach me such wit; who'd be a fool then?' And seeing the giant beginning to weary and fail in his blows, Tom thought best to make hay whilst the sun shone, and, laying on as fast as though he had been mad, he brought the giant to the ground. In vain were the giant's roars and prayers and promises to yield himself and be Tom's servant. Tom laid at him till he was dead, and then, cutting off his head, he went into the cave, and found a great store of silver and gold, which made his heart leap. So he loaded his cart, and after delivering his beer at Wisbeach, he came home and told his master what had befallen him. And on the morrow he and his master and more of the towns-folk of Lynn set out for the giant's cave. Tom showed them the head, and what silver and gold there was in the cave, and not a man but leapt for joy, for the giant was a great enemy to all the country.

The news was spread all up and down the countryside how Tom Hickathrift had killed the giant. And well was he that could run to see the cave; all the folk made bonfires for joy, and if Tom was respected before, he was much more so now. With common consent he took possession of the cave and everyone said, had it been twice as much, he would have deserved it. So Tom pulled down the cave, and built himself a brave house. The ground that the giant kept by force for himself, Tom gave part to the poor for their common land, and part he turned into good wheat-land to keep himself and his old mother, Jane Hickathrift. And now he was become the chiefest man in the countryside; 'twas no longer plain Tom, but Mr Hickathrift, and he was held in due respect I promise you. He kept men and maids and lived most bravely; made him a park to keep deer, and time passed with him happily in his great house till the end of his days.

The Blacksmith and the Horseman

THERE was a man one time, and he was very strong. He was full of money, and one day he put about twenty pounds of it into a purse.

'I'll set out on my travels now,' said he, 'and I'll keep on going until I meet a man who is stronger than myself. If I meet him, he'll get this purse.'

So on he travelled, asking everyone if they knew of any strong man, until at last he was directed to a certain smith. When he reached the forge, he pulled up his horse outside the window without dismounting.

'Have you anything in there to "redden" my pipe for me?' he shouted to the smith.

The smith picked up a live coal with the tongs, placed it on top of the great anvil, took up the anvil by its snout with one hand and reached it out through the window to the horseman. The horseman took hold of the other end of the anvil, let the live coal slip into his pipe, and handed the anvil back to the smith. The smith put the anvil back on the block.

'My horse needs a shoe. Have you any made?' asked the horseman.

'I have,' replied the smith, picking out a horseshoe. 'This may do you,' said he.

'Give it here to me,' said the horseman. When he got it, he pulled it apart with his two hands. 'That shoe was no good,' said he.

The smith gave him another shoe, but he broke it in two in the same way.

'That one was no good either,' said he. 'Give me another.'

'What's the use in giving them to you?' asked the smith.

'I'll try one more,' said the horseman.

The smith passed another shoe to him.

'This will do,' said the horseman.

The smith put the shoe on the horse, and when he had the last nail driven, 'How much do I owe you?' asked the horseman.

'A half crown,' said the smith. When the horseman handed him a half crown, the smith took it between his fingers and broke it in two.

'That was no good,' said the smith. The horseman gave him a second half crown, and the smith broke it in two again.

'That was no good either. Give me another,' said he.

'What's the use in giving them to you?' asked the horseman.

'I'll try one more,' said the smith. 'This will do,' said he when he got the third half crown.

The horseman took the purse out of his pocket. 'Take this,' said he. 'You deserve it, for you are a stronger man than I am. I had a good hold on the shoes to break them, but you had hardly any hold on the half crowns that you broke.'

The History of
Jack and the Bean-Stalk

IN THE DAYS of King Alfred, there lived a poor woman, whose cottage was situated in a remote country village, a great many miles from London.

She had been a widow some years, and had an only child, named Jack, whom she indulged to a fault; the consequence of her blind partiality was, that Jack did not pay the least attention to any thing she said, but was indolent, careless, and extravagant. His follies were not owing to a bad disposition, but that his mother had never checked him. By degrees, she disposed of all she possessed – scarcely any thing remained but a cow.

The poor woman one day met Jack with tears in her eyes; her distress was great, and, for the first time in her life, she could not help reproaching him, saying, 'Indeed, dear son, you have at last brought me to beggary and ruin; I have not money enough to purchase food for another day – nothing remains for me but to sell my cow. I am very sorry to part with her; it grieves me sadly, but we must not starve.'

For five minutes Jack felt a degree of remorse, but it was soon over, and he importuned his mother to let him sell the cow at the next village. As he was going along, he met a butcher, who enquired why he was driving the cow from home? Jack replied, it was his intention to sell it. The butcher held some curious beans in his hat; they were of various colours, and attracted Jack's notice: this did not pass unnoticed by the butcher, who, knowing Jack's easy temper, thought now was the time to take advantage of it, and determined not to let slip so good an opportunity, asked what was the price of the cow, offering at the same time all the beans in his hat for her. The silly boy could not express his pleasure at what he supposed so great an offer: the bargain was struck instantly, and the cow exchanged for a few paltry beans. Jack made the best of his way home, calling aloud to his mother before he reached the house, thinking to surprise her.

When she saw the beans, and heard Jack's account, her patience quite forsook her, she kicked the beans away in a passion – they flew in all directions, some were scattered into the garden. The poor woman reflected on her great loss, and was quite in despair. Not having any thing to eat, they both went supperless to bed.

Jack awoke very early in the morning, and, seeing something uncommon from the window of his bedchamber, ran downstairs into the garden, where he soon discovered that some of the beans had taken root, and sprung up surprisingly: the stalks were of an immense thickness, and had so entwined, that they formed a ladder nearly like a chain in appearance.

Looking upwards, he could not discern the top, it appeared to be lost in the clouds: he tried it, found it firm, and not to be shaken. He quickly formed the resolution of endeavouring to climb up to the top, in order to seek his fortune, and ran to communicate his intention to his mother, not doubting but she would be equally pleased with himself. She declared he should not go; said he would break her heart, entreated, and threatened, but all in vain. Jack set out, and, after climbing for some hours, reached the top of the bean-stalk, fatigued and quite exhausted. Looking around, he found himself in a strange country: it appeared to be a desert, quite barren: not a tree, shrub, house, or living creature to be seen; here and there were scattered fragments of unhewn stone, and, at unequal distances, small heaps of earth were loosely thrown together. Jack seated himself pensively upon a block of stone, thought of his mother, and reflected with sorrow on his disobedience in climbing the bean-stalk against her inclination: he concluded that he must now die with hunger.

However he walked on, hoping to see a house where he might beg something to eat and drink: presently an infirm looking woman appeared at a distance; as she approached, he saw that she was old, her skin much wrinkled, and her tattered garments proved poverty. She accosted Jack, enquiring how he came there; he related the circumstance of the bean-stalk. She then asked if he recollected his father? he replied he did not; and added, that there must be some mystery relating to him, for he had frequently asked his mother who his father was, but that she always burst into tears, and appeared violently agitated, nor did she recover herself for some days after; one thing, however, he could not avoid observing upon those occasions, which was, that she always carefully avoided answering him, and even seemed afraid of speaking, as if there were some secret connected with his father's history which she must not disclose.

The old woman replied, 'I will reveal the whole story, your mother must not; but, before I begin, I require a solemn promise on your part to do what I command: I am a fairy, and if you do not perform exactly what I desire, your mother and yourself shall both be destroyed.'

Jack was frightened at the old woman's menaces, and promised to fulfil her injunctions exactly, and the fairy thus addressed him:

'Your father was a rich man, his disposition remarkably benevolent; he was very good to the poor, and constantly relieving them: he made it a rule never to let a day pass without doing a kindness to some person. On one particular day in the week he kept open house, and invited only those who were reduced and had lived well. He always presided himself, and did all in his power to render his guests comfortable; the rich and the great were not invited. The servants were all happy, and greatly attached to their master and mistress. Your father, though only a private gentleman, was as rich as a prince, and he deserved all he possessed, for he only lived to do good. Such a man was soon known and talked of. A giant lived a great many miles off; this man was altogether as wicked as your father was good: he was in his heart envious, covetous, and cruel; but he had the art of concealing those vices. He was poor, and wished to enrich himself at any rate.

'Hearing your father spoken of, he was determined to become acquainted with him, hoping to ingratiate himself into your father's favour. He removed quickly into your neighbourhood, caused it to be reported that he was a gentleman who had just lost all he possessed by an earthquake, and found it difficult to escape with his life; his wife was with him. Your father gave credit to his story and pitied him; he gave him handsome apartments in his own house, and caused himself and his wife to be treated like visitors of consequence, little imagining that the giant was meditating a horrid return for all his favours. Things went on in this way some time, the giant becoming daily more impatient to put his plan into execution; at last a favourable opportunity presented itself. Your father's house was at some distance from the sea-shore, but with a good glass the coast could be seen distinctly. The giant was one day using the telescope; the wind was very high; he saw a fleet of ships in distress off the rocks; he hastened to your father, mentioned the circumstance, and eagerly requested he would send all the servants he could spare to relieve the sufferers. Everyone was instantly dispatched, except the porter and your nurse; the giant then joined your father in the study, and appeared to be delighted – he really was so. Your father recommended a favourite book, and was handing it down: the giant took the opportunity and stabbed him, he instantly fell dead; the giant left the body, found the porter and nurse, and presently dispatched them. You were then only three months old; your mother had you in her arms in a remote part of the house, and was ignorant of what was going on; she went into the study, but how was she shocked, on discovering your father a corpse, and weltering in his blood! She was stupified with horror and grief, and was motionless. The giant, who was seeking her, found her in that state, and hastened to serve her and you as he had done her husband, but she fell at his feet, and in a pathetic manner besought him to spare your life and hers.

'The cruel giant, for a short time, was struck with remorse, and spared your life and hers; but first he made her swear solemnly, that she never would inform you who your father was, or answer any questions concerning him: assuring her, that if she did he would certainly discover her, and put both of you to death in the most cruel manner. Your mother took you in her arms, and fled as quick as possible; she was scarcely gone, when the giant repented that he had suffered her to escape; he would have pursued her instantly, but he had his own safety to provide for, as it was necessary he should be gone before the servants returned. Having gained your father's confidence, he knew where to find all his treasure: he soon loaded himself and his wife, set the house on fire in several places, and when the servants returned the house was burnt down to the ground.

'Your poor mother, forlorn, abandoned, and forsaken, wandered with you a great many miles from this scene of desolation; fear added to her haste: she settled in the cottage where you were brought up, and it was entirely owing to her fear of the giant that she has never mentioned your father to you.

'I became your father's guardian at his birth; but fairies have laws to which they are subject as well as mortals. A short time before the giant went to your father's, I transgressed; my punishment was a total suspension of power for a limited time: an unfortunate circumstance, as it prevented my succouring your father. The day on which you met the butcher, as you went to sell your mother's cow, my power was restored. It was I who secretly prompted you to take the beans in exchange for your cow. By my power, the bean-stalk grew to so great a height and formed a ladder. I need not add, that I inspired you with a strong desire to ascend the ladder.

'The giant lives in this country; you are the person appointed to punish him for all his wickedness. You will have dangers and difficulties to encounter, but you must persevere in avenging the death of your father, or you will not prosper in any of your undertakings, but always be miserable. As to the giant's possessions, you may seize upon all with impunity; for everything he has is yours, though now you are unjustly deprived of it. One thing I strictly charge you – never let your mother be made acquainted with your journeys beforehand; the thought of it would kill her, for she has not yet thoroughly overcome the fright she encountered at your father's death. Go along the direct road, you will soon see the house where your cruel enemy lives. Remember the severe punishment that awaits you if you disobey my commands.' So saying the fairy disappeared, leaving Jack to pursue his journey.

He walked until after sunset, and soon, to his great joy, espied a large mansion. A plain looking woman was standing at the door, he accosted her, begging she would give him a morsel of bread and a night's lodging. She expressed great surprise on seeing him, said it was quite uncommon to see a human being near their house, for it was well known that her husband was a large and powerful giant, and that he would never eat any thing but human flesh, if he could possibly get it; that he did not think any thing of walking fifty miles to procure it, usually being out all day for that purpose.

This account terrified Jack, but still he hoped to elude the giant, and therefore again he entreated the woman to take him in for one night only, and hide him in the oven. The good woman at last suffered herself to be persuaded, for she was of a compassionate disposition. She gave him plenty to eat and drink, and took him into the house. First they entered a large hall, magnificently furnished; they then passed through several spacious rooms, all in the same style of grandeur, though they appeared to be forsaken and desolate.

A long gallery was next; it was very dark, just light enough to shew that instead of a wall on one side, there was a grating of iron which parted off a dismal dungeon, from whence issued the groans of those poor victims whom the giant reserved in confinement for his own voracious appetite. Poor Jack was half dead with fear, and would have given the world to be with his mother again, but that he feared could never be; for he gave himself up for lost, and now mistrusted the good woman.

At the farther end of the gallery there was a winding staircase, which led them into a spacious kitchen; a very good fire was burning in the grate, and Jack, not seeing any thing to make him uncomfortable, soon forgot his fears, and was just beginning to enjoy himself, when he was aroused by a loud knocking at the street door; the giant's wife ran to secure him in the oven, and then made what haste she could to let her husband in, and Jack heard him accost her in a voice like thunder, saying, 'Wife, I smell fresh meat.'

'Oh! my dear,' she replied, 'it is nothing but the people in the dungeon.'

The giant appeared to believe her, and walked down stairs into the very kitchen, where poor Jack was, who shook, trembled, and was more terrified than he had yet been.

At last, the monster seated himself quietly by the fire-side, whilst his wife prepared supper. By degrees Jack recovered himself sufficiently to look at the giant through a crevice; he was astonished to see how much he devoured, and thought he never would have done eating and drinking. When supper was ended, the giant desired his wife to bring him his hen. A very beautiful hen was brought, and placed upon the table before him. Jack's curiosity was very great to see what would happen; he observed that every time the giant said 'lay', the hen laid an egg of solid gold. The giant amused himself a long time with the hen, meanwhile his wife went to bed. At length the giant fell asleep

271

by the fireside, and snored like the roaring of a cannon. At daybreak, Jack finding the giant not likely to be soon roused, crept softly out of his hiding-place, seized the hen, and ran off with her.

He met with some difficulty in finding his way out the house, but at last he reached the road in safety, without fear of pursuit: he easily found the way to the bean-stalk, and descended it better and quicker than he expected. His mother was overjoyed to see him; he found her crying bitterly, and lamenting his fate, for she concluded he had come to some shocking end through his rashness.

Jack was impatient to shew his hen, and inform his mother how valuable it was.

'And now, mother,' said Jack, 'I have brought home that which will quickly make you rich without any trouble: I hope I have made you some amends for the affliction I have caused you through my idleness, extravagance, and folly.'

The hen produced them as many eggs as they desired; they sold them, and in a little time became very rich.

For some months Jack and his mother lived happily together; but he being very desirous of travelling, longed to climb the bean-stalk and pay the giant another visit, in order to carry off some more of his treasures; for during the time Jack was in the giant's mansion, whilst he lay concealed in the oven, he learned from the conversation which took place between the giant and his wife, that he possessed some great curiosities. Jack thought on his journey again and again; but still he could not determine how to break it to his mother, being well assured that she would be quite resolved to prevent his going. One day, he told her boldly that he must take a journey up the bean-stalk; she begged he would not think of it, and tried all in her power to dissuade him, saying, that the giant could not fail of knowing him, and would desire no better than to get him into his power, that he might put him to a cruel death, in order to be revenged for the loss of his hen.

Jack finding that all his arguments were useless, pretended to give up the point, though resolved to go at all events. He had a dress prepared, which would disguise him, and with something to discolour his skin, he thought it impossible for anyone to recollect him. In a few mornings after discoursing with his mother, he rose very early, put on his disguise, changed his complexion, and, unperceived by anyone, climbed the bean-stalk. He was greatly fatigued when he reached the top, and very hungry. Having rested some time on one of the stones, he pursued his journey to the giant's mansion. He reached it late in the evening, the woman was standing at the door as usual; Jack accosted her, at the same time telling her a pitiful tale, and requested she would give him some victuals and drink; and a night's lodging. She told him what he knew before full well, concerning her husband, and also that she one night admitted a poor, hungry, distressed boy, who was half dead with travelling; that he stole one of the giant's treasures, and, ever since that, her husband was worse than before, and used her very cruelly, continually upbraiding her with being the cause of his loss.

Jack was at no loss to discover that he was attending to the account of a story in which he was the principal actor: he did his best to persuade the good woman to admit him, but he found it a very hard task.

At last she consented, and as she led the way, Jack observed that everything was just as he had found it before; she took him into the kitchen, and hid him in an old lumber-closet. The giant returned at the usual time, and walked in so heavily that the house was shaken to the foundation. He seated himself by a good fire, saying, 'I smell fresh meat;' the wife replied it was the crows, who had brought a piece of carrion, and laid it at the top of the house upon the leads.

Whilst supper was preparing, the giant was very ill-tempered and impatient, frequently lifting up his hand to strike his wife for not being quick enough; she, however, was always so fortunate as to elude the blow: he was also continually upbraiding her with the loss of his hen.

The giant, at last, having finished his voracious supper, and eaten till he was quite satisfied, said to his wife – 'I must have something to amuse me – either my bags of money or my harp.' After a great deal of ill-humour, and having teased his wife some time, he commanded her to bring his bags of gold and silver. Jack, as before, peeped out of his hiding-place, and presently the woman brought two bags into the room; they were of an immense size, one was filled with new guineas, the other with new shillings. They were both placed before the giant, he reprimanded his wife most severely for staying so long; the poor woman replied, trembling with fear, that they were so heavy she could scarcely lift them, and concluded, at last, that she never could bring them down stairs, adding, that she had nearly fainted owing to their weight. This so exasperated the giant, that he raised his hand to strike her; she, however, escaped and went to bed, leaving him to count over his treasures by way of amusement.

First, the bag containing the silver was emptied, and the contents placed upon the table. Jack viewed the glittering heaps with delight, and most heartily wished the contents in his own possession. The giant (little thinking himself so narrowly watched) reckoned the silver over and over again, then put it all carefully into the bag, which he made very secure. The other bag was opened next, and the guineas placed upon the table. If Jack was pleased at sight of the silver, how much more delighted he felt when he saw such a heap of gold: he had the boldness even to think of gaining it; but soon recollecting himself, he feared the giant would feign sleep, in order the better to entrap anyone who might be concealed. The gold was put up as the silver had been before, and, if possible, more securely. The giant snored aloud; Jack could compare his noise to nothing but the roaring of the sea in a high wind, when the tide is coming in. At last Jack, concluding him to be asleep, and therefore secure, stole out of his hiding place, and approached the giant, in order to carry off the two bags of money; but, just as he laid his hand upon one of the bags, a little dog, whom he had not perceived before, started out from under the giant's chair, and barked at Jack most furiously, who gave himself up for lost; fear riveted him to the spot – instead of running he stood still, though expecting his enemy to awake every minute. Contrary, however, to expectation, the giant continued in a sound sleep – the dog grew weary of barking; Jack, looking round, saw a large piece of meat, which he threw to the dog, who took it into the lumber-closet which Jack had just left.

He found himself thus delivered from a noisy and troublesome enemy; and, as the giant did not awake, Jack seized both the bags, and carried them away; he reached the street door in safety, and found it quite daylight. In his way to the top of the bean-stalk the only difficulty he had to encounter arose from the weight of the bags, and really they were so heavy he could hardly carry them. Jack was overjoyed when he found himself near the bean-stalk; he soon reached the bottom, and immediately ran to seek his mother. To his great surprise, the cottage was deserted, he went from one room to another, without being able to find any one; he then went out into the street, hoping to see some of the neighbours, who could inform him where he might find his mother. An old woman said she was at a neighbour's, ill of a fever, and directed him to the house where she was. He was shocked on finding her apparently dying, and could scarcely bear his own reflections on knowing himself to be the cause. On being told of his return, by degrees she revived, and began to recover gradually. Jack presented her with his two valuable bags; they lived happily and comfortably: the cottage was repaired and well furnished.

For three years Jack heard no more of the bean-stalk, but he could not forget it; though he feared making his mother unhappy; she would not mention the bean-stalk, lest it might remind him of taking another journey. Notwithstanding the comforts Jack enjoyed, his mind dwelt upon the bean-stalk; he could not think of anything else, it was in vain endeavouring to amuse himself. His mother found that something preyed upon his mind, and endeavoured to discover the cause; but Jack knew too well what the consequence would be to disclose the cause of his melancholy to her. He did his utmost therefore to conquer the great desire he felt for another journey up the bean-stalk; however, finding the inclination grew too powerful for him, he began to make secret preparations for his journey, and, on the longest day, arose as soon as it was light, ascended the bean-stalk, and reached the top with some trouble.

He found the road, journey, etc. much as it had been the two former times; he arrived at the giant's mansion in the evening, and found his wife standing at the door. Jack had disguised himself so completely, that she did not appear to have the least recollection of him; however, when he pleaded hunger and poverty in order to gain admittance, he found it very difficult indeed to persuade her. At last he prevailed, and was concealed in the copper. When the giant returned in the evening, he said, 'I smell fresh meat,' but Jack felt quite composed, as he had said so before, and was soon satisfied; however, the giant started up suddenly, and, notwithstanding all his wife could say, he searched all around the room. Whilst this was going on, Jack was terrified exceedingly, and ready to die with fear, wishing himself at home a thousand times; but when the giant approached the oven, and put his hand upon the lid, Jack thought his death-warrant was signed. The giant ended his search there, without moving the lid of the copper, and seated himself quietly. This fright nearly overcame poor Jack; he was afraid of moving or even breathing, lest he should be heard.

The giant at last ate a great supper; when he had finished, he commanded his wife to fetch down his harp. Jack peeped under the copper-lid, and soon saw the most beautiful harp that could be imagined; it was placed by the giant, he said 'play', and it instantly played of its own accord, without being touched. The music was very fine, Jack was delighted, and felt more anxious to get the harp into his possession, than either of the former treasures. The giant's soul was not attuned to harmony, and the music lulled him into a sound sleep. Now therefore was the time to carry off the harp, and the giant appeared to be in a more profound sleep than usual. Jack quickly determined, got out of the oven, and took the harp. The harp was a fairy; it called out loudly 'Master! Master! Master!'

The giant awoke, stood up, and tried to pursue Jack, but he had drunk so much that he could not stand. Poor Jack ran as fast as he could; in a little time the giant was sufficiently recovered to walk slowly, or rather to reel, after him; had he been sober he must have overtaken Jack instantly; but, as he then was, Jack contrived to be first at the top of the bean-stalk, the giant calling to him all the way he went, and sometimes he was very near him. The moment Jack set his foot on the bean-stalk, he called for a hatchet; one was brought directly; he soon reached the ground, just at that instant the giant was beginning to come down; but Jack with his hatchet cut the bean-stalk close off to the root, which made the giant fall into the garden – the fall killed him.

Jack's mother was delighted when she saw the bean-stalk destroyed; he heartily begged his mother's pardon for all the sorrow and affliction he had caused her, promising faithfully to be very dutiful and obedient to her for the future. He proved as good as his word, and was a pattern of affectionate behaviour and attention to his parent. His mother and he lived together a great many years, and continued to be always very happy.

ISTORICAL

Historical

In *English Hours*, Henry James said of his future homeland that 'you feel local custom and tradition – another tone of things – pressing on you from every side'. A people with so pronounced a sense of their own past as the British and the Irish naturally tell many tales about it (tales that in turn foster their sense of history). The traveller through the British Isles may sometimes feel that there is scarcely a river or a ruin, a tumulus or a venerable tree that does not have some story, some curious amalgam of fact and fantasy associated with it; he may discover that almost innumerable past events and people well-known and unknown are still present in folk-tale, and even now alluded to in the more remote parts of the country as if they had happened or lived the day before yesterday. Another discerning American student of our manners and modes, Ralph Waldo Emerson, put his finger on it when he spoke of Britain as 'this all-preserving island'.

The tale of *Garlatha*, from Harris in the Outer Hebrides, is in essence a grimmer version of the one in Ariosto's *Orlando Furioso* in which a bride playfully hides herself in a trunk only to be trapped in it when the lid closes with a spring lock, and for her skeleton to be discovered there fifty years later. There is no way of telling whether this tradition reached Harris in the Italian original, in Sir John Harington's elegant Elizabethan translation, in Thomas Haynes Bayly's (1797-1839) reworking of the motif in his ballad 'The Mistletoe Bough', or through some other (and possibly pre-Ariostan) source.

The tale was collected by John Gregorson Campbell (1836-91), an important figure in the history of Scottish folklore whose source was his own parishioners on the Gaelic-speaking islands of Coll and Tiree. Most of Campbell's work was published

281

posthumously and *Garlatha* appeared in the last of five volumes known collectively as *Waifs and Strays of the Celtic Tradition, Argyllshire Series,* inspired by Campbell of Islay and introduced by their publisher, the formidable Alfred Nutt (1856-1912). Three times President of the Folk-Lore Society, and scholarly and prolific writer on Scottish and Irish folklore, John Gregorson Campbell's skill as a translator was praised by Nutt, who wrote perceptively about the kind of problems he faced:

> The difficulty of rendering Gaelic into English does not lie in the fact of its possessing a rude simplicity which the more sophisticated language is incapable of reproducing, but rather in that, whilst the emotions and conceptions are close to the primitive passions of nature in a degree that our civilisation has long forsworn, the mode of expression has the richness of colour and elaborate artificiality of a pattern in the Book of Kells.

The origins of *Beth Gêlert* are not at all easy to establish. What is sure is that William Robert Spencer, author of the poem printed here, was following a false late eighteenth-century trail in noting that 'The story of this ballad is traditionary in a village at the foot of Snowdon where Llewellyn the Great had a house. The Greyhound named Gêlert was given to him by his father-in-law, King John, in the year 1205, and the place to this day is called Beth-Gêlert, or the grave of Gêlert.' The tale greatly interested William Alexander Clouston, Joseph Jacobs and Sabine Baring-Gould and between them they established that the legend of a man who rashly slays the dog that has saved his own child has parallels in Asia and Europe, including those in the *Fables of Bidpai* and *The Book of Sindibad*, and was well known in Wales long before it was connected either with Llewellyn the Great or with Beth Gêlert in Caernarfonshire.

The celebrated tale of *Whittington* is not unlike *Beth Gêlert* in associating a well-documented medieval figure with a motif to be found in countries east and west. What is tantalising is how so prosaic a figure as Richard Whittington, a rich mercer who was four times Mayor of London between 1397 and 1419, should come to be associated with a lucky cat (a tradition already current in a 16th century chapbook). Some readers will believe that this tradition has a historical foundation, some will point to similar traditions in Persia and Denmark and Italy, and some may think with Max Müller that the cat owes his presence to a misunderstanding of the French *achat* and that Whittington derived his wealth not from some feline accomplice but from his trading partners.

William Carew Hazlitt (1834-1913), grandson of William Hazlitt, included this story in his *Tales and Legends*. His version is rather too wordy but pleasingly redoubtable. In his introduction, Hazlitt relates *Whittington* to the 'Blind Beggar of Bethnal Green', 'Tom o' Lincoln' and 'Thomas of Reading' as being 'examples of romantic inventions originating in the early mercantile enterprise of our country and its relations with others'.

In a brief entry in his *Chronicon Anglicanum*, the late twelfth-century chronicler Ralph of Coggeshall says that a merman was caught at Orford in Suffolk during the reign of Henry II, and was imprisoned there in the newly-built castle that still looks out over the Alde estuary and the saltmarshes. He did not recognise the Cross, would not talk despite being subjected to torture, returned voluntarily into captivity having eluded three rows of nets, and then disappeared never to be seen again. The version printed here develops these bare facts into a tale told by the anguished Wildman himself.

Ivar and Matilda similarly puts flesh on a terse sentence in the *Chronicon Manniae* that 'In the year 1249 Reginald began to reign on 6th May, and on 30th May of the same year was slain by the Knight Ivar and his accomplices.' It was collected by A. W. Moore who worked in the Isle of Man with Sir John Rhys (see p.11) but its distinctly literary, not to say melodramatic tone indicates it was communicated to Moore in written form. The hero's retreat from the world into monastic orders is a measure reminiscent of the world of medieval Romance. In *The Folk-Lore of the Isle of Man* (1891), A. W. Moore assembled a valuable collection of myths, legends, superstitions, customs and proverbs, some personally collected, some drawn from the earlier visitors to the island, George Waldron and Joseph Train (see p.12 and 85).

The tale of *Cromwell and O'Donnell* was recorded in County Galway in 1935. For all its sprightliness, it is not difficult to detect the underlying bitterness that gave rise to this and many similar tales after Cromwell's repression of Ireland in 1649-50. Sean O'Sullivan, who includes this tale in *Folktales of Ireland*, notes that 'Some versions tell that Cromwell dies in Ireland, that the Irish soil refused to receive his body, and that it drifted on the sea until it finally sank to the bottom of the Irish Sea, causing it to be very rough ever since!' Although *Cromwell and O'Donnell* contains several powerful motifs, such as the manifestation of the devil in human form and the appearance of the wild hunt, it is not a particularly well-rounded tale. And this is true of a great many historical folk-tales: they are not so much aesthetically satisfying as interesting for the social sidelight they throw on people and moments and episodes in the past, and as illustrations of the way in which folk memory works.

Garlatha

AT ONE TIME it is said the outermost of the western isles formed three separate and independent possessions; the northern part of the Long Island (*an t-eilean fada*), Lewis (*Leòdhais*), was held by one Cenmal (*Ceannamhaol* [baldhead]), who was a king, while the southern portion, Harris (*na h-Earra*), was owned by a prince; and another king, one named Keligan [thin one], possessed Uist, which is further south. In this way Lewis and Uist had each a king, while there was only a prince in Harris.

This prince, who was famed for his courage and bravery, was held in great esteem by those on his land for the good advice (*na comhairlean dealbhach*) they readily got from him and the benefits he conferred on them. He discouraged bickerings and jealousy (*farmad*) among his subordinates and neighbours, and spread among them a knowledge of many useful arts. He encouraged manual labour as well as manly exercise and the recitation of poems, romance, etc. His wife, Garlatha, was not less namely for her goodness to those around her, among whom she promoted thrifty and industrious habits, and taught the use and methods of preparing different kinds of roots, grain and plants, for food and healing, and to be kind and tender to the weak and infirm, and to live good lives. In this way the people on their land were contented with their condition and sought no change.

Garlatha died, it is said, about 800 AD – a long time ago, but whatever it was, she went away (and it was not to be helped), leaving an infant daughter who was named after her mother, Garlatha. As the girl grew up it was seen that she inherited her mother's good gifts, and the people were equally well pleased with her. In time she began to be spoken about and heard of, and was sought in marriage by numerous suitors. The king who ruled in Lewis was eager in pursuit of her (*'an tòir oirre*), and crossed over to see her. The ruler (*fear-riaghlaidh*) of Uist came on the same errand.

One day then her father said to her, 'Daughter, I wish to see you married, before the end of my life comes, to a good man, and I am looking to see which of those men who come to see you is the most suitable, and I see that it will suit you best to take him who is in Lewis.'

His daughter preferred the one who owned Uist, but by her father's advice word was sent to the possessor of Lewis to come and that he would get her. He came, and being well pleased with his reception every arrangement was made, and they were married.

Afterwards the bride said to a maid, 'You will go in to the entertainment (*fleadh*) and among the company: I am going to hide myself.'

This was done, and the company sat at the feast without the bride, for whose coming a long delay was made. When it was seen that she would not return, the question of what had become of her or where she was, was asked of everyone but no one knew. The maid was asked, but she had not any knowledge or tale (*fios no sgeul*) to tell of where the lost one was to be found.

The time was passing (*bha 'n ùineachd 'ruith*) and search was made outside for her, but she was not found. Then they looked for her from place to place, where it was possible to find her, but without success. The night passed, leaving the feast untouched

286

and the guests cheerless. Next day the search was renewed along the shores and among the hills, and in every direction from day to day, till there was not a spot between Barra Head and the Butt of Lewis where a bird could sleep, that was not searched, but there was no trace of her (*cha d' fhuaireadh riamh i, cha d' fhuaireadh idir i*). The father continued to wander about, searching in vain, for many years after all hope of finding her was dead, till at last he was seen to turn every leaf he met with the staff in his hand, and even to look under ragweed (*buagh-allan*). He died, and she was not found.

The place, Harris, was then two hundred years without any one to own it (*thug an t-àite sin dà cheud bliadhna gun duine ann*). MacLeod (*fear Mac Leòid*) then took possession of the country and began to build new houses; the old dwellings had become uninhabitable (*air dol fàs*); the roof had fallen in (*thuit an ceann 'n am broinn*). When clearing out one of these an old chest was found, and on lifting it the lower part remained on the ground, with the skeleton of a woman resting in it, each bone according to its place (*cnàimh a réir cnàimh*), and by its side the wedding-ring, as new as it was on the day it was put on her finger, with the name 'Garlatha' engraved on it, and from that the story came.

Beth Gêlert

The spearmen heard the bugle sound,
  And cheerily smiled the morn;
And many a brach, and many a hound
  Obeyed Llewellyn's horn.

And still he blew a louder blast,
  And gave a lustier cheer,
'Come, Gêlert, come, wert never last
  Llewellyn's horn to hear.

'O where does faithful Gêlert roam
  The flower of all his race;
So true, so brave – a lamb at home,
  A lion in the chase?'

In sooth, he was a peerless hound,
  The gift of royal John;
But now no Gêlert could be found,
  And all the chase rode on.

Historical

That day Llewellyn little loved
   The chase of hart and hare;
And scant and small the booty proved,
   For Gêlert was not there.

Unpleased, Llewellyn homeward hied,
   When, near the portal seat,
His truant Gêlert he espied
   Bounding his lord to greet.

But when he gained the castle door,
   Aghast the chieftain stood;
The hound all o'er was smeared with gore;
   His lips, his fangs, ran blood.

Llewellyn gazed with fierce surprise;
   Unused such looks to meet,
His favourite checked his joyful guise,
   And crouched, and licked his feet.

Onward, in haste, Llewellyn passed,
   And on went Gêlert too;
And still, where'er his eyes he cast,
   Fresh blood-gouts shocked his view.

O'erturned his infant's bed he found,
   With blood-stained covert rent;
And all around the walls and ground
   With recent blood besprent.

He called his child – no voice replied –
   He searched with terror wild;
Blood, blood he found on every side,
   But nowhere found his child.

Historical

'Hell-hound! My child's by thee devoured,'
  The frantic father cried;
And to the hilt his vengeful sword
  He plunged in Gêlert's side.

Aroused by Gêlert's dying yell,
  Some slumberer wakened nigh;
What words the parent's joy could tell
  To hear his infant's cry!

Concealed beneath a tumbled heap
  His hurried search had missed,
All glowing from his rosy sleep
  The cherub boy he kissed.

Nor scathe had he, nor harm, nor dread,
  But, the same couch beneath,
Lay a gaunt wolf, all torn and dead,
  Tremendous still in death.

Ah, what was then Llewellyn's pain!
  For now the truth was clear;
His gallant hound the wolf had slain
  To save Llewellyn's heir.

Whittington

RICHARD WHITTINGTON was so obscurely bred that he could scarce say who his parents were; and being well-nigh starved in the country, it appears that he came up to London, where he expected to meet with greater charity.

He was ashamed to beg, and the thought of stealing he abhorred; and during two days he wandered about the streets, gazing on the shops, with next to nought to eat.

At length he waxed so faint, that he seated himself on a bench beside a merchant's gateway in Leadenhall Street, and had not rested there long when the merchant himself, going forth for his occasions into the city, looked on him, and, not knowing his hard case, demanded why he loitered there sooner than busy himself with earning his living in some lawful vocation; and he threatened him with the stocks or the whipping-post.

But Whittington made legs to his worship, and shewed how it stood with him, saying that there was no employment, how mean and poor soever, that he would not take, if it should offer.

The merchant, thereupon eyeing him more favourably, called to one of his servants, and desired him to give the youth victual such as the house afforded, and on his return he would have further speech with him. And the servant did so.

While the merchant, then, was absent at the exchange in Lombard Street, Whittington sat by the fire in the kitchen to warm himself (for it was the winter season), and plenty of good food being presently brought, he fed like a farmer, and the colour returned into his cheeks; so that when the merchant's daughter, learning that a new visitor had arrived, came into the place where he was, she was greatly taken by his fair looks and by his honest answers to the questions she put to him concerning the country whence he had travelled up.

The dinner hour arrived, and Master Fitzwarren (for this was the merchant's name) brought home one or two friends to partake of his good cheer; and the servants' table was also set out, at which Whittington was prayed to sit, albeit he had so newly broken his fast; for all liked his company well, some being pleased with his country speech, and others entertained by his simplicity.

II

Now when Master Fitzwarren's guests had departed, and he and his daughter remained alone, she commended his charity in that he had befriended the poor fellow that now sat in the kitchen. To whom: 'God-a-mercy! daughter,' quoth he, 'right glad am I that thou hast remembered me thereof: for I commanded my servants to care for him, and I marvel if they have so done.'

His daughter answered and said: 'Father, I even bad them let him stay dinner, nor dismiss him, till you could have conference with him.'

Master Fitzwarren rose, and with his daughter passed into the hall, where they called Whittington to them. Whose address was so lowly and modest, that he enlisted in his favour that gentle lady, the merchant's daughter; and in the end he was admitted into the household to do what labour was enjoined to him, and to have bed and board, and clothing.

Wages he had as yet none; yet with a penny, that some kind man gave him for a service, he bought a young cat, which he made his companion; and it had the leaving of his plate, and slept in the same garret with its master.

The merchant was accustomed from time to time to adventure ships upon the sea to distant lands with merchandise and goods; and it entered into his practice (for he was a generous man) to suffer all his household and servants to put in somewhat; and now it was the case that a ship was in course of fitting out for a long voyage, and all had license to join to their power.

Only Whittington, albeit Master Fitzwarren gave him leave, had nought to send; and when his kind mistress, the merchant's daughter, made offer to lend him money out of her purse, her father replied, saying that each must give out of his own proper chattels. So he prayed Whittington to consider well if he had anything his very own which he might put to hazard, for the *Unicorn* was lying at Blackwall, and was ready to set sail.

Whittington could only offer his cat, and loth enough he was to part with so dear a playmate; yet, because he was urged, he let it go, and right glad the captain was of it, for it destroyed the rats and mice wherewith the ship abounded, and which damaged the cargo and other commodities.

III

Meanwhile, it happened that Whittington and the kitchenmaid at Master Fitzwarren's proved no good friends, and she so evil-intreated him, because he was too honest to plunder, that at last he could bear his life no longer, and, gathering up the few clothes he had, ran away. He ran toward Bun Hill, and it being All Hallows' Day, the bells of Bow Church began to ring, and they were, as it seemed to him, tuned to this ditty:

> *Turn again, Whittington,*
> *Lord Mayor of London:*

Turn again, Whittington,
Lord Mayor of London!

This made a deep impression on his mind, and because it was so early, that he might return ere the family had risen, he resolved to go back, and found everything as he had left it, and none cognizant of his departure and flight.

Let us leave Whittington, who grew to be beloved of all, save the shrewd kitchen-wench, and speak of what befell the *Unicorn*, which, driven by contrary winds, was enforced to land on the shores of Barbary, where no Englishman had ever traded before; and the Moors, when they perceived such an unwonted sight, hastened down in great numbers, and bought all the rich goods which Master Fitzwarren had despatched by his factor; and the king of that country, when he understood the matter, sent for the Englishmen, and likewise purchased from them, and bad them to a great feast.

The custom was among his people, which were not Christians, but heathens, worshipping Mahomet, to sit at meat, not round a table as our use is, but on a carpet, like tailors on a shop-board; and when the viands were spread, and all were prepared to partake of the good cheer, a swarm of rats and mice settled upon the dishes and consumed everything, to the meat on the trenchers of the king and the queen.

This spectacle annoyed the Englishmen, and the king to their asking replied that he would gladly give half the revenues of his dominion, if he might be quit of this terrible visitation, since he could not lay down his head on his pillow at night, unless a watch were set to guard him from destruction.

The factor thereupon made known to the king that, it being so, they had a strange beast on board their ship which would speedily rid the kingdom of this plague; and his grace said that he would lade the vessel with gold, silver and pearls to have so rare a treasure. The Englishmen doubted if they might spare the beast from the ship, for that, while they slept, it kept the vermin from their merchandise and their diet.

All the more the king desired to see and possess such a blessing; and at last the Englishmen went and fetched the cat, which, when the dishes that had been devoured were renewed, and the rats and mice again made their entrance, no sooner shewed itself, and seized on such as were nighest, but they all fled, and were seen no more.

Greatly the king and the nobility rejoiced when they had witnessed this sport, and vowed that the hunting of the lion was not comparable with it; and because the cat looked to have kittens, which would in short time people the whole realm, the king made it so, that the price of the cat by far exceeded all the other lading of the ship.

When they had set sail from Barbary, and safely arrived at Blackwall once again, Master Fitzwarren, when he learned what fortune poor Whittington had met withal, sent for him when he was scouring the pots in the kitchen; and whereas he at first excused himself, saying that his shoes were soiled, and the floor of the parlour but newly rubbed, to the repeated calls of the merchant he in the end answered, and presented himself before Master Fitzwarren, with whom were his daughter, the factor of the ship, and her pilot.

Whereupon to Whittington making humble obeisance as before, the good merchant spake graciously and heartily, saluting him by the title of Master Whittington; and he caused chairs to be brought, and placed Master Whittington by his side. But he, moved by this strange exaltation, wept, and asked the meaning thereof. To whom his master replied, that he was now a better and richer man than himself, and exhibited to him the prodigious wealth that he had gotten through his cat in such unlooked for sort.

IV

Master Whittington bestowed of his exceeding great substance on the factor, and all others that had shown him courtesy; and when he was sumptuously clothed, and went in all things like a gentleman, the merchant's daughter, that before had pitied him, began to cast an eye upon him, as upon one whom she would fain have for a suitor, and to her father's singular content, who designed a match between these two.

Now it was not long ere Master Whittington sought that lady, his kind mistress when he was poor and hungry, in marriage; and Master Fitzwarren spared no cost at the wedding, whereto were bidden the lord mayor and aldermen, and all the chief merchants of the city of London, and shortly after he was pricked for sheriff, and acquitted himself in that office with infinite credit.

At length, that the words which the bells of Bow Church had rung out might be fulfilled, in the one and twentieth year of King Richard II, Master Whittington was chosen mayor, and was knighted by the king's grace. During the term of whose mayoralty there arose great discord and trouble in England, and grievous pride and riotous excess in living by reason, as it was deemed, of the singular growth of commerce with foreign countries through Sir Richard Whittington and other merchants his very friends encouraging strange new fashions and vain wantonness in diet.

Which Sir Richard Whittington was four times mayor of London, and as in his life he founded divers noble charities in remembrance of the gratitude that he owed to Almighty God for having raised him, so mean a creature, to so great a fortune and dignity, so his executors by his ordinance after his death continued that good work for the souls' health of the said Sir Richard and Dame Alice his wife.

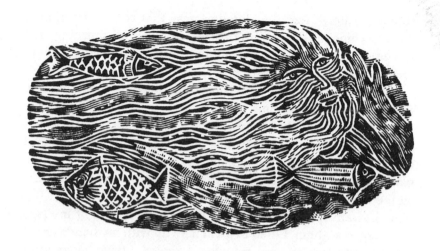

The Wildman

DON'T ask me my name. I've heard you have names. I have no name.

They say this is how I was born. A great wave bored down a river, and at the mouth of the river it ran up against a great wave of the sea. The coupled waves kicked like legs and whirled like arms and swayed like hips. sticks in the water snapped like bones and the seaweed bulged like gristle and muscle. In this way the waves rose. When they fell, I was there.

My home is water as your home is earth. I rise to the surface to breathe air, I glide down through the darkening rainbow. The water sleeks my hair as I swim. And when I stand on the sea-bed, the currents comb my waving hair; my whole body seems to ripple.

Each day I go to the land for food. I swim to the shore, I'm careful not to be seen. Small things, mice, shrews, moles, I like them to eat. I snuffle and grub through the growth and undergrowth and grab them, and squeeze the warm blood out of them, and chew them.

Always before sunset I'm back in the tugging, laughing,

sobbing water. Then the blue darkness that comes down over the sea comes inside me too. I feel heavy until morning. If I stayed too long on the land I might be found, lying there, heavy, unable even to drag myself back to the water.

My friends are seals. They dive as I do, and swim as I do. Their hair is like my hair. I sing songs with their little ones. They've shown me their secret place, a dark grotto so deep that I howled for the pain of the water pressing round me there and rose to the surface, gasping for air. My friends are the skimming plaice and the flickering eel and the ticklish trout. My friends are all the fishes.

As I swam near the river mouth, something caught my legs and tugged at them. I tried to push it away with my hands and it caught my hands and my arms too. I kicked; I flailed; I couldn't escape. I was dragged through the water, up out of the darkness into the indigo, the purple, the pale blue. I was lifted into the air, the sunlight, and down into a floating thing.

Others. There were others in it, others, others as I am. But their faces were not covered with hair. They had very little hair I could see except on their heads, but they were covered with animal skins and furs. When they saw me they were afraid and trembled and backed away and one fell into the water.

I struggled and bit but I was caught in the web they had made. They took me to land and a great shoal gathered round me there. Then they carried me in that web to a great high place of stone and tipped me out into a gloomy grotto.

One of them stayed by me and kept making noises; I couldn't understand him. I could tell he was asking me things. I would have liked to ask him things. How were you born? Why do you have so little hair? Why do you live on land? I looked at him, I kept looking at him, and when the others came back, I looked at them: their hairless hands, their legs, their shining eyes. There were so many of them almost like me, and I've never once seen anyone in the sea like me.

They brought me two crossed sticks. Why? What are they? They pushed them into my face, they howled at me. One of them smacked my face with his hand. Why was that? It hurt. Then another with long pale hair came and wept tears over me. I licked my lips; the tears tasted like the sea. Was this one like me? Did this one come from the sea? I put my arms round its waist but it shrieked and pushed me away.

They brought me fish to eat. I wouldn't eat fish. Later they brought me meat; I squeezed it until it was dry and then I ate it.

I was taken out into sunlight, down to the river mouth. The rippling, rippling water. It was pink and lilac and grey; I shivered with longing at the sight of it. I could see three rows of webs spread across the river from bank to bank. Then they let me go, they let me dive into the water. It coursed through my long hair. I laughed and passed under the first net and the second net and the third net. I was free. But why am I only free away from those who are like me, with those who are not like me? Why is the sea my home?

They were all shouting and waving their arms, and jumping up and down at the edge of the water. They were all calling out across the grey wavelets. Why? Did they want me to go back after all? Did they want me to be their friend?

I wanted to go back, I wanted them as friends. So I stroked back under the nets again and swam to the sandy shore. They fell on me then, and twisted my arms, and hurt me. I howled. I screamed. They tied long webs round me and more tightly round me, and carried me back to the place of stone, and threw me into the gloomy grotto.

I bit through the webs. I slipped through the window bars. It was almost night and the blue heaviness was coming into me. I staggered away, back to the water, the waiting dark water.

Ivar and Matilda

THERE was a young and gallant knight, named Ivar, who was enamoured of a very beautiful maiden, named Matilda. He loved her ardently, and she reciprocated his affection. From childhood they had been companions, and as they grew up in years, the firmer became they attached to each other. Never, indeed, were two beings more indissolubly bound by the fetters of love than Ivar and Matilda. But storms will overcast the serenest sky. At this period Reginald was King of the Isle of Man; and, according to ancient custom, it was incumbent upon Ivar to present his betrothed at the court of the monarch, and obtain his consent, prior to becoming linked in more indissoluble fetters with her. The nuptial day had already been fixed, the feast had been prepared, and it was noised abroad that the great and noble of the Island were to be present at the celebration of the marriage. King Reginald resided in Rushen Castle, in all the barbaric pomp which was predominant in those olden times; and thither Ivar, accompanied by Matilda, proceeded to wait upon him.

Dismounting from their horses at the entrance of the keep,

they were conducted to the presence of the king. Ivar doffed his jewelled cap, and made obeisance; then, leading forward Matilda, he presented her to him. Reginald was greatly enraptured with the maiden's beauty from the first moment she had met his gaze, and swore inwardly that he would possess her for himself, and spoil the knight of his affianced bride. To carry into effect his wicked purpose, he accused Ivar of pretended crimes; and, ordering in his guards, banished him from his presence; detaining, however, the maiden.

Vain would it be to depict Matilda's anguish at this barbarous treatment. Reginald endeavoured to soothe her agitation, but it was to no purpose. He talked to her of his devoted love, but the maiden spurned his impious offers with contempt. Exasperated at her resistance, he had her confined in one of the most solitary apartments in the castle.

In the meantime, Ivar exerted himself to avenge the deep injury which he had received; but Reginald had such despotic sway, that all his endeavours proved abortive. At length he resolved to retire from the world, to assume the monastic habit, and to join the pious brotherhood of the Monastery of St Mary's of Rushen.

The brethren received him with joy, commiserating the bereavement which he had sustained. Ivar was now devoted to acts of piety; but still he did not forget his Matilda. Sometimes he would ascend the hill, and gaze towards the castle, wondering if Matilda were yet alive.

One day, matin prayers having been offered up, Ivar wandered as usual through the woods, thinking of his betrothed, and bowed down with sorrow. At last he reclined on the grass to rest; when, looking around, he beheld a fissure in a rock which abutted from an eminence immediately opposite. Curiosity induced him to go near; and he discovered that it was the entrance to a subterranean passage. Venturing in, he proceeded for some distance. Onward he went, till a great door arrested his progress. After some difficulty it yielded to his endeavours, and he passed through. Suddenly a piercing shriek, which

301

reverberated along the echoing vaults, fixed him horror-struck for a moment to the place. It was repeated faintly several times. A faint glimmer of light now broke in upon his path, and he found himself in a vaulted chamber. Passing through it, another cry met his ear; and rushing impetuously forward, he heard a voice in a state of exhaustion exclaim, 'Mother of God, save Matilda!' whilst, through a chink in the barrier, he beheld his long lost love, with dishevelled hair and throbbing bosom, in the arms of the tyrant Reginald.

Ivar instantly sprang through the barrier, rushed upon the wretch, and, seizing his sword, which lay carelessly on the table, plunged it into Reginald's bosom. Ivar, carrying Matilda in his arms, continued on through the subterranean passage, which brought them to the seaside where they met with a boat, which conveyed them to Ireland. There they were united in holy matrimony, and passed the remainder of their days in the raptures of a generous love, heightened by mutual admiration and gratitude.

Cromwell and O'Donnell

THERE was a man here in Ireland long ago. He was a gentleman by the name of O'Donnell and he was very friendly with a monk in the district. One day the monk told him that there was a great change to come over Ireland; that England would take over Ireland, and that a leader of the name of Cromwell would be throwing the Irish people, who had land, out on the road and would be settling his own people from England in their place.

'The best plan for you', said the monk to O'Donnell, 'is to go off over to England. The man they call Cromwell is a cobbler. You must travel around England, with a notebook, and ask every man you meet to sign his name in the book, promising that he won't ever take your land or dwelling-place off you. Keep on travelling like that until you go to where Cromwell is living.'

That was that! O'Donnell crossed over to England and he was travelling around with his book, pretending to be a bit simple, asking everyone he met to sign his book that he would never take his land or dwelling-place off him. He kept going till he came to Cromwell's house. He went in and asked Cromwell to put a side-patch on one of his shoes. When the job was done, he handed a guinea to Cromwell.

'A thousand thanks to you! That's good payment,' said Cromwell.

'Now,' said O'Donnell, 'I hope that you will sign this book that you will never take my land or dwelling-place off me.'

'Why wouldn't I promise you that?' said Cromwell.

He took hold of the book and signed in it that he would never take his land or dwelling-place off O'Donnell in Ireland. When he had done that, O'Donnell went back to Ireland.

Some years later, there was a great change in England. Cromwell rose up high and took the power from the king. Then he came to Ireland. He was throwing the people out of their land, whether they were noble or lowly, and killing them. He arrived at O'Donnell's house and struck a blow on the door.

'Out with you from here!' he shouted. 'You're here long enough!'

'I hope you won't put me out until you and myself have dinner together,' said O'Donnell.

'What sort of dinner have you?' asked Cromwell.

'Roast duck,' said O'Donnell.

'That's very good,' said Cromwell. 'I like that.'

Cromwell went into the house and the two of them started eating the dinner. When they had it eaten, O'Donnell took out his book and showed it to Cromwell.

'Do you recognise that writing?' said O'Donnell.

'I do, 'tis mine,' said Cromwell. 'How did you know that I'd be coming to Ireland or that I'd rise so high?'

It was no use for O'Donnell to hide it; he had to tell the truth to Cromwell.

'There was a holy monk in this place,' said he, 'and it was he that told me that a great change would come in Ireland and that it was a cobbler in England by the name of Cromwell who would come here and put me out of my land.'

'You must send for that holy monk for me,' said Cromwell, 'and if he doesn't come, I'll cut the head off him!'

O'Donnell went off and found the monk and brought him back to Cromwell.

'How did you get this knowledge?' asked Cromwell.

'I got it from Heaven,' replied the monk.

'Now you must tell me how long I will live,' said Cromwell.

'You will live as long as you wish to,' said the holy monk.

'I'll live for ever then!' said Cromwell.

There was another big gentleman from England along with Cromwell.

'And how long will I live? Will I get a long life?' he asked.

'If you pass the door of the next forge you meet on the road alive,' said the monk, 'you'll live a long time.'

'Ah, I'll live for ever so!' said the gentleman.

That was that! Cromwell didn't evict O'Donnell; he left him where he was, and went away. Himself and the English gentleman and their troop of soldiers went along, and when they were passing by a forge, Cromwell said:

'There's a shoe loose on one of our horses. But luckily we're near this forge!'

He jumped off his horse and entered the forge. The smith was inside.

'Hurry up and put a shoe on this horse for us!' said Cromwell.

The poor smith was trembling with terror. He hurried here and there about the forge, looking for a good piece of iron. He was afraid that he wouldn't be able to get a piece good enough for Cromwell and his army. Cromwell himself was searching around also, and he spied an old gun-barrel stuck above one of the rafters of the forge.

'Here's a piece of iron that's good!' said he.

He pulled down the old gun and shoved the barrel of it into the fire – he was well used to working in forges too, for his father was a smith. He started to blow the bellows. The English gentleman was standing outside the door. It wasn't long till the shot went off through the mouth of the gun and it struck the gentleman on his vest pocket and went out through his body at the other side. It killed him. Cromwell ran out when he heard the noise outside, jumped up on his horse, dug the spurs into it and raced for Dublin. As he was galloping along the road, whom did he see, walking ahead of him, but the holy monk! When the monk saw Cromwell coming towards him, he tried to run down and hide himself under the arch of a bridge.

'Come up out of that, you devil!' shouted Cromwell. 'If I have to go down to you, I'll cut the head off you!'

The monk came up to him.

"Tisn't from you I was hiding at all,' said the monk, 'but from the man behind you.'

'What man is behind me?' asked Cromwell.

'He's sitting behind you on the horse,' said the monk.

Cromwell looked behind him and he saw the Devil at his back. All he did was dig his spurs into his horse and race for Dublin. He went back to England and never returned to Ireland again. After spending a while in England, he grew restless. The King of Spain died, and his son, who hadn't much sense or knowledge about ruling a country, took his place. Cromwell decided on a plan which seemed very good to him. He wrote a letter to the young Spanish king, inviting him to England and offered him his daughter in marriage. When the king got the letter, he sent for his advisers and told them about it.

'That's a plan of Cromwell's', said they, 'to try to get into this country and take over the kingdom. Write a letter back to him and say that you'd like such a marriage arrangement, but you want a year to think the matter over; when the year is out, you might like the offer very much. You must be strengthening your army during the year, and at the end of it, write to him and say that you don't wish to marry the Devil's daughter!'

Cromwell happened to be shaving himself when he got the letter at the end of the year. He had one side of his face shaved, when the letter was handed to him. When he read the piece about the Devil's daughter, he cut his throat with the razor and fell dead.

About the time when Cromwell killed himself, a ship was

entering Liverpool, and the captain saw, coming towards him in the air, a fiery coach drawn by dogs, and they crying out: 'Clear the way for Oliver Cromwell!'

AINTS AND

DEVILS

Saints and Devils

Several British folk-tales tell how a human woman is required to assist as midwife or nurse to the fairies. Robert Hunt collected one in Cornwall, others are localised in Somerset and Northumberland, while Robert Cromek included the particularly haunting tale of 'The Woman who Suckled a Fairy' in his *Remains of Galloway and Nithsdale Songs* (1810). The taboo on the use of fairy ointment, the suggestions that the human woman is a captive and the show of fairy gratitude present in these tales all occur in *The Fiend Master* in which we are translated from the Otherworld to the Underworld.

The tale was collected in Wales by Wirt Sikes, United States Consul to the Principality, and published by him in his delightfully-named *British Goblins* (1880), a compendium of tales and information diplomatically dedicated to the Prince of Wales. In his preamble, Sikes alludes to French and German versions of the tale and makes a telling comparison between *The Fiend Master* and the legend of Cupid and Psyche, in which Psyche disobeys Cupid's command that she should never try to find out who he is, and lights a lamp only to spill a drop of hot oil on to Cupid's shoulder.

Samuel Lover (1797-1868), a man of letters who also won a small reputation as a painter and composer, published two series of *Legends and Stories of Ireland* in 1831 and 1834. These literary adaptations of tales collected in Ireland by Lover himself find little favour with folklorists and Richard Dorson dismisses Lover as author of 'the cloyingly comic Anglo-Irish sketch'. More useful, perhaps, are W. B. Yeats's observations in his introduction to *Fairy and Folk Tales of the Irish Peasantry*:

Croker and Lover, full of the ideas of harum-scarum Irish

311

gentility, saw everything humorised. The impulse of the Irish literature of their time came from a class that did not – mainly for political reasons – take the populace seriously, and imagined the country as a humorist's Arcadia; its passion, its gloom, its tragedy, they knew nothing of. What they did was not wholly false; they merely magnified an irresponsible type, found oftenest among boatmen, carmen and gentlemen's servants, into the type of a whole nation, and created the stage Irishman.

Certainly, there is no denying the natural exuberance and marvellous ear on display in *King O'Toole and his Goose*, a tale that carries memories of the time when early Irish kings granted land to the Celtic church for the foundation of monasteries, and reads like a deliberate parody of the charming fresh legends associating many Celtic saints with birds and beasts.

The Man that Sold his Soul to the Devil is in effect a folk-Faust in which drunken stupidity is substituted for damning complicity. The tale was collected by Hamish Henderson of the School of Scottish Studies in 1956 from the son of a man who had heard it from Rosie Powers herself – and it is not difficult to imagine Rosie using her sharp tongue to ease the lives of her neighbours by warning their menfolk of the end that awaited them if they persisted with 'the demon drink'. Wullie's fate illustrates the danger of saying things that may be overheard by supernatural beings and used against the speaker, a motif that occurs in a number of British folk-tales.

'Thirty five years since,' writes Robert Hunt in his introduction to *Popular Romances of the West of England* (1865), 'on a beautiful spring morning, I landed at Saltash, from the very ancient passage-boat which in those days conveyed men and women, carts and cattle, across the River Tamar . . . Sending my box forward to Liskeard by a van, my wanderings commenced; my purpose being to visit each relic of Old Cornwall, and to gather up every existing tale of its ancient people. Ten months were delightfully spent in this way . . . ' Hunt was the first of the English folklorists to concentrate on a single county; he printed tales as he heard them, unembellished; and later in his introduction he offered an invaluable account of the 'droll teller':

> The wandering minstrel, story-teller and newsmonger appears to have been an old institution amongst the Cornish . . . The only wandering droll-teller whom I well remember was an old blind man, from the parish of Cury . . . He neither begged nor offered anything for sale, but was sure of a welcome to bed and board in every house he called at . . . Soon after he reached my father's house, he would stretch himself on the 'chimney-stool', and sleep until supper-time. When the old man had finished his frugal meal of bread and milk, he would tune his fiddle and ask if 'missus' would like to hear him sing her favourite ballad . . . Yet the grand resource was the stories in which the supernatural bore great part.

Hunt's amusing aetiological tale of *The Crowza Stones* illustrates how folk memory on occasion translates spiritual strength or technical ability into bodily strength (in much the same way, the Anglo-Saxons marvelled at the remains of Roman stone buildings in England and called the Romans 'giants'). In British folk-tales, it is usually the devil or a giant who is responsible for features of the landscape but this is one of two tales collected by Hunt – the other concerns St Just and St Sennen – in which saints take their place.

Both the hell hound in *The Bewitched Sixareen* (p.196) and the huge black cat in *The Demon Cat* portray the devil as a shape-changer and in each case he has to give way to the superior power of those who invoke or act in Christ's name. The tale was collected by Lady Jane Francesca 'Speranza' Wilde and included by her in *Ancient Legends, Mystic Charms, and Superstitions of Ireland* (1887), a miscellany of tales and superstitions and opinion that Yeats praised as 'the most poetical and ample collection of Irish folk-lore yet published'. Scarcely less celebrated in Dublin society than their son Oscar, glamorous Speranza and her husband Sir William, an eye surgeon, between them collected three volumes of folk material. Like several contemporaries, Speranza saw her work as part of an effort to give back to the Irish an awareness of their own history and traditions largely ignored or destroyed by the English.

The Fiend Master

A RESPECTABLE young Welshwoman of the working class, who lived with her parents, went one day to a hiring fair. Here she was addressed by a very noble-looking gentleman all in black, who asked her if she would be a nursemaid, and undertake the management of his children. She replied that she had no objection; when he promised her immense wages, and said he would take her home behind him, but that she must, before they started, consent to be blindfolded. This done, she mounted behind him on a coal-black steed, and away they rode at a great rate.

At length they dismounted, when her new master took her by the hand and led her on, still blindfolded, for a considerable distance. The handkerchief was then removed, when she beheld more grandeur than she had ever seen before; a beautiful palace lighted up by more lights than she could count, and a number of little children as beautiful as angels; also many noble-looking ladies and gentlemen. The children her master put under her charge, and gave her a box containing ointment, which she was to put on their eyes. At the same time he gave her strict orders always to wash her hands immediately after using the ointment, and be particularly careful never to let a bit of it touch her own eyes. These injunctions she strictly followed, and was for some time very happy; yet she sometimes thought it odd that they should always live by candle-light; and she wondered, too, that grand and beautiful as the palace was, such fine ladies and gentlemen as were there should never wish to leave it. But so it was; no one ever went out but her master.

One morning, while putting the ointment on the eyes of the children, her own eye itched, and forgetting the orders of her master she touched one corner of it with her finger which was covered with ointment. Immediately, with the vision of that corner of her eye, she saw herself surrounded by fearful flames; the ladies and gentlemen looked like devils, and the children appeared like the most hideous imps of hell. Though with the other parts of her eyes she beheld all grand and beautiful as before, she could not help feeling much frightened at all this; but having great presence of mind she let no one see her alarm. However, she took the first opportunity of asking her master's leave to go and see her friends. He said he would take her, but she must again consent to be blindfolded. Accordingly a handkerchief was put over her eyes; she was again mounted behind her master, and was soon put down in the neighbourhood of her own house.

It will be believed that she remained quietly there, and took good care not to return to her place; but very many years afterwards, being at a fair, she saw a man stealing something from a stall, and with one corner of her eye beheld her old master pushing his elbow. Unthinkingly she said, 'How are you master? How are the children?'

He said, 'How did you see me?'

She answered, 'With the corner of my left eye.'

From that moment she was blind in her left eye, and lived many years with only her right.

316

King O'Toole and his Goose

BY GOR, I thought all the world, far and near, heerd o' King
O'Toole – well, well, but the darkness of mankind is ontellible!
Well, sir, you must know, as you didn't hear it afore, that there
was a king, called King O'Toole, who was a fine ould king in the
ould ancient times, long ago; and it was him that owned the
churches in the early days. The king, you see, was the right sort;
he was the rale boy, and loved sport as he loved his life, and
huntin' in partic'lar; and from the risin' o' the sun, up he got,
and away he wint over the mountains beyant afther the deer;
and the fine times them wor.

Well, it was all mighty good, as long as the king had his
health; but, you see, in coorse of time the king grew ould, by
raison he was stiff in his limbs, and when he got sthriken in
years, his heart failed him, and he was lost intirely for want o'
divarshin, bekase he couldn't go a huntin' no longer; and, by
dad, the poor king was obleeged at last for to get a goose to divart
him. Oh, you may laugh, if you like, but it's truth I'm tellin' you;
and the way the goose divarted him was this-a-way: You see, the
goose used for to swim acrass the lake, and go divin' for throut,

and cotch fish on a Friday for the king, and flew every other day round about the lake, divartin' the poor king. All went on mighty well, antil, by dad, the goose got sthriken in years like her master, and couldn't divart him no longer, and then it was that the poor king was lost complate.

The king was walkin' one mornin' by the edge of the lake, lamentin' his cruel fate, and thinkin' o' drownin' himself, that could get no divarshun in life, when all of a suddint, turnin' round the corner beyant, who should he meet but a mighty dacent young man comin' up to him.

'God save you,' says the king to the young man.

'God save you kindly, King O'Toole,' says the young man.

'Thrue for you,' says the king. 'I am King O'Toole,' says he, 'prince and plennypennytinchery o' these parts,' says he; 'but how kem ye to know that?' says he.

'Oh, never mind,' says Saint Kavin.

You see it was Saint Kavin, sure enough – the saint himself in disguise, and nobody else. 'Oh, never mind,' says he, 'I know more than that. May I make bowld to ax how is your goose, King O'Toole?' says he.

'Blur-an-agers, how kem ye to know about my goose?' says the king.

'Oh, no matther; I was given to understand it,' says Saint Kavin.

After some more talk the king says, 'What are you?'

'I'm an honest man,' says Saint Kavin.

'Well, honest man,' says the king, 'and how is it you make your money so aisy?'

'By makin' ould things as good as new,' says Saint Kavin.

'Is it a tinker you are?' says the king.

'No,' says the saint; 'I'm no tinker by thrade, King O'Toole; I've a betther thrade than a tinker,' says he – 'what would you say,' says he, 'if I made your ould goose as good as new?'

My dear, at the word o' making his goose as good as new, you'd think the poor ould king's eyes was ready to jump out iv his head. With that the king whistled, and down kem the poor goose, all as one as a hound, waddlin' up to the poor cripple, her masther, and as like him as two pays.

The minute the saint clapt his eyes on the goose, 'I'll do the job for you,' says he, 'King O'Toole.'

'By *Jaminee*!' says King O'Toole, 'if you do, bud I'll say you're the cleverest fellow in the sivin parishes.'

'Oh, by dad,' says Saint Kavin, 'you must say more nor that – my horn's not so soft all out,' says he, 'as to repair your ould goose for nothin'; what'll you gi' me if I do the job for you? – that's the chat,' says Saint Kavin.

'I'll give you whatever you ax,' says the king; 'isn't that fair?'

'Divil a fairer,' says the saint; 'that's the way to do business. Now,' says he, 'this is the bargain I'll make with you, King O'Toole: will you gi' me all the ground the goose flies over, the first offer, afther I make her as good as new?'

'I will,' says the king.

'You won't go back o' your word?' says Saint Kavin.

'Honor bright!' says King O'Toole, howldin' out his fist.

'Honor bright!' says Saint Kavin, back agin, 'it's a bargain. Come here!' says he to the poor ould goose – 'come here, you unfort'nate ould cripple, and it's I that'll make you the sportin' bird.'

With that, my dear, he took up the goose by the two wings – 'Criss o' my crass an you,' says he, markin' her to grace with the blessed sign at the same minute – and throwin' her up in the air, 'whew,' says he, jist givin' her a blast to help her; and with that, my jewel, she tuk to her heels, flyin' like one o' the aigles themselves, and cuttin' as many capers as a swallow before a shower of rain.

Well, my dear, it was a beautiful sight to see the king standin' with his mouth open, lookin' at his poor ould goose flyin' as light as a lark, and betther nor ever she was: and when she lit at his fut, patted her an the head, and, '*Ma vourneen*,' says he, 'but you are the *darlint* o' the world.'

'And what do you say to me,' says Saint Kavin, 'for making' her the like?'

'By gor,' says the king, 'I say nothin' bates the art o' man, barrin' the bees.'

'And do you say no more nor that?' says Saint Kavin.

'And that I'm behoulden to you,' says the king.

'But will you gi'e me all the ground the goose flew over?' says Saint Kavin.

'I will,' says King O'Toole, 'and you're welkim to it,' says he, 'though it's the last acre I have to give.'

'But you'll keep your word thrue?' says the saint.

'As thrue as the sun,' says the king.

'It's well for you, King O'Toole, that you said that word,' says he; 'for if you didn't say that word, *the devil receave the bit o' your goose id ever fly agin.*'

Whin the king was as good as his word, Saint Kavin was *plazed* with him, and thin it was that he made himself known to the king. 'And,' says he, 'King O'Toole, you're a decent man, for I only kem here to *thry you*. You don't know me,' says he, 'bekase I'm disguised.'

'Musha! thin,' says the king, 'who are you?'

'I'm Saint Kavin,' said the saint, blessin' himself.

'Oh, queen iv heaven!' says the king, makin' the sign 'o the crass betune his eyes, and fallin' down on his knees before the saint; 'is it the great Saint Kavin,' says he, 'that I've been discoorsin' all this time without knowin' it,' says he, 'all as one as if he was a lump iv a *gossoon*? – and so you're a saint?' says the king.

'I am,' says Saint Kavin.

'By gor, I thought I was only talking to a dacent boy,' says the king.

'Well, you know the differ now,' says the saint. 'I'm Saint Kavin,' says he, 'the greatest of all the saints.'

And so the king had his goose as good as new, to divart him as long as he lived: and the saint supported him afther he kem into his property, as I tould you, until the day iv his death – and that was soon afther; for the poor goose thought he was ketchin' a throut one Friday; but, my jewel, it was a mistake he made – and instead of a throut, it was a thievin' horse-eel; and by gor, instead iv the goose killin' a throut for the king's supper – by dad, the eel killed the king's goose – and small blame to him; but he didn't ate her, bekase he darn't ate what Saint Kavin laid his blessed hands on.

The Man that Sold his Soul
to the Devil

THERE was a man called Wullie Powers, a kind of pedlar, who was a terrible man for drink. One night he asked his wife for five shillings to go drinking. Porter only cost twopence a bottle, so she wouldn't give it him, and he said, 'If you don't give me money for a drink, I'll sell myself to the Devil for it.'

Next night he was crossing Craig Avon Bridge when he met a man who gave him five shillings. 'I've not seen you before,' he said to the man, and the man said, 'No; but you'll see me again'; but next day he was full of remorse, and went to the priest, and took the pledge. The priest told him never to say such a thing again.

For a while Wullie kept his pledge, but presently he slipped back and was worse than ever. One night he asked his wife for money, and she wouldn't give him any, and again he pledged himself to the Devil. He went out, and met the same man again, who gave him five shillings. He went on his way, and met another man, who offered him a job if he'd bring his cart along.

322

He said he'd do any job if he was paid for it.

So he took his cart along and was given a long box covered in black velvet. He was to leave it in a certain place, and say nothing about it. So he had a double amount to drink and went home to beat his wife up. He was so dangerous that she ran away, taking the children with her. But she came back when she thought he was asleep, and lay down in the next room. At midnight the door of Wullie's room opened and a man came in.

'Who are you?' said Wullie, still half drunk.

'Don't you know me?'

'You're the man that gave me the five shillings.'

'Yes, and I'm the man that gave you the black box. Don't you know who I am?'

'No.'

'I'm the one that you sold your soul to for five shillings. There was another soul in the black box, that never saw the light of day, nor ever will.'

With that, Wullie gave a screech like an animal. Rosie, his wife, heard him in the next room, and she ran out and fetched the neighbours. Wullie was lying on the bed like a piece of scorched bread. They buried him, but a child could have carried the coffin. There was nothing there but some black ashes.

The Crowza Stones

St Just, from his home in Penwith, being weary of having little to do, except offering prayers for the tinners and fishermen, went on to visit to the hospitable St Keverne, who had fixed his hermitage in a well-selected spot, not far from the Lizard headland. The holy brothers rejoiced together, and in full feeding and deep drinking they pleasantly passed the time. St Just gloried in the goodly chalice from which he drank the richest of wines, and envied St Keverne the possession of a cup of such rare value. Again and again did he pledge St Keverne; their holy bond of brotherhood was to be for ever; Heaven was to witness the purity of their friendship, and to the world they were to become patterns of ecclesiastical love.

The time came when St Just felt he must return to his flock; and repeating over again his vows, and begging St Keverne to return his visit, he departed – St Keverne sending many a blessing after his good brother.

The saint of the west had not left his brother of the south many hours before the latter missed his cup. Diligent search was made in every corner of his dwelling, but no cup could be found. At length St Keverne could not but feel that he had been robbed of his treasure by his western friend. That one in whom he had placed such confidence – one to whom he had opened his heart, and to whom he had shown the most unstinting hospitality – should have behaved so treacherously, overcame the serenity of the good man. His rage was excessive. After the first burst was over, and reason reasserted her power, St Keverne felt that his wisest course was to pursue the thief, inflict summary punishment on him, and recover his cup. The thought was followed by a firm resolve, and away St Keverne started in pursuit of St Just. Passing over Crowza Down, some of the boulders of 'Ironstone' which are scattered over the surface caught his eye, and presently he whipped a few of these stone pebbles into his pockets, and hastened onward.

When he drew near Tre-men-keverne he spied St Just. St Keverne worked himself up into a boiling rage, and toiled with increased speed up the hill, hallooing to the saintly thief, who pursued his way for some time in the well-assumed quiet of conscious innocence.

Long and loud did St Keverne call on St Just to stop, but the latter was deaf to all calls of the kind – on he went, quickening, however, his pace a little.

At length St Keverne came within a stone's throw of the dissembling culprit, and calling him a thief – adding thereto some of the most choice epithets from his holy vocabulary – taking a stone from his pocket, he let it fly after St Just.

The stone falling heavily by the side of St Just convinced him that he had to deal with an awkward enemy, and that he had best make all the use he could of his legs. He quietly untied the chalice, which he had fastened to his girdle, and let it fall to the ground. Then, still as if unconscious of his follower, he set off to run as fast as his ponderous body would allow his legs to carry him. St Keverne came up to where his cup glistened in the sunshine. He had recovered his treasure, he should get no good out of the false friend, and he was sadly jaded with his long run. Therefore he took, one by one, the stones from his pockets – he hurled them, fairly aimed, after the retreating culprit, and cursed him as he went.

There the pebbles remained where they fell – the peculiarity of the stone being in all respects unlike anything around, but being clearly the Crowza stones – attesting the truth of the legend; and their weights, each one being several hundred pounds, proving the power of the giant saint.

Many have been the attempts made to remove these stones. They are carried away easily enough by day, but they ever return to the spot on which they now repose, at night.

The Demon Cat

THERE was a woman in Connemara, the wife of a fisherman, and as he always had very good luck, she had plenty of fish at all times stored away in the house ready for market. But to her great annoyance she found that a great cat used to come in at night and devour all the best and finest fish. So she kept a big stick by her and determined to watch.

One day, as she and a woman were spinning together, the house suddenly became quite dark; and the door was burst open as if by the blast of a tempest, when in walked a huge black cat, who went straight up to the fire, then turned round and growled at them.

'Why, surely this is the devil!' said a young girl, who was by, sorting the fish.

'I'll teach you how to call me names,' said the cat; and, jumping at her, he scratched her arm till the blood came. 'There now,' he said, 'you will be more civil another time when a gentleman comes to see you.' And with that he walked over to the door and shut it close to prevent any of them going out, for the poor young girl, while crying loudly from fright and pain, had made a desperate rush to get away.

Just then a man was going by, and hearing the cries he pushed open the door and tried to get in, but the cat stood on the threshold and would let no one pass. On this, the man attacked him with his stick, and gave him a sound blow; the cat, however, was more than his match in the fight, for it flew at him and tore his face and hands so badly that the man at last took to his heels and ran away as fast as he could.

'Now it's time for my dinner,' said the cat, going up to examine the fish that was laid out on the tables. 'I hope the fish is good today. Now don't disturb me, nor make a fuss; I can help myself.' With that he jumped up and began to devour all the best fish, while he growled at the woman.

'Away, out of this, you wicked beast!' she cried, giving it a blow with the tongs that would have broken its back, only it was a devil; 'out of this! No fish shall you have today.'

But the cat only grinned at her, and went on tearing and spoiling and devouring the fish, evidently not a bit the worse for the blow. On this, both the women attacked it with sticks, and struck hard blows enough to kill it, on which the cat glared at them, and spit fire; then making a leap, it tore their hands and arms till the blood came, and the frightened women rushed shrieking from the house.

But presently the mistress returned, carrying with her a bottle of holy water; and looking in, she saw the cat still devouring the fish, and not minding. So she crept over quietly and threw the holy water on it without a word. No sooner was this done than a dense black smoke filled the place, through which nothing was seen but the two red eyes of the cat, burning like coals of fire. Then the smoke gradually cleared away, and she saw the body of the creature burning slowly till it became shrivelled and black like a cinder, and finally disappeared. And from that time the fish remained untouched and safe from harm, for the power of the Evil One was broken, and the demon cat was seen no more.

NCHANTMENT

Enchantment

Here are tales that are sometimes described as Folk Narratives or Märchen. The characters and events within them often reflect deeply-held folk beliefs but the tales themselves, with the possible exceptions of *Bewitched Butter* and *The Soul as a Butterfly*, are fictional concoctions, not recitals of things as they are believed to have happened. Within them, the everyday and the magical co-exist as easily as they do within a child's mind.

The tradition of *Three Heads of the Well*, which is broadly similar to Perrault's 'Diamonds and Toads', was known in England at least as early as the 16th century; in George Peele's comedy, *The Old Wives Tale* (1595), two daughters, one fair and one foul, go separately to a well and listen to the head that appears and says:

> *Gently dip, but not too deepe*
> *For feare you make the golden birde to weepe,*
> *Faire maiden white and red,*
> *Stroke me smoothe, and combe my head:*
> *And thou shalt have some cockell bread.*

The power of the severed head is of course a familiar motif in both primitive and civilised societies. Earlier this century, head-hunters in the Philippines needed heads to guarantee the success of their rice crops; in the *Tain*, we read how Irish warriors carried off the heads of their enemies, tied to their saddles; Odin cherishes and speaks to the head of wise Mimir; and Keats made use of the motif in *Isabella*.

The version printed here was abridged by James Orchard Halliwell (1820–89) from an unknown chapbook called the *Three Kings of Colchester*, and was one of the nineteen tales included in his *Popular Tales and Nursery Rhymes* (1849). Despite (or perhaps because of) a turbulent personal life, Halliwell made significant contributions to the saving and study of popular literature, sometimes working from earlier sources, sometimes collecting in the field, as well as being an expert on dialect and a Shakespearean scholar.

The Story of Tom Thumb is another tale that has been popular in England for several centuries. In *The Classic Fairy Tales*, Iona and Peter Opie survey its history from its first appearance in 1621 as a forty-page booklet, *The History of Tom Thumbe*, which they advance as 'the earliest extant printing of an English fairy tale'.

Tom himself, conjured up by Merlin, the enchanter-bard of Arthurian Romance, has his counterparts in the French tales of 'Le petit Poucet' and the German tales of 'Daumling', but shares only the isolated adventure with them. His picaresque adventures are here recounted by James Reeves whose *English Fables and Folk Stories* (1954) is probably, with Sybil Marshall, the best set of retellings in recent times.

It would be difficult to find an example of sheer gab to surpass Thomas Crofton Croker's *Daniel O'Rourke*. After a sober first paragraph, full of circumstantial detail, he rapidly accelerates into a power of enchanting nonsense, with marvellous exchanges between the imperious eagle and poor flummoxed Daniel. Crofton Croker (see p.9) commented in a footnote that 'The Castle of Carrigphooka, or the Phooka's Rock, beneath the walls of which O'Rourke was discovered by his wife, is doubtless the one of that name situated about two miles west of Macroom': it is a timely reminder that for all the tale's entertaining tissue of fantasy, its point of departure is that enduring folk belief that certain places (like certain times) have supernatural assocations.

We return to the world of the heroine with a cruel stepmother in *Rashin Coatie*, one of no less than 345 variants of the Cinderella-tale discussed by Marian Roalfe Cox in *Cinderella* (1893), the first comparative study of a folk-tale to be published in Great Britain. Perhaps the most striking feature of this version is the way in which the dying queen gives her daughter a red calf who will act as her surrogate mother, surely an echo of primitive belief in reincarnation in animal form.

Andrew Lang (1844–1912) collected the tale from Margaret Craig of Elgin and printed it in the quarterly review *Folk-Lore* in 1890. Lang was an energetic and brilliant polymath – a poet, Greek scholar, historian, biographer, novelist, critic and editor – whose greatest loves were folklore and anthropology. At his best in the cut and thrust of a debate, he was primarily a theorist out to show as a 'survivalist' (see p.137) how 'All peoples notoriously tell the same myths, fairy tales, fables, and improper stories, repeat the same proverbs, are amused by the same riddles or devinettes, and practise the same, or closely analogous, religious rites and mysteries'; and interested in exploring how the study of such material led directly to a better understanding of prehistoric and primitive cultures. His most influential work in the field of folklore was probably *Custom and Myth* (1901), his most popular the twelve colour *Fairy Books* in which so great a number of folk-tales were translated into English for the first time.

John Sampson (see p.136) collected *Frosty* in Romani, and the translation printed here is taken from *Gypsy Folk-Tales* (1948) compiled by Dora Yates, sometime Honorary Secretary of The Gypsy Lore Society. Miss Yates writes that 'an English rendering often fails to reflect the dignity and severe simplicity of the original tongue, and to reproduce in an uninflected vernacular the narrative style peculiar to most Gypsy idioms in Europe: a succession of short crisp sentences each consisting sometimes of but a single word strongly accented'. Nevertheless, this is a robust and convincing version of a tale of the same kind as Grimm's 'Die Bremen Musikanter' in which a small band of travelling animals or humans combines its wide range of talents to defeat the opposition at the end of the road.

That W. B. Yeats long made use of folklore in his poetry should not blind one to the fact that he has a distinguished place in the annals of Irish folklore. He had psychic experiences himself, he contributed to *Folk-Lore*, he mused on folk beliefs in *The Celtic Twilight*, with Lady Gregory he collected many tales in Galway and wrote sustained essays to accompany her subsequent publication of them, and he edited *Fairy and Folk Tales of the Irish Peasantry* (1888) and *Irish Fairy Tales* (1892).

I have included his *Bewitched Butter*, a tale from the county of Leix, in this section because it is clear that Yeats did not reproduce the tale as he heard it but added to it and made of it something more literary than oral. It was certainly believed as early as the twelfth century (Giraldus Cambrensis) that witches could turn themselves into hares and Christina Hole writes that 'Witch-hares were supposed to steal the milk of cows and sheep lying out in the fields'. The events described here must once have been taken at face value but here they are seen in transition, half way between legend and entertainment.

The same applies to the haunting tale of *The Soul as a Butterfly* (printed in Sean O'Sullivan's *Folktales of Ireland)* in which Peig Sayers (see p.110) displays wonderful artifice in building a brief fiction on the foundations of a folk belief also mentioned by her fellow Blasket-islander Maurice O'Sullivan in his *Twenty Years A'Growing*. The shamanistic idea that the spirit or soul can leave and return to the body is of course shared by many peoples.

Although the tale of the 'The Frog Prince' seems to have been known in Scotland for as long as *Three Heads of the Well* and *The Story of Tom Thumb* in England, it was first recorded by the Brothers Grimm ('Der Froschkönig'). The tale later attracted the attention of W. A. Clouston (see p.163) who turned up Icelandic, Gaelic, Turkish, Sanskrit and Kaffir analogues, and argued the connection between 'The Frog Prince' and the loathly lady of medieval Romance – the hag who could only be turned back into a beautiful maiden when a knight agreed to marry her and gave her a kiss. The tale also has much in common with 'Beauty and the Beast'. The version printed here, *The Paddo*, was collected by Robert Chambers (see p.138) from the antiquary Charles Sharpe who had heard it from his Annandale nurse in 1784.

Black Annis, says Ruth Tongue (see p.190) was 'told by an evacuee Leicester girl on 24 December 1941, as we ate our lunch of wartime sandwiches, sitting on a haymow in Hillfield Barn'. It is an admirably vivid and urgent tale that interestingly brings together elements encountered earlier in the anthology. It is a wicked stepmother, as in *Three Heads of the Well* and *Rashin Coatie*, who precipitates the action; the Christmas bells here play the same role as the invocation to Jesus in *The Bewitched Sixareen* and the holy water in *The Demon Cat*. Of the witch herself, Ruth Tongue notes that 'Black Annis is credited with being an early goddess. Traditionally she was a supernatural cannibal hag, but the *bleeding of the witch* places her well in mortal witch lore'. A stone with a hole in it (sometimes called a hag-stone or witch-stone) has long been considered a protection against witchcraft.

The last tale in the section is *The King o' the Cats*. This version was compiled by Joseph Jacobs from five variants, including one by Halliwell, and appears in his *More English Fairy Tales*. One can seldom look to Jacobs for sources recorded as they were heard, but always for cleverly-made versions and thoroughly helpful critical notes. Amongst folklorists, he is the supreme cobbler. Your editor has little time for cats and even less for their worshippers but, of all the many British folk-tales concerning the species, he finds this the most atmospheric and startling!

The Three Heads of the Well

LONG before Arthur and the Knights of the Round Table, there reigned in the eastern part of England a king who kept his court at Colchester. He was witty, strong, and valiant, by which means he subdued his enemies abroad, and secured peace among his subjects at home.

Nevertheless, in the midst of his glory, his queen died, leaving behind her an only daughter, about fifteen years of age. This lady, from her courtly carriage, beauty and affability, was the wonder of all that knew her; but, as covetousness is said to be the root of all evil, so it happened in this instance. The king, hearing of a lady who had likewise an only daughter, for the sake of her riches had a mind to marry; though she was old, ugly, hook-nosed, and humpbacked, yet all this could not deter him from marrying her. Her daughter, also, was a yellow dowdy, full of envy and ill-nature; and, in short, was much of the same mould as her mother. This signified nothing, for in a few weeks the king, attended by the nobility and gentry, brought his intended bride to his palace, where the marriage rites were performed.

336

They had not been long in the court before they set the king against his own beautiful daughter, which was done by false reports and accusations. The young princess, having lost her father's love, grew weary of the court, and one day meeting with her father in the garden, she desired him, with tears in her eyes, to give her a small subsistence, and she would go and seek her fortune; to which the king consented, and ordered her mother-in-law to make up a small sum according to her discretion. She went to the queen, who gave her a canvas bag of brown bread and hard cheese, with a bottle of beer. Though this was but a very pitiful dowry for a king's daughter, she took it, returned thanks, and proceeded on her journey, passing through groves, woods, and valleys, till at length she saw an old man sitting on a stone at the mouth of a cave, who said, 'Good morrow, fair maiden, whither away so fast?'

'Aged father,' says she, 'I am going to seek my fortune.'

'What hast thou in thy bag and bottle?'

'In my bag I have got bread and cheese, and in my bottle good small beer; will you please to partake of either?'

'Yes,' said he, 'with all my heart.'

With that the lady pulled out her provisions, and bid him eat and welcome. He did so, and gave her many thanks, saying thus: 'There is a thick thorny hedge before you, which will appear impassable; but take this wand in your hand, strike three times, and say, "Pray, hedge, let me come through," and it will open immediately; then, a little further, you will find a well; sit down on the brink of it, and there will come up three golden heads, which will speak: pray do whatever they require.'

Promising she would follow his directions, she took her leave of him. Arriving at the hedge, and pursuing the old man's directions, it divided, and gave her a passage: then, going to the well, she had no sooner sat down than a golden head came up singing –

'Wash me, and comb me,
And lay me down softly,

337

And lay me on a bank to dry,
That I may look pretty
When somebody comes by.'

'Yes,' said she, and putting forth her hand, with a silver comb performed the office, placing it upon a primrose bank.

Then came up a second and a third head, making the same request, which she complied with. She then pulled out her provisions and ate her dinner.

Then said the heads one to another, 'What shall we do for this lady who hath used us so kindly?'

The first said, 'I will cause such addition to her beauty as shall charm the most powerful prince in the world.'

The second said, 'I will endow her with such perfume, both in body and breath, as shall far exceed the sweetest flowers.'

The third said, 'My gift shall be none of the least, for, as she is a king's daughter, I'll make her so fortunate that she shall become queen to the greatest prince that reigns.'

This done, at their request she let them down into the well again, and so proceeded on her journey. She had not travelled long before she saw a king hunting in the park with his nobles; she would have avoided him, but the king having caught a sight of her, approached, and what with her beauty and perfumed breath, was so powerfully smitten, that he was not able to subdue his passion, but commenced his courtship immediately, and was so successful that he gained her love, and, conducting her to his palace, he caused her to be clothed in the most magnificent manner.

This being ended, and the king finding that she was the King of Colchester's daughter, ordered some chariots to be got ready, that he might pay the king a visit. The chariot in which the king and queen rode was adorned with rich ornamental gems of gold. The king, her father, was at first astonished that his daughter had been so fortunate as she was, till the young king made him sensible of all that happened. Great was the joy at court amongst all, with the exception of the queen and her club-footed daughter, who were ready to burst with malice, and envied her happiness; and the greater was their madness because she was now above them all. Great rejoicings, with feasting and dancing, continued many days. Then at length, with the dowry her father gave her, they returned home.

The deformed daughter perceiving that her sister had been so happy in seeking her fortune, would needs do the same; so disclosing her mind to her mother, all preparations were made, and she was furnished not only with rich apparel, but sweet-meats, sugar, almonds, etc., in great quantities, and a large bottle of Malaga sack. Thus provided, she went the same road as her sister, and coming near the cave, the old man said, 'Young woman, whither so fast?'

'What is that to you?' said she.

'Then', said he, 'what have you in your bag and bottle?'

She answered, 'Good things, which you shall not be troubled with.'

'Won't you give me some?' said he.

'No, not a bit, nor a drop, unless it would choke you.'

The old man frowned, saying, 'Evil fortune attend thee.'

Going on, she came to the hedge, through which she espied a gap, and thought to pass through it, but, going in, the hedge closed, and the thorns ran into her flesh, so that it was with great difficulty that she got out. Being now in a painful condition, she searched for water to wash herself, and, looking round, she saw the well; she sat down on the brink of it, and one of the heads came up, saying, 'Wash me, comb me, and lay me down softly, etc.' but she banged it with her bottle, saying, 'Take this for your washing.'

So the second and third heads came up, and met with no better treatment than the first; whereupon the heads consulted among themselves what evils to plague her with for such usage.

The first said, 'Let her be struck with leprosy in her face.'

The second, 'Let an additional smell be added to her breath.'

The third bestowed on her a husband, though but a poor country cobbler.

This done she goes on till she came to a town, and it being market day, the people looked at her, and seeing such an evil face, fled out of her sight, all but a poor country cobbler (who not long before had mended the shoes of an old hermit, who having no money, gave him a box of ointment for the cure of the leprosy, and a bottle of spirits for a bad breath). Now the cobbler having a mind to do an act of charity, was induced to go up to her and ask her who she was.

'I am', said she, 'the King of Colchester's daughter-in-law.'

'Well,' said the cobbler, 'if I restore you to your natural complexion, and make a sound cure both in face and breath, will you in reward take me for a husband?'

'Yes, friend,' replied she, 'with all my heart.'

With this the cobbler applied the remedies, and they worked the effect in a few weeks, and then they were married, and after a few days they set forward for the court of Colchester.

When the queen understood she had married a poor cobbler, she fell into distraction, and hanged herself for vexation. The death of the queen was not a source of sorrow to the king, who had only married her for her fortune, and bore her no affection; and shortly afterwards he gave the cobbler £100 to take the daughter to a remote part of the kingdom, where he lived many years mending shoes, while his wife assisted the housekeeping by spinning, and selling the results of her labour at the country market.

The Story of Tom Thumb

IN THE DAYS of King Arthur there lived a famous magician called Merlin. One day, when he was travelling the country disguised as a beggar, he stopped at the cottage of a poor ploughman to ask for food. The ploughman had just come in from work, and was sitting down to supper. He was very tired, but he welcomed the stranger, even though this was only a ragged beggar man; and the ploughman's wife said he could sit down and share their supper.

Now Merlin noticed that the ploughman and his wife, though they had a snug cottage and enough to eat, did not seem happy.

'What is the matter?' he asked. 'What is it you lack?'

'Why,' said the ploughman's wife, 'my husband and I have lived here happily enough for nearly twenty years, but we have no child. This is a great sorrow to us. How I should love to have had a son – yes, even a little son no bigger than my husband's thumb. However small he was, I should not mind, just so as I could call him my own and look after him.'

Well, the beggar said nothing, and soon afterwards took his

leave. But thinking over what the poor woman had said, Merlin said to himself, 'What a good idea to give this woman just what she wants.' So by magic he brought it about that the plough-man's wife had a little boy no bigger than the ploughman's thumb. They loved him dearly and named him Tom Thumb, and he never grew an inch bigger, but was always just the same size as his father's thumb.

One moonlight night the Fairy Queen happened to look in at the window of the cottage. She flew inside and kissed Tom, and ordered her fairies to make him a suit of clothes. They made him a shirt of spider's web, a jacket of thistledown, trousers of feathers, stockings of apple peel, and a little pair of shoes of mouse-skin, with the fur on the inside. Then on top of his head was placed an oak-leaf cap; and these were the clothes that Tom wore, winter and summer, greatly to the admiration of his mother and all the neighbours round about.

As he grew older, Tom was full of tricks. He used to play at cherry-stones with the boys from the village. When he had no stone of his own, he would creep into the bags belonging to the boys and steal their stones. One sharp-eyed lad caught sight of him doing this, and just as Tom had got his head inside the boy's bag, he pulled the string tight and made Tom howl with pain.

'That'll serve you right for stealing!' said the boy with the bag.

'I'll never steal again!' cried Tom. 'Only let me out, and I'll never steal again!'

So Tom was let out; and – for a time at least – he stole no more cherry-stones.

Tom was so small that, although his mother loved him dearly, she sometimes lost sight of him, especially when she was busy. One day she was making a batter pudding and chanced to leave the kitchen for a moment. Tom climbed on to the edge of the basin to see what was inside; his foot slipped, and splash! he fell right into the batter. His mother poured the mixture into the pan and began cooking it. Tom's mouth was so full of the pudding that he could not call out, but he kicked and struggled for all he was worth.

'Well, now,' said Tom's mother, 'I do declare that pudding is bewitched. An evil spirit has got into it, and it's good for nothing.'

So she tipped the pudding out of the window. Just then a tinker happened to be passing, and being hungry, he thought the pudding would do for his dinner. So he picked it up and put it in his wallet. But by this time Tom had got his mouth free of the batter and began to hollo out loud.

'Oh, my!' said the tinker. 'Now what's got into my bag, I wonder? 'Tis some evil spirit come to frighten me for picking up that pudding.'

So without looking into his wallet, he opened it as quickly as he could and tipped everything out, Tom and pudding and all. Shaking the rest of the batter from his clothes and picking up his oak-leaf cap, which had fallen off, Tom ran home as fast as he could. His mother was overjoyed at seeing him again, gave him a good wash in a teacup full of warm water, kissed him, and put him to bed.

Next day his mother took him out to the field with her when she went to milk the cow. It was a windy day, and she was afraid the little boy would get blown away. So while she did her milking, she tied him to a thistle. But the cow, seeing only his oak-leaf cap, thought she would like a tasty mouthful, so she gobbled up the thistle and Tom as well. Inside the cow's mouth Tom was terrified of the two great rows of teeth, so he called out with all his might:

'Mother, mother! Help, help!'

'Where are you?' cried his mother, getting up from her milking-stool and looking round for the thistle where she had tied her son for safety.

'Here!' called Tom. 'Inside the cow's mouth!'

But the cow was so surprised to hear a shrill voice coming from inside her own mouth that she opened her jaws and let Tom fall. As luck would have it, his mother held out her apron and caught Tom just in time.

Tom's next adventure happened when he was out in the fields

driving the cattle along with a whip which his father had made him of a barley straw. He slipped on some rough ground and fell into a furrow. Before he could pick himself up, a great black raven flew down and carried him off in her beak. Away she flew over hills and valleys until she came to the sea – and there she dropped him.

Down and down fell Tom Thumb, till at last he struck the water. Then snap! – a great fish with wide-open jaws swallowed him up in a moment and carried him out to sea. But a fishing-boat caught up the fish in its nets, and next day this very fish, and Tom inside, was brought to the court of King Arthur himself. When the cook cut open the fish to prepare it for the King's dinner, how surprised she was to find Tom inside! Alive and well he was, though a little frightened at his adventure; and all the scullions and the kitchen-maids gathered round to look at him. Then the cook took him up to the King himself; and there stood Tom, on the King's own table, bowing and taking off his oak-leaf hat to all the ladies and the knights of the Round Table. Everyone laughed and clapped hands, and Tom was made the King's dwarf and became a great favourite. They all wondered where he had come from. Only Merlin, the magician, could tell, but he said nothing.

'Tell me what your parents are like,' said the King to Tom one day. 'Are they little folk, just like yourself?'

'Why, no,' said Tom, 'my father and mother are poor labouring folk, just like those who work in your fields. They are no bigger and no smaller than others are; but perhaps they are poorer than most.'

'Well,' said the King, who was very fond of Tom, 'go into my treasury, where I keep all my money, and take as much gold or silver as you can carry. Go home with it, and give it to your poor father and mother.'

So Tom went to King Arthur's treasury with a bag made from a water bubble. But all he could get into the bag was a silver threepenny piece, and even this was almost too heavy for him. Away he trudged with his load on his back, and it took him two days and two nights to reach home. His mother and father were delighted to see him, and they cooked a fine meal and made much of him, for he was nearly dead with weariness after carrying the silver piece so far. They were proud to have the silver piece, especially when they knew it was a present from King Arthur himself; and many an evening he spent telling them of his adventures at court and what a great favourite he was with all the lords and ladies.

After a few weeks, he kissed them goodbye and went back to the King's castle, for he was afraid the King would be missing his dwarf; and very pleased they all were at court to see him again. There is no time to tell all the adventures that befell him after that; but we will finish by describing how King Arthur made him one of his knights.

First he must have a new suit, for his other clothes, that he had had from the Fairy Queen, had become torn and ragged from his adventures in the batter pudding and the cow's mouth and the great fish. So the court tailors were ordered to make him a new coat of butterflies' wings, and the royal boot-maker made him a pair of boots of chicken hide. Then he was knighted before the assembled court and given a needle for a sword and a sleek white mouse for a horse. And on fine days he would go hunting with all the courtiers, his sword by his side, and his mouse steed trotting beneath him.

The King also had a chair of state made for him so that he might sit on the royal table and amuse the Queen at meal times; and a little gold palace was made for him to live in with a great door an inch wide. But for all his finery Sir Thomas Thumb, as he was now called, never forgot his humble parents. Once a month he rode off on his white mouse to their cottage in the country and amused the old folks with tales and talk from the court of King Arthur. So that the poor ploughman and his wife had good cause to be proud of the little son they had been given through the magic of the great Merlin, whom they had entertained unknown, years ago, in the form of an old and tattered beggar.

Daniel O'Rourke

PEOPLE may have heard of the renowned adventures of Daniel O'Rourke, but how few are there who know that the cause of all his perils, above and below, was neither more nor less than his having slept under the walls of the Phooka's tower. I knew the man well: he lived at the bottom of Hungry Hill, just at the right-hand side of the road as you go towards Bantry. An old man was he, at the time that he told me the story, with grey hair and a red nose; and it was on 25 June 1813 that I heard it from his own lips, as he sat smoking his pipe under the old poplar tree, on as fine an evening as ever shone from the sky. I was going to visit the caves in Dursey Island, having spent the morning at Glengariff.

'I am often *axed* to tell it, sir,' said he, 'so that this is not the first time. The master's son, you see, had come from beyond foreign parts in France and Spain, as young gentlemen used to go, before Buonaparte or any such was heard of; and sure enough there was a dinner given to all the people on the ground, gentle and simple, high and low, rich and poor. The *ould* gentlemen were the gentlemen after all, saving your honour's presence. They'd swear at a body a little, to be sure, and, may be, give one a cut of a whip now and then, but we were no losers by it in the end; and they were so easy and civil, and kept such rattling houses, and thousands of welcomes – and there was no grinding for rent, and few agents; and there was hardly a tenant on the estate that did not taste of his landlord's bounty often and often in a year; but now it's another thing: no matter for that, sir, for I'd better be telling you my story.

'Well, we had everything of the best, and plenty of it; and we ate, and we drank, and we danced, and the young master by the same token danced with Peggy Barry, from the Bohereen – a lovely young couple they were, though they are both low enough now. To make a long story short, I got, as a body may say, the same thing as tipsy almost, for I can't remember ever at all, no ways, how it was I left the place; only I did leave it, that's certain. Well, I thought, for all that, in myself, I'd just step to Molly Cronohan's, the fairy woman, to speak a word about the bracket heifer that was bewitched; and so as I was crossing the stepping-stones of the ford at Ballyashenogh, and was looking up at the stars and blessing myself – for why? it was Lady Day – I missed my foot, and souse I fell into the water. "Death alive!" thought I, "I'll be drowned now!" However, I began swimming, swimming, swimming away for the dear life, till at last I got ashore, somehow or other, but never the one of me can tell how, upon a *dissolute* island.

'I wandered and wandered about there, without knowing where I wandered, until at last I got into a big bog. The moon was shining as bright as day, or your fair lady's eyes, sir (with your pardon for mentioning her), and I looked east and west, and north and south, and every way, and nothing did I see but bog, bog, bog – I could never find out how I got into it; and my heart grew cold with fear, for sure and certain I was that it would be my *berrin* place. So I sat down upon a stone which, as good luck would have it, was close by me, and I began to scratch my head, and sing the *Ullagone* – when all of a sudden the moon grew black, and I looked up, and saw something for all the world as if it was moving down between me and it, and I could not tell

347

what it was. Down it came with a pounce, and looked at me full in the face; and what was it but an eagle? as fine a one as ever flew from the kingdom of Kerry. So he looked at me in the face, and says he to me, "Daniel O'Rourke," says he, "how do you do?"

'"Very well, I thank you, sir," says I: "I hope you're well;" wondering out of my senses all the time how an eagle came to speak like a Christian.

'"What brings you here, Dan?" says he.

'"Nothing at all, sir," says I: "only I wish I was safe home again."

'"Is it out of the island you want to go, Dan?" says he.

'"'Tis, sir," says I: so I up and told him how I had taken a drop too much, and fell into the water; how I swam to the island; and how I got into the bog and did not know my way out of it.

'"Dan," says he, after a minute's thought, "though it is very improper for you to get drunk on Lady Day, yet as you are a decent sober man, who 'tends mass well, and never flings stones at me or mine, nor cries out after us in the fields – my life for yours," says he; "so get up on my back, and grip me well for fear you'd fall off, and I'll fly you out of the bog."

'"I am afraid," says I, "your honour's making game of me; for who ever heard of riding a horseback on an eagle before?"

'"'Pon the honour of a gentleman," says he, putting his right foot on his breast, "I am quite in earnest: and so now either take my offer or starve in the bog – besides, I see that your weight is sinking the stone."

'It was true enough as he said, for I found the stone every minute going from under me. I had no choice; so thinks I to myself, faint heart never won fair lady, and this is fair persuadance: "I thank your honour," says I, "for the loan of your civility; and I'll take your kind offer."

'I therefore mounted upon the back of the eagle, and held him tight enough by the throat, and up he flew in the air like a lark. Little I knew the trick he was going to serve me. Up – up – up, God knows how far up he flew. "Why then," said I to him – thinking he did not know the right road home – very civilly, because why? – I was in his power entirely – "sir," says I, "please your honour's glory, and with humble submission to your better judgment, if you'd fly down a bit, you're now just over my cabin, and I could be put down there, and many thanks to your worship."

'"*Arrah*, Dan," said he, "do you think me a fool? Look down in the next field, and don't you see two men and a gun? By my word it would be no joke to be shot this way, to oblige a drunken blackguard that I picked up off of a *could* stone in a bog."

'"Bother you," said I to myself, but I did not speak out, for where was the use? Well, sir, up he kept, flying, flying, and I asking him every minute to fly down, and all to no use. "Where in the world are you going, sir?" says I to him.

'"Hold your tongue, Dan," says he: "mind your own business, and don't be interfering with the business of other people."

'"Faith, this is my business, I think," says I.

'"Be quiet, Dan," says he: so I said no more.

'At last where should we come to, but to the moon itself. Now you can't see it from this, but there is, or there was in my time, a reaping-hook sticking out of the side of the moon, this way, (drawing the figure thus ⟲ on the ground with the end of his stick.)

'"Dan," said the eagle, "I'm tired with this long fly; I had no notion 'twas so far."

'"And my lord, sir," said I, "who in the world *axed* you to fly so far – was it I? Did not I beg, and pray, and beseech you to stop half an hour ago?"

'"There's no use talking, Dan," said he; "I'm tired bad enough, so you must get off, and sit down on the moon until I rest myself."

'"Is it sit down on the moon?" said I; "is it upon that little round thing, then? why, then, sure I'd fall off in a minute, and be *kilt* and split, and smashed all to bits: you are a vile deceiver – so you are."

'"Not at all, Dan," said he: "you can catch fast hold of the reaping-hook that's sticking out of the side of the moon, and 'twill keep you up."

'"I won't, then," said I.

'"May be not," said he, quite quiet. "If you don't, my man, I shall just give you a shake, and one slap of my wing, and send you down to the ground, where every bone in your body will be smashed as small as a drop of dew on a cabbage-leaf in the morning."

'"Why, then, I'm in a fine way," said I to myself, "ever to have come along with the likes of you;" and so giving him a hearty curse in Irish, for fear he'd know what I said, I got off his back with a heavy heart, took hold of the reaping-hook, and sat down upon the moon, and a mighty cold seat it was, I can tell you that.

'When he had me there fairly landed, he turned about on me, and said, "Good morning to you, Daniel O'Rourke," said he: "I think I've nicked you fairly now. You robbed my nest last year," ('twas true enough for him, but how he found it out is hard to say,) "and in return you are freely welcome to cool your heels dangling upon the moon like a cockthrow."

'"Is that all, and is this the way you leave me, you brute, you?" says I. "You ugly unnatural *baste*, and is this the way you serve me at last? Bad luck to yourself, with your hook'd nose, and to all your breed, you blackguard." 'Twas all to no manner of use: he spread out his great big wings, burst out a laughing, and flew away like lightning. I bawled after him to stop; but I might have called and bawled for ever, without his minding me. Away he went, and I never saw him from that day to this – sorrow fly away with him! You may be sure I was in a disconsolate condition, and kept roaring out for the bare grief, when all at once a door opened right in the middle of the moon, creaking on its hinges as if it had not been opened for a month before, I suppose they never thought of greasing 'em, and out there walks – who do you think but the man in the moon himself? I knew him by his bush.

350

'"Good morrow to you, Daniel O'Rourke," said he: "how do you do?"

'"Very well, thank your honour," said I. "I hope your honour's well."

'"What brought you here, Dan?" said he. So I told him how I was a little overtaken in liquor at the master's, and how I was cast on a *dissolute* island, and how I lost my way in the bog, and how the thief of an eagle promised to fly me out of it, and how instead of that he had fled me up to the moon.

'"Dan," said the man in the moon, taking a pinch of snuff when I was done, "you must not stay here."

'"Indeed, sir," says I, "'tis much against my will I'm here at all; but how am I to go back?"

'"That's your business," said he, "Dan: mine is to tell you that here you must not stay, so be off in less than no time."

'"I'm doing no harm," says I, "only holding on hard by the reaping-hook, lest I fall off."

'"That's what you must not do, Dan," says he.

'"Pray, sir," says I, "may I ask how many you are in family, that you would not give a poor traveller lodging: I'm sure 'tis not so often you're troubled with strangers coming to see you, for 'tis a long way.'

'"I'm by myself, Dan," says he; "but you'd better let go the reaping-hook "

'"Faith, and with your leave," says I, "I'll not let go the grip, and the more you bids me, the more I won't let go – so I will."

'"You had better, Dan," says he again.

'"Why, then, my little fellow," says I, taking the whole weight of him with my eye from head to foot, "there are two words to that bargain; and I'll not budge, but you may if you like."

'"We'll see how that is to be," says he; and back he went, giving the door such a great bang after him (for it was plain he was huffed) that I thought the moon and all would fall down with it.

'Well, I was preparing myself to try strength with him, when back again he comes, with the kitchen cleaver in his hand, and without saying a word he gives two bangs to the handle of the reaping-hook that was keeping me up, and *whap!* it came in two. "Good morning to you, Dan," says the spiteful little old black-guard, when he saw me cleanly falling down with a bit of the handle in my hand; "I thank you for your visit, and fair weather after you, Daniel."

I had not time to make any answer to him, for I was tumbling over and over, and rolling and rolling at the rate of a fox-hunt.

"God help me," says I, "but this is a pretty pickle for a decent man to be seen in at this time of night: I am now sold fairly." The word was not out of my mouth, when whiz! what should fly by close to my ear but a flock of wild geese; all the way from my own bog of Ballyasheenough, else how should they know *me*? The *ould* gander, who was their general, turning about his head, cried out to me, "Is that you, Dan?"

'"The same," said I, not a bit daunted now at what he said, for I was by this time used to all kinds of *bedevilment*, and, besides, I knew him of *ould*.

'"Good morrow to you," says he, "Daniel O'Rourke: how are you in health this morning?"

'"Very well, sir," says I, "I thank you kindly," drawing my breath, for I was mightily in want of some. "I hope your honour's the same."

'"I think 'tis falling you are, Daniel," says he.

'"You may say that, sir," says I.

'"And where are you going all the way so fast?" said the gander. So I told him how I had taken the drop, and how I came on the island, and how I lost my way in the bog, and how the thief of an eagle flew me up to the moon, and how the man in the moon turned me out. "Dan," said he, "I'll save you: put out your hand and catch me by the leg, and I'll fly you home."

'"Sweet is your hand in a pitcher of honey, my jewel," says I, though all the time I thought within myself that I don't much trust you; but there was no help, so I caught the gander by the leg, and away I and the other geese flew after him as fast as hops.

'We flew, and we flew, and we flew, until we came right over the wide ocean. I knew it well, for I saw Cape Clear to my right hand, sticking up out of the water. "Ah my lord," said I to the goose, for I thought it best to keep a civil tongue in my head any way, "fly to land if you please."

'"It is impossible, you see, Dan," said he, "for a while, because you see we are going to Arabia."

'"To Arabia!" said I; "that's surely some place in foreign parts, far away. Oh! Mr Goose: why then, to be sure, I'm a man to be pitied among you."

'"Whist, whist, you fool," said he, "hold your tongue; I tell you Arabia is a very decent sort of place, as like West Carbery as one egg is like another, only there is a little more sand there."

'Just as we were talking, a ship hove in sight, scudding so beautiful before the wind: "Ah! then, sir," said I, "will you drop me on the ship, if you please?"

'"We are not fair over it," said he.

'"We are," said I.

'"We are not," said he: "If I dropped you now you would go splash into the sea."

'"I would not," says I: "I know better than that, for it is just clean under us, so let me drop now at once."

'"If you must, you must," said he; "there, take your own way;" and he opened his claw, and faith he was right – sure enough I came down plump into the very bottom of the salt sea! Down to the very bottom I went, and I gave myself up then for ever, when a whale walked up to me, scratching himself after his night's sleep, and looked me full in the face, and never the word did he say, but lifting up his tail, he splashed me all over again with the cold salt water till there wasn't a dry stitch upon my whole carcass; and I heard somebody saying – 'twas a voice I knew too – "Get up, you drunken brute, off of that;" and with that I woke up, and there was Judy with a tub full of water, which she was splashing all over me – for, rest her soul! though she was a good wife, she never could bear to see me in drink, and had a bitter hand of her own.

'"Get up," said she again: "and of all places in the parish would no place *sarve* your turn to lie down upon but under the *ould* walls of Carrigaphooka? an uneasy resting I am sure you had of it." And sure enough I had; for I was fairly bothered out of my senses with eagles, and men of the moons, and flying ganders, and whales, driving me through bogs, and up to the moon, and down to the bottom of the green ocean. If I was in drink ten times over, long would it be before I'd lie down in the same spot again, I know that.'

Rashin Coatie

THERE was a king and a queen, as mony ane's been few have we seen and as few may we see, and the queen she deeit, and left a bonnie little lassie; and she had naething tae gie the wee lassie but a little red calfy, and she tellt the lassie whatever she wanted the calfy would gie her.

The king married again, an ill-natured wife, wi' three ugly dochters o' her ain. They didna like the little lassie, because she was bonnie; they took awa' a' her braw claes that her ain mither had geen her, and put a rashen coatie on her, and gart her sit in the kitchen neuk, an' a'body ca'd her Rashin Coatie. She didna get anything to eat but what the rest left, but she didna care, for she went to her red calfie, and it gave her everything she asked for. She got good meat from the calfy, but her ill stepmother gart the calfie be killed, because it was good to Rashin Coatie. She was very sorry for the calfie, and sat down and grat. The dead calfy said to her:

> 'Tak me up, bane by bane,
> And pit me aneath yon grey stane,

355

and whatever you want, come and seek it frae me, and I will
give you it.'

Yuletide came, and the rest put on their braw claes, and was
gaen awa' to the kirk. Rashin Coatie said, 'Oh, I would like to
gang to the kirk too!' but the others said, 'What would you do at
the kirk, you nasty thing? You must bide at hame and make the
dinner.'

When they were gone to the kirk, Rashin Coatie did na ken
how to make the dinner, but she went up to the grey stone, and
she told the calf that she could not make the dinner, and she
wanted to win to the kirk. The calfie gave her braw claes, and
bade her gang into the house and say:

> '*Every peat gar ither burn,*
> *Every spit gar ither turn,*
> *Every pot gar ither play,*
> *Till I come frae the kirk this guid Yule day.*'

Rashin Coatie put on the braw claes that the calfy gave her,
and went awa' to the kirk, and she was the grandest and the
brawest lady there. There was a young prince in the kirk, and he
fell in love with her. She cam' awa' before the blessing, and she
was home before the rest, and had off her braw claes, and had
on her rashin coatie, and the calfy had covered the table, and the
dinner was ready and everything in good order when the rest
cam' hame. The three sisters said to Rashin Coatie, 'Oh, lassie, if
you had only seen the braw lady that was in the kirk today, that
the young prince fell in love with!'

She said: 'Oh, I wish ye would let me gang with you to the
kirk tomorrow!' For they used to gang three days after ither to
the kirk.

They said: 'What should the like o' you do at the kirk, nasty
thing? The kitchen work is good enough for you.'

The next day they went away and left her, but she went back
to her calfy, and he bade her repeat the same words as before,
and he gave her braver claes, and she went back to the kirk, and
a' the world was looking at her, and wondering where sic a

grand lady came from; and as for the young prince, he fell more in love with her than ever, and bade somebody watch where she went back to. But she was back afore anybody saw her, and had off her braw claes, and on her rashin coatie, and the calfy had the table covered, and everything ready for the dinner.

The next day the calfy dressed her in brawer claes than ever, and she went back to the kirk. The young prince was there, and he put a guard at the door to keep her, but she jumped over their heads, and lost one of her beautiful satin slippers. She got hame before the rest, and had on the rashin coatie, and the calfy had all things ready. The young prince put out a proclamation that he would marry whoever the satin slipper would fit. All ladies of the land went to try on the slipper, and with the rest the three sisters, but none would it fit, for they had ugly broad feet. The henwife took in her daughter, and cut off her heels and her toes, and the slipper was forced on her, and the prince was to marry her, for he must keep his promise. As he rode along to the kirk with her behind him, a bird began to sing, and ever it sang:

> 'Minched fit and pinched fit
> Beside the King she rides,
> But braw fit, and bonny fit,
> In the kitchen neuk she hides.'

The prince said, 'What is that the bird sings?'

And the henwife said: 'Nasty lying thing! Never mind what it says;' but the bird sang ever the same words. The prince said: 'Oh, there must be someone that the slipper has not been tried on.'

But they said, 'There is none but a poor thing that sits in the kitchen neuk, and wears a rashin coatie.'

But the prince was determined to try it on Rashin Coatie, and she ran awa' to the grey stone, where the red calfy dressed her yet brawer than ever, and she went to the prince, and the slipper jumped out of his pocket and on to her foot, and the prince married her, and they lived happily all their days.

357

Frosty

AN OLD man was strolling along the road with his hat cocked on one side. His name was Frosty. He had walked half a mile, when he met another man. This man was lying on his belly with his ear to the ground.

'What are thou doing here, thou fool?' asked Frosty.

'I am no fool. I am listening to the Members of Parliament making speeches in London.'

'Thou wilt be of use, come with me. Thou has excellent hearing.'

The two walked on down the road. They met another man with a gun on his shoulder

'What are thou doing there?'

'Dost thou not see what I am doing? There is a fly upon a rock in America: I am going to shoot it.'

'Thou wilt be of use, come with us.'

And the three went on until they met another man.

'What are thou doing there?' asked Frosty.

'There is a mill far away over yonder, and there is no wind: I am blowing the sails round.'

'Thou wilt be of use. Wilt thou come with us?' The man went with them.

They walked along until they met another man carrying one of his legs under his arm.

'Why dost thou do that?'

'I have pulled my leg off lest I should run too fast.'

'Oh, thou must come with us.'

They went on, and presently saw another man carrying a huge tree upon his shoulder: a great powerful man was he.

At last they came to a town. They heard the talk of the king's court – that he had an old witch who was a swift runner, and that a great reward was offered to whatever man could beat her. 'Let us go up to the palace', said Frosty.

They went up to the palace, and Frosty and the king had a parley about the race. 'I have a man who will run with her', said he. The whole band slept in the palace that night.

They arose betimes. This was the morning on which Run-well and the witch were to have their race. They began to run. 'Wait a bit, the old witch is beating him,' exclaimed Shoot-well to Frosty. So he shot a dart into her knee, and Run-well beat the witch.

The king was furious at this. 'Who are these men?' said he to himself.

The old witch counselled the king: 'Tomorrow, proclaim that thou desirest the lake in front of the palace to be drained dry.' Now the six were sleeping in the palace again that night, and Hear-well overheard this talk. He told Frosty what was going to happen.

They arose betimes. The king came and told them that he wanted the lake drained on the following morning. The day dawned, and out they went, every one of them. Frosty summoned Blow-well. Blow-well blew the lake dry; he blew all the mud and stones out of it and left it bare.

The old king did not know how to deal with them. They had beaten the witch hollow. 'I will lodge them in my old iron chamber and kindle a great fire beneath it until it grows as hot as an oven, and I will burn them to death.'

Night fell. The old king summoned the six men, and threw open the door of this chamber. 'Wouldst thou like to sleep here tonight, Frosty?'

Frosty entered. 'Yes, we will sleep here; it seems a warm room.'

The old King smiled. 'Yes, it is a warm room, and it will be warmer still presently.'

In went Frosty and his men.

'We shall sleep snugly here.'

They sat down, and talked a little before settling to sleep. The room grew hotter and hotter. Presently it became too hot to stop in. So Frosty cocked his hat on the other side. The men were chilled to the bone, and began to shiver. When they were half dead with cold, Frosty tilted his hat up a very little. Then the room grew cool, and the six lay down and slept.

The old King came in the morning to look for them. He was amazed to find them alive. He called them outside. 'Go over there and get your breakfast', said he. When they had finished their meal, he returned, and said: 'I want a ship built upon that lake. I want to see it before the door tomorrow morning.'

Morning dawned, and the ship had been built. 'I want the ship to sail with no water beneath it.' Frosty summoned Blowwell. He blew the ship out of sight, until none could see it.

The king asked Frosty: 'How much money dost thou want to be off?'

'As much as one of my servants can carry.'

'Thou shalt have it', quoth the king.

And here comes Strong-man with a huge sack. He opened the mouth of the sack. He half filled it. 'That is as much as thou canst carry', said the King.

Strong-man lifted the sack in his hand. 'Dost thou call this trifle heavy? Fill it.'

The old king looked angrily at him. He filled the sack. 'I have filled it now: there, take it, and be off, and do ye never come here any more.' They took the gold and departed.

When they had gone the old king was beside himself with

grief at the loss of all this treasure. He sent his soldiers after them. Hear-well heard them coming. 'Wait a moment, I hear an army pursuing us.' The men halted and looked behind them. 'Do not fear,' said Frosty. The soldiers drew near to them. Frosty cocked his hat on one side. The soldiers were rooted to the spot: they were so benumbed with cold, they could not stir.

Then old Frosty paid off all his men. He went home alone to his native village, and bought a little house for himself.

And there he lives to this day, and is doing well. And the Woods went there and played the fiddle for him.

Bewitched Butter

ABOUT the commencement of the last century there lived in the vicinity of the once famous village of Aghavoe* a wealthy farmer, named Bryan Costigan. This man kept an extensive dairy and a great many milch cows, and every year made considerable sums by the sale of milk and butter. The luxuriance of the pasture lands in this neighbourhood has always been proverbial; and, consequently, Bryan's cows were the finest and most productive in the country, and his milk and butter the richest and sweetest, and brought the highest price at every market at which he offered these articles for sale.

Things continued to go thus prosperously with Bryan Costigan, when, one season, all at once, he found his cattle declining in appearance, and his dairy almost entirely profitless. Bryan, at first, attributed this change to the weather, or some such cause, but soon found or fancied reasons to assign it to a far different source. The cows, without any visible disorder, daily declined, and were scarcely able to crawl about on their pasture: many of

*The field of kine.

362

them, instead of milk, gave nothing but blood; and the scanty quantity of milk which some of them continued to supply was so bitter that even the pigs would not drink it; whilst the butter which it produced was of such a bad quality, and stunk so horribly, that the very dogs would not eat it. Bryan applied for remedies to all the quacks and 'fairy-women' in the country – but in vain. Many of the impostors declared that the mysterious malady in his cattle went beyond *their* skill; whilst others, although they found no difficulty in tracing it to superhuman agency, declared that they had no control in the matter, as the charm under the influence of which his property was made away with, was too powerful to be dissolved by anything less than the special interposition of Divine Providence. The poor farmer became almost distracted; he saw ruin staring him in the face; yet what was he to do? Sell his cattle and purchase others! No; that was out of the question, as they looked so miserable and emaciated, that no one would even take them as a present, whilst it was also impossible to sell to a butcher, as the flesh of one which he killed for his own family was as black as a coal, and stunk like any putrid carrion.

The unfortunate man was thus completely bewildered. He knew not what to do; he became moody and stupid; his sleep forsook him by night, and all day he wandered about the fields, amongst his 'fairy-stricken' cattle like a maniac.

Affairs continued in this plight, when one very sultry evening in the latter days of July, Bryan Costigan's wife was sitting at her own door, spinning at her wheel, in a very gloomy and agitated state of mind. Happening to look down the narrow green lane which led from the high road to her cabin, she espied a little old woman barefoot, and enveloped in an old scarlet cloak, approaching slowly, with the aid of a crutch which she carried in one hand, and a cane or walking-stick in the other. The farmer's wife felt glad at seeing the odd-looking stranger; she smiled, and yet she knew not why, as she neared the house. A vague and indefinable feeling of pleasure crowded on her imagination; and, as the old woman gained the threshold, she bade her 'welcome' with a warmth which plainly told that her lips gave utterance but to the genuine feelings of her heart.

'God bless this good house and all belonging to it,' said the stranger as she entered.

'God save you kindly and you are welcome, whoever you are,' replied Mrs Costigan.

'Hem, I thought so,' said the old woman with a significant grin. 'I thought so, or I wouldn't trouble you.'

The farmer's wife ran, and placed a chair near the fire for the stranger; but she refused, and sat on the ground near where Mrs C. had been spinning. Mrs Costigan had now time to survey the old hag's person minutely. She appeared of great age; her countenance was extremely ugly and repulsive; her skin was rough and deeply embrowned as if from long exposure to the effects of some tropical climate; her forehead was low, narrow, and indented with a thousand wrinkles; her long grey hair fell in matted elf-locks from beneath a white linen skull-cap; her eyes were bleared, blood-shotten, and obliquely set in their sockets, and her voice was croaking, tremulous, and at times, partially inarticulate. As she squatted on the floor, she looked round the house with an inquisitive gaze; she peered pryingly from corner to corner, with an earnestness of look, as if she had the faculty, like the Argonaut of old, to see through the very depths of the earth, whilst Mrs C. kept watching her motions with mingled feelings of curiosity, awe, and pleasure.

'Mrs,' said the old woman, at length breaking silence, 'I am dry with the heat of the day; can you give me a drink?'

'Alas!' replied the farmer's wife, 'I have no drink to offer you except water, else you would have no occasion to ask me for it.'

'Are you not the owner of the cattle I see yonder?' said the old hag, with a tone of voice and manner of gesticulation which plainly indicated her foreknowledge of the fact.

Mrs Costigan replied in the affirmative, and briefly related to her every circumstance connected with the affair, whilst the old woman still remained silent, but shook her grey head repeatedly;

and still continued gazing round the house with an air of importance and self-sufficiency.

When Mrs C. had ended, the old hag remained a while as if in a deep reverie: at length she said –

'Have you any of the milk in the house?'

'I have,' replied the other.

'Show me some of it.'

She filled a jug from a vessel and handed it to the old sybil, who smelled it, then tasted it, and spat out what she had taken on the floor.

'Where is your husband?' she asked.

'Out in the fields,' was the reply.

'I must see him.'

A messenger was despatched for Bryan, who shortly after made his appearance.

'Neighbour,' said the stranger, 'your wife informs me that your cattle are going against you this season.'

'She informs you right,' said Bryan.

'And why have you not sought a cure?'

'A cure!' re-echoed the man; 'why, woman, I have sought cures until I was heart-broken, and all in vain; they get worse every day.'

'What will you give me if I cure them for you?'

'Anything in our power,' replied Bryan and his wife, both speaking joyfully, and with a breath.

'All I will ask from you is a silver sixpence, and that you will do everything which I will bid you,' said she.

The farmer and his wife seemed astonished at the moderation of her demand. They offered her a large sum of money.

'No,' said she, 'I don't want your money; I am no cheat, and I would not even take sixpence, but that I can do nothing till I handle some of your silver.'

The sixpence was immediately given her, and the most implicit obedience promised to her injunctions by both Bryan and his wife, who already began to regard the old beldame as their tutelary angel.

The hag pulled off a black silk ribbon or fillet which encircled her head inside her cap, and gave it to Bryan, saying –

'Go, now, and the first cow you touch with this ribbon, turn her into the yard, but be sure don't touch the second, nor speak a word until you return; be also careful not to let the ribbon touch the ground, for, if you do, all is over.'

Bryan took the talismanic ribbon, and soon returned, driving a red cow before him.

The old hag went out, and, approaching the cow, commenced pulling hairs out of her tail, at the same time singing some verses in the Irish language in a low, wild, and unconnected strain. The cow appeared restive and uneasy, but the old witch still continued her mysterious chant until she had the ninth hair extracted. She then ordered the cow to be drove back to her pasture, and again entered the house.

'Go, now,' said she to the woman, 'and bring me some milk from every cow in your possession.'

She went, and soon returned with a large pail filled with a frightful-looking mixture of milk, blood, and corrupt matter. The old woman got it into the churn, and made preparations for churning.

'Now,' she said, 'you both must churn, make fast the door and windows, and let there be no light but from the fire; do not open your lips until I desire you, and by observing my directions, I make no doubt but, ere the sun goes down, we will find out the infernal villain who is robbing you.'

Bryan secured the doors and windows, and commenced churning. The old sorceress sat down by a blazing fire which had been specially lighted for the occasion, and commenced singing the same wild song which she had sung at the pulling of the cow hairs, and after a little time she cast one of the nine hairs into the fire, still singing her mysterious strain, and watching, with intense interest, the witching process.

A loud cry, as if from a female in distress, was now heard approaching the house; the old witch discontinued her incantations, and listened attentively. The crying voice approached the door.

'Open the door quickly,' shouted the charmer.

Bryan unbarred the door, and all three rushed out in the yard, when they heard the same cry down the *boreheen*, but could see nothing.

'It is all over,' shouted the old witch; 'something has gone amiss, and our charm for the present is ineffectual.'

They now turned back quite crest-fallen, when, as they were entering the door, the sybil cast her eyes downwards, and perceiving a piece of horse-shoe nailed on the threshold, she vociferated –

'Here I have it; no wonder our charm was abortive. The person that was crying abroad is the villain who has your cattle bewitched; I brought her to the house, but she was not able to come to the door on account of that horseshoe. Remove it instantly, and we will try our luck again.'

Bryan removed the horse-shoe from the doorway, and by the hag's directions placed it on the floor under the churn, having previously reddened it in the fire.

They again resumed their manual operations. Bryan and his wife began to churn, and the witch again to sing her strange verses, and casting her cow-hairs into the fire until she had them all nearly exhausted. Her countenance now began to exhibit evident traces of vexation and disappointment. She got quite pale, her teeth gnashed, her hand trembled, and as she cast the ninth and last hair into the fire, her person exhibited more the appearance of a female demon than of a human being.

Once more the cry was heard, and an aged red-haired woman* was seen approaching the house quickly.

'Ho, ho!' roared the sorceress, 'I knew it would be so; my charm has succeeded; my expectations are realised, and here she comes, the villain who has destroyed you.'

'What are we to do now?' asked Bryan.

'Say nothing to her,' said the hag; 'give her whatever she demands, and leave the rest to me.'

* Red-haired people are thought to possess magic power.

The woman advanced screeching vehemently, and Bryan went out to meet her. She was a neighbour, and she said that one of her best cows was drowning in a pool of water – that there was no one at home but herself, and she implored Bryan to go rescue the cow from destruction.

Bryan accompanied her without hesitation; and having rescued the cow from her perilous situation, was back again in a quarter of an hour.

It was now sunset, and Mrs Costigan set about preparing supper.

During supper they reverted to the singular transactions of the day. The old witch uttered many a fiendish laugh at the success of her incantations, and inquired who was the woman whom they had so curiously discovered.

Bryan satisfied her in every particular. She was the wife of a neighbouring farmer; her name was Rachel Higgins; and she had been long suspected to be on familiar terms with the spirit of darkness. She had five or six cows; but it was observed by her sapient neighbours that she sold more butter every year than other farmers' wives who had twenty. Bryan had, from the commencement of the decline in his cattle, suspected her for being the aggressor, but as he had no proof, he held his peace.

'Well,' said the old beldame, with a grim smile, 'it is not enough that we have merely discovered the robber; all is in vain, if we do not take steps to punish her for the past, as well as to prevent her inroads for the future.'

'And how will that be done?' said Bryan.

'I will tell you; as soon as the hour of twelve o'clock arrives tonight, do you go to the pasture, and take a couple of swift-running dogs with you; conceal yourself in some place convenient to the cattle; watch them carefully; and if you see anything, whether man or beast, approach the cows, set on the dogs, and if possible make them draw the blood of the intruder; then ALL will be accomplished. If nothing approaches before sunrise, you may return, and we will try something else.'

Convenient there lived the cowherd of a neighbouring squire. He was a hardy, courageous young man, and always kept a pair of very ferocious bulldogs. To him Bryan applied for assistance, and he cheerfully agreed to accompany him, and, moreover, proposed to fetch a couple of his master's best greyhounds, as his own dogs, although extremely fierce and bloodthirsty, could not be relied on for swiftness. He promised Bryan to be with him before twelve o'clock, and they parted.

Bryan did not seek sleep that night; he sat up anxiously awaiting the midnight hour. It arrived at last, and his friend, the herdsman, true to his promise, came at the time appointed. After some further admonitions from the *Collough*, they departed. Having arrived at the field, they consulted as to the best position they could choose for concealment. At last they pitched on a small brake of fern, situated at the extremity of the field, adjacent to the boundary ditch, which was thickly studded with large, old white-thorn bushes. Here they crouched themselves, and made the dogs, four in number, lie down beside them, eagerly expecting the appearance of their as yet unknown and mysterious visitor.

Here Bryan and his comrade continued a considerable time in nervous anxiety, still nothing approached, and it became manifest that morning was at hand; they were beginning to grow impatient, and were talking of returning home, when on a sudden they heard a rushing sound behind them, as if proceeding from something endeavouring to force a passage through the thick hedge in their rear. They looked in that direction, and judge of their astonishment, when they perceived a large hare in the act of springing from the ditch, and leaping on the ground quite near them. They were now convinced that this was the object which they had so impatiently expected, and they were resolved to watch her motions narrowly.

After arriving to the ground, she remained motionless for a few moments, looking around her sharply. She then began to skip and jump in a playful manner; now advancing at a smart pace towards the cows, and again retreating precipitately, but still drawing nearer and nearer at each sally. At length she advanced up to the next cow, and sucked her for a moment; then on to the next, and so respectively to every cow on the field – the cows all the time lowing loudly, and appearing extremely frightened and agitated. Bryan, from the moment the hare commenced sucking the first, was with difficulty restrained from attacking her; but his more sagacious companion suggested to him, that it was better to wait until she would have done, as she would then be much heavier, and more unable to effect her escape than at present. And so the issue proved; for being now done sucking them all, her belly appeared enormously distended, and she made her exit slowly and apparently with difficulty. She advanced towards the hedge where she had entered, and as she arrived just at the clump of ferns where her foes were couched, they started up with a fierce yell, and hallooed the dogs upon her path.

The hare started off at a brisk pace, squirting up the milk she had sucked from her mouth and nostrils, and the dogs making after her rapidly. Rachel Higgins's cabin appeared, through the grey of the morning twilight, at a little distance; and it was evident that puss seemed bent on gaining it, although she made a considerable circuit through the fields in the rear. Bryan and his comrade, however, had their thoughts, and made towards the cabin by the shortest route, and had just arrived as the hare came up, panting and almost exhaustèd, and the dogs at her very scut. She ran round the house, evidently confused and disappointed at the presence of the men, but at length made for the door. In the bottom of the door was a small, semi-circular aperture, resembling those cut in fowl-house doors for the ingress and egress of poultry. To gain this hole, puss now made a last and desperate effort, and had succeeded in forcing her head and shoulders through it, when the foremost of the dogs made a spring and seized her violently by the haunch. She uttered a loud and piercing scream, and struggled desperately to free herself from his gripe, and at last succeeded, but not until she left a piece of her rump in his teeth.

The men now burst open the door; a bright turf fire blazed on the hearth, and the whole floor was streaming with blood. No hare, however, could be found, and the men were more than ever convinced that it was old Rachel, who had, by the assistance of some demon, assumed the form of the hare, and they now determined to have her if she were over the earth. They entered the bedroom, and heard some smothered groaning, as if proceeding from some one in extreme agony. They went to the corner of the room from whence the moans proceeded, and there, beneath a bundle of freshly-cut rushes, found the form of Rachel Higgins, writhing in the most excruciating agony, and almost smothered in a pool of blood.

The men were astounded; they addressed the wretched old woman, but she either could not, or would not answer them. Her wound still bled copiously; her tortures appeared to increase, and it was evident that she was dying. The aroused family thronged around her with cries and lamentations; she did not seem to heed them, she got worse and worse, and her piercing yells fell awfully on the ears of the bystanders. At length she expired, and her corpse exhibited a most appalling spectacle, even before the spirit had well departed.

Bryan and his friend returned home. The old hag had been previously aware of the fate of Rachel Higgins, but it was not known by what means she acquired her supernatural knowledge. She was delighted at the issue of her mysterious operations. Bryan pressed her much to accept of some remuneration for her services, but she utterly rejected such proposals. She remained a few days at his house, and at length took her leave and departed, no one knew whither.

Old Rachel's remains were interred that night in the neighbouring churchyard. Her fate soon became generally known, and her family, ashamed to remain in their native village, disposed of their property, and quitted the country for ever. The story, however, is still fresh in the memory of the surrounding villagers; and often, it is said, amid the grey haze of a summer twilight, may the ghost of Rachel Higgins, in the form of a hare, be seen scudding over her favourite and well-remembered haunts.

The Soul as a Butterfly

THERE were two men searching for sheep one time in a glen. There was a stream running through it. They were tired and exhausted from their travels, so in the evening they stretched themselves down in the glen-side. The evening was delightful, and one of them fell fast asleep. The other remained awake. As he was watching the sleeper, he noticed his mouth widening, and out of it came a white butterfly! It went down along his body and along one of his legs, before alighting on the grass, and then went on for about six yards. The man who was awake rose to his feet and followed the butterfly until it reached a small, uneven pathway. It went along the pathway until it came to the edge of the stream. There was a stone flag, under which the water flowed, across the stream, and the butterfly went across by the flag to the other side. It continued on until it came to a small clump of sedges, and it went in and out through the clump several times. The man followed it for twenty yards or so further, until the butterfly came to an old horse-skull, which was white and weather-beaten. The butterfly went in through one of the

373

eye-sockets, and the man watched as it went into, and searched, every corner of the skull. It then went out again through the other socket.

The butterfly then went back by the same route: in and out through the clump of sedges, across the stream by the stone flag; then along the uneven pathway, until it reached the sleeper's body. It made its way up along his right leg, and never stopped until it went into the sleeper's mouth. When it did this, the sleeping man closed his mouth. The next moment he sighed and yawned and opened his eyes. He glanced around and saw his companion looking at him.

'It must be late in the evening by now,' said he.

'Whether 'tis late or early,' replied his companion, 'I have seen some wonders just now.'

"'Tis I who have seen the wonders!' said the sleeper. 'I dreamt that I was going along a fine, wide road, with trees and flowers at either side of me, until I came to a great river. Across the river was the finest and most ornamental bridge I had ever seen. Soon after crossing the bridge, I came to the most wonderful wood I had ever seen. I walked through it for a long time, until at the other side of it I came to a splendid palace. I went into it. There was nobody to be seen. I walked from one room to another until I grew tired. I was making up my mind to stay there, when an eerie feeling came over me. I left the palace and travelled along the same route home. I felt very hungry when I arrived, and then when I was going to eat some food, I woke up.'

'It looks as if the soul wanders around while the body is sleeping,' said his companion. 'Come with me now, and I'll show you all the fine places you passed through in your sleep.'

He told him about the butterfly, and showed him the uneven, little pathway, the stone flag across the stream, the clump of sedges and the horse-skull.

'That skull,' said he, 'is the fine palace you were in a while ago. That clump of sedges is the wonderful wood you saw, and that stone flag is the ornamental bridge you crossed. And that rough, little path is the fine, wide road you travelled, with flowers at every side!'

Both of them had seen wonders.

Black Annis

BLACK ANNIS lived in the Danehills.

She was ever so tall and had a blue face and had long white teeth and she ate people. She only went out when it was dark.

My mum says, when she ground her teeth people could hear her in time to bolt their doors and keep well away from the one window. That's why we don't have a lot of big windows in Leicestershire cottages, she can't only get an arm inside.

My mum says that's why we have the fire and chimney in a corner.

The fire used to be on the earth floor once and people slept all round it until Black Annis grabbed the babies out the window. There wasn't any glass in that time.

When Black Annis howled you could hear her five miles away and then even the poor folk in the huts fastened skins across the window and put witch-herbs above it to keep her away safe.

My mum told us there was a wicked stepmother who sent her three little children out near Christmastide to gather wood when it got dark earlier than this is (a dark lunchtime, Christmas Eve

376

1941). They were ever so cold and frightened and little Dicky he cried.

'Don't cry, Dicky lad,' says Jim. 'Don't be frighted. 'Tis Christmas Eve. You can't be hurted noways.'

'Why?' says Dicky.

'There's no bad'uns about,' says Jen.

'Why?' says Dicky.

"Tis Our Lord's birthday and the bells ring,' they said. 'If the bad'uns hear them they die.'

So off they went to the wood and picked a big load each. It was getting dark and they had a long way back and they were so tired and little Dicky cried and so did Jen. 'It's getting dark and she may not have gone under the earth yet. I'm going to run.'

But she couldn't with all her load of firewood.

Then Jim said, 'I've got a holed stone and if you like I'll look through it and see. But she'll be right underground with the covers over her ears till after Christmas.'

But she wasn't, she'd forgotten the day and Jim saw her five miles off.

It wasn't quite dark yet and they tried to make haste. Then Jim looked again. 'She's only a mile away,' he whispered, but they couldn't go any faster until they heard a yell.

Then they did run till they dropped.

'She won't come now,' says Jim. 'She'll stop to eat that ragged, drunken old woman I saw – I think it was Stepmother come to look for us.'

'I hope it were,' says Jen and little Dicky. 'We're nearly home now.'

So they rested just a bit longer and then little Dicky says, 'It's coming on near dark,' and Jen says. 'There's something grinding teeth. Look through the stone, Jim.'

So Jim looked and it was Black Annis only half a mile behind them. She hadn't liked the taste of that beery old stepmother, so she only snapped off her head and come on again.

'Drop your faggot across the path, little Dicky, and run for home!' says Jim.

So Black Annis bruised her legs and ran back to her cave to get an ointment to stop the bleeding. My mum says if a witch bleeds she loses all her power and dies.

And didn't Jim and Jen run too! But she wasn't scratched bad and back she come. She was only a quarter mile away when Jim looked, so they both dropped their faggots to trip her and ran for it.

Black Annis fell flat on her face over the firing but she caught up with them at their cottage door where their dad stood with an axe. And he threw it right in her face and her nose bled like a pig and she yelled and ran for her cave crying, 'Blood! Blood!' but the Christmas bells started pealing and she fell down far away and died.

Then the children kissed their dad and he'd brought a great load of firewood himself, and the stepmother was dead, and it was Christmas Eve so they made a big fire and had kippers and butter for tea. ('*Butter?*' said a rationed boy listener, 'Coo! what a feast!')

'It was Christmas Eve,' said the tale teller firmly, 'and the old stepmother had been hiding all their rations to sell to the grocer's man so she could buy beer.'

('Did they find Black Annis?' I asked.)

'The crows picked her bones – but one of my uncles he found a long tooth – ever so sharp it is – that's how I know it's quite true.'

The Paddo

A POOR widow was one day baking bannocks, and sent her dochter wi' a dish to the well to bring water. The dochter gaed, and better gaed, till she came to the well, but it was dry. Now, what to do she didna ken, for she couldna gang back to her mother without water, sae she sat down by the side o' the well, and fell a-greeting. A Paddo* then came loup-loup-louping out o' the well, and asked the lassie what she was greeting for; and she said she was greeting because there was nae water in the well. 'But,' says the Paddo, 'an ye'll be my wife, I'll gie ye plenty o' water.' And the lassie, no thinking that the poor beast could mean anything serious, said she wad be his wife, for the sake o' getting the water.

So she got the water into her dish, and gaed away hame to her mother, and thought nae mair about the Paddo, till that night, when, just as she and her mother were about to go to their beds, something came to the door, and when they listened, they heard this sang:

* A frog.

379

> *'Oh open the door, my hinnie, my heart,*
> *Oh open the door, my ain true love;*
> *Remember the promise that you and I made,*
> *Down i' the meadow, where we twa met.'*

Says the mother to the dochter: 'What noise is that at the door?'

'Hout,' says the dochter, 'it's naething but a filthy Paddo.'

'Open the door,' says the mother, 'to the poor Paddo.'

So the lassie opened the door, and the Paddo came loup-loup-louping in, and sat down by the ingle-side. Then he sings:

> *'Oh gie me my supper, my hinnie, my heart,*
> *Oh gie me my supper, my ain true love;*
> *Remember the promise that you and I made,*
> *Down i' the meadow, where we twa met.'*

'Hout,' quo' the dochter, 'wad I gie a filthy Paddo his supper?'

'Oh ay,' said the mother, 'e'en gie the poor Paddo his supper.'

So the Paddo got his supper; and after that he sings again:

> *'Oh put me to bed, my hinnie, my heart,*
> *Oh put me to bed, my ain true love;*
> *Remember the promise that you and I made,*
> *Down i' the meadow, where we twa met.'*

'Hout,' quo' the dochter, 'wad I put a filthy Paddo to bed?'

'Oh ay,' says the mother, 'put the poor Paddo to bed.' And so she put the Paddo to his bed. Then the Paddo sang again:

> *'Now fetch me an axe, my hinnie, my heart,*
> *Now fetch me an axe, my ain true love;*
> *Remember the promise that you and I made,*
> *Down i' the meadow, where we twa met.'*

The lassie wasna lang o'fetching the axe; and then the Paddo sang:

> *'Now chap aff my head, my hinnie, my heart,*
> *Now chap aff my head, my ain true love;*

Enchantment

Remember the promise that you and I made,
Down i' the meadow, where we twa met.'

Well, the lassie chappit aff his head; and no sooner was that done, than he started up the bonniest young prince that ever was seen. And the twa lived happy a' the rest o' their days.

The King o' the Cats

ONE winter's evening the sexton's wife was sitting by the fireside with her big black cat, Old Tom, on the other side, both half asleep and waiting for the master to come home. They waited and they waited, but still he didn't come, till at last he came rushing in, calling out, 'Who's Tommy Tildrum?' in such a wild way that both his wife and his cat stared at him to know what was the matter.

'Why, what's the matter?' said his wife. 'And why do you want to know who Tommy Tildrum is?'

'Oh, I've had such an adventure. I was digging away at old Mr Fordyce's grave when I suppose I must have dropped asleep, and only woke up by hearing a cat's *Miaou*.'

'*Miaou!*' said Old Tom in answer.

'Yes, just like that! So I looked over the edge of the grave, and what do you think I saw?'

'Now, how can I tell?' said the sexton's wife.

'Why, nine black cats all like our friend Tom here, all with a white spot on their chestesses. And what do you think they were carrying? Why, a small coffin covered with a black velvet pall, and on the pall was a small coronet all of gold, and at every third step they took they cried all together, *Miaou* ——'

'Miaou!' said Old Tom again.

'Yes; just like that!' said the sexton. 'And as they came nearer and nearer to me I could see them more distinctly, because their eyes shone out with a sort of green light. Well, they all came towards me, eight of them carrying the coffin and the biggest cat of all walking in front for all the world like . . . But look at our Tom, how he's looking at me. You'd think he knew all I was saying.'

'Go on, go on,' said his wife; 'never mind Old Tom.'

'Well, as I was a-saying, they came towards me slowly and solemnly, and at every third step crying all together, *Miaou* ——'

'Miaou!' said Old Tom again.

'Yes; just like that; till they came and stood right opposite Mr Fordyce's grave, where I was, when they all stood still and looked straight at me. I did feel queer, that I did! But look at Old Tom; he's looking at me just like they did.'

'Go on, go on,' said his wife; 'never mind Old Tom.'

'Where was I? Oh, they all stood still looking at me, when the one that wasn't carrying the coffin came forward and staring straight at me, said to me – yes, I tell 'ee, *said* to me – with a squeaky voice, "Tell Tom Tildrum that Tim Toldrum's dead," and that's why I asked you if you knew who Tom Tildrum was, for how can I tell Tom Tildrum Tim Toldrum's dead if I don't know who Tom Tildrum is?'

'Look at Old Tom! Look at Old Tom!' screamed his wife.

And well he might look, for Tom was swelling, and Tom was staring, and at last Tom shrieked out, 'What – old Tim dead! Then I'm the King o' the Cats!' and rushed up the chimney and was never more seen.

NVOI

Envoi

One of the last great storytellers was Angus MacLellan (Aonghus Beag), an old sheep-shearer on the island of South Uist in the Outer Hebrides. Between 1949 and 1960, John Lorne Campbell, highly-regarded folklorist and Laird of Canna, collected from him 130 stories – heroic tales about Fionn mac Cumhaill and his warriors, ghost stories, and humorous and adventure stories. About one third of this remarkable and wide repertoire appears in *Stories from South Uist* (1961) which broke new ground in folklore studies by being the first occasion on which 'translations of Gaelic stories into English have been made for publication direct from tape recordings without the intervention and use of a transcribed Gaelic text'.

It seems fitting to end this anthological survey with so confident and skilful a piece of storytelling as *Why Everyone Should be Able to Tell a Story*; to end with a tale that is about storytelling; and with words that come from a corner of our islands where the ancient storytelling tradition is still just alive, 'better preserved' in the words of John Lorne Campbell, 'and more carefully cultivated ... than anywhere else in Western Europe'.

Why Everyone Should be Able
to Tell a Story

ONCE there was an Uistman who was travelling home, at the time when the passage wasn't as easy as it is today. In those days travellers used to come by the Isle of Skye, crossing the sea from Dunvegan to Lochmaddy. This man had been away working at the harvest on the mainland. He was walking through Skye on his way home, and at nightfall he came to a house, and thought he would stay there till morning, as he had a long way to go. He went in, and I'm sure he was made welcome by the man of the house, who asked him if he had any tales or stories. He replied that he had never known any.

'It's very strange you can't tell a story,' said his host. 'I'm sure you've heard plenty.'

'I can't remember one,' said the Uistman.

His host himself was telling stories all night, to pass the night, until it was time to go to bed. When they went to bed, the Uistman was given the closet inside the front door to sleep in. What was there hanging in the closet but the carcass of a sheep!

The Uistman hadn't been long in bed when he heard the door being opened, and two men came in and took away the sheep.

The Uistman said to himself that it would be very unfortunate for him to let those fellows take the sheep away, for the people of the house would think that he had taken it himself. He went after the thieves, and he had gone some way after them when one of them noticed him, and said to the other:

'Look at that fellow coming after us to betray us; let's go back and catch him and do away with him.'

They turned back, and the Uistman made off as fast as he could to try to get back to the house. But they got between him and the house. The Uistman kept going, until he heard the sound of a big river; then he made for the river. In his panic he went into the river, and the stream took him away. He was likely to be drowned. But he got ahold of a branch of a tree that was growing on the bank of the river, and clung on to it. He was too frightened to move; he heard the two men going back and forth along the banks of the river, throwing stones wherever the trees cast their shade; and the stones were going past him.

He remained there until dawn. It was a frosty night, and when he tried to get out of the river, he couldn't do it. He tried to shout, but he couldn't shout either. At last he managed to utter one shout, and made a leap; and he woke up, and found himself on the floor beside the bed, holding on to the bedclothes with both hands. His host had been casting spells on him during the night! In the morning when they were at breakfast, his host said:

'Well, I'm sure that wherever you are tonight, you'll have a story to tell, though you hadn't one last night.'

That's what happened to the man who couldn't tell a story; everyone should be able to tell a tale or a story to help pass the night!

BIBLIOGRAPHY

SOURCES

ADDY, SIDNEY OLDALL. *Household Tales with other Traditional Remains.* London and Sheffield, 1895.

Athenaeum, The. London, 1847.

BARRETT, W.H. *More Tales from the Fens.* London, 1964.

BRIGGS, KATHARINE M. *A Dictionary of British Folk-Tales.* 4 volumes. London, 1970-71.

BURNE, CHARLOTTE. *Shropshire Folk-Lore: A Sheaf of Gleanings* edited from the Collections of Georgina F. Jackson. London, Shrewsbury and Chester, 1883.

CAMPBELL OF ISLAY, JOHN FRANCIS. *Popular Tales of the West Highlands.* 4 volumes. Edinburgh, 1860-62.

CAMPBELL, JOHN GREGORSON. *Clan Traditions and Popular Tales of the Western Highlands and Islands.* (Waifs and Strays of the Celtic Tradition V). Edited by Jessie Wallace and Duncan MacIsaac. London, 1895.

CAMPBELL, JOHN LORNE. *See under MacLellan.*

CHAMBERS, ROBERT. *The Popular Rhymes of Scotland.* Edinburgh and London, 1826.

CLODD, EDWARD. *Tom Tit Tot.* London, 1898.

CLOUSTON, WILLIAM ALEXANDER. *The Book of Noodles.* London, 1888.

CROKER, THOMAS CROFTON. *Fairy Legends and Traditions from the South of Ireland.* London, 1825; Parts II and III, 1828.

CROSSLEY-HOLLAND, KEVIN. *The Wildman.* London, 1976.

CUNDALL, JOSEPH. *A Treasury of Pleasure Books for Young People.* London, 1856.

CURTIN, JEREMIAH. *Myths and Folk-Lore of Ireland.* Boston, 1890.

DENHAM, MICHAEL AISLABIE. *The Denham Tracts.* Edited by James Hardy. 2 volumes. London, 1891–95.

ELDER, ABRAHAM. *Tales and Legends of the Isle of Wight.* London, 1839.

EMERSON, P.H. *Welsh Fairy-Tales and Other Stories.* London, 1894.

Folk-Lore, I, iii. 'English and Scotch Fairy Tales' collected by Andrew Lang. London, 1890.

GARNER, ALAN, (editor). *The Hamish Hamilton Book of Goblins.* London, 1969.

GROOME, FRANCIS HINDES. *Gypsy Folk-Tales.* London, 1899.

Bibliography

HALLIWELL-PHILLIPS, JAMES ORCHARD. *Popular Rhymes and Nursery Tales of England*. London, 1849.

HARE, AUGUSTUS. *Memorials of a Quiet Life*. London, 1871.

HAZLITT, WILLIAM CAREW. *Fairy Tales, Legends and Romances*. London, 1875.

HENDERSON, HAMISH. *See under* Scottish Studies.

HUNT, ROBERT. *Popular Romances of the West of England*. 2 volumes. London, 1865.

HYDE, DOUGLAS. *Beside the Fire*. London, 1890.

JACOBS, JOSEPH. *Celtic Fairy Tales*. London, 1892.

JACOBS, JOSEPH. *More English Fairy Tales*, London, 1894.

JONES, T. GWYNN. *Welsh Folklore and Folk-Custom*. London, 1930.

KEIGHTLEY, THOMAS. *The Fairy Mythology*. London, 1828.

KENNEDY, PATRICK. *Legendary Fictions of the Irish Celts*. London, 1866.

LANG, ANDREW. *The Lilac Fairy Book*. London, 1910.

LOVER, SAMUEL. *Legends and Stories of Ireland*. Dublin, 1831. 2nd series, London, 1834.

MACLELLAN, ANGUS and CAMPBELL, JOHN LORNE. *Stories from South Uist*. London, 1961.

MARSHALL, SYBIL. *Everyman's Book of English Folk Tales*. London, 1981.

MARWICK, ERNEST W. *The Folklore of Orkney and Shetland*. London, 1975.

MILLER, HUGH. *Old Red Sandstone*. Edinburgh, 1841.

MOORE, ARTHUR W. *The Folk-Lore of the Isle of Man*. London, 1891.

NORTON, F.J. *Collection*. MS 6 volumes. Reprinted in *A Dictionary of British Folk-Tales* edited by Katharine M.Briggs.

O'SULLIVAN, SEAN. *Folktales of Ireland*. With a foreword by Richard M.Dorson. London, 1966.

OWEN, ELIAS. *Welsh Folk-Lore, A collection of the Folk-Tales and Legends of North Wales*. Oswestry and Wrexham, 1896.

REEVES, JAMES. *English Fables and Fairy Stories*. London, 1954.

RHYS, JOHN. *Celtic Folklore, Welsh and Manx*. 2 volumes. Oxford, 1901.

SCOTT, WALTER. *Minstrelsy of the Scottish Border*. 2 volumes. Kelso, 1802-03.

Scottish Studies, II, i. Edinburgh, 1958.

SIKES, WILLIAM WIRT. *British Goblins: Welsh Folk-Lore, Fairy Mythology, Legends, and Traditions*. London, 1880.

SIMPSON, JACQUELINE. *British Dragons*. London, 1980.

SOUTHEY, ROBERT. *The Doctor, IV*. London, 1837.

SPENCER, W.R. *Beth Gêlert, or the Grave of the Greyhound*. Dolymalynllyn, 1800.

TABART, BENJAMIN. *The History of Jack and the Bean-Stalk*, printed from the Original Manuscript. Edited by William Godwin. London, 1807.

Bibliography

TONGUE, RUTH. *Forgotten Folk-Tales of the English Counties*. London, 1970.

TRAIN, JOSEPH. *An Historical and Statistical Account of the Isle of Man*. 2 volumes. Douglas, Isle of Man, 1845.

WADDELL, HELEN. *The Princess Splendour and Other Stories*. London, 1969.

WALLACE, JESSIE AND MACISAAC, DUNCAN. *See under Campbell, John Gregorson*.

WARING, ELIJAH. *Recollections and Anecdotes of Edward Williams*. London, 1850.

WILDE, JANE F. 'SPERANZA'. *Ancient Legends, Mystic Charms, and Superstitions of Ireland*. 2 volumes. London, 1887.

YATES, DORA E. *A Book of Gypsy Folk-Tales*. London, 1948.

YEATS, WILLIAM BUTLER. *Fairy and Folk Tales of the Irish Peasantry*. London, 1888.

FURTHER READING

BRIGGS, KATHARINE. *A Dictionary of Fairies*. London, 1976.

DORSON, RICHARD M. *The British Folklorists. A History*. London, 1968.

OPIE, IONA AND PETER. *The Classic Fairy Tales*. London, 1974.

THOMPSON, STITH. *Motif-Index of Folk Literature*. 6 volumes. Bloomington, Indiana, 1955-58.

THOMPSON, DAVID. *The People of the Sea*. London, 1954.

Kevin Crossley-Holland is a well-known poet, writer for children (his *Storm* was awarded the Library Association's Carnegie Medal 1985 for an outstanding children's book), broadcaster and interpreter of the northern world. Much of his work is infused with a knowledge and love of north-west European literature, myth and folklore, and he is the author of *The Dead Moon*, a collection of folk-tales from East Anglia and the Fens.